SOUTHERN LITERARY STUDIES

FRED HOBSON, EDITOR

The FAMILY SAGA *in the* SOUTH

The FAMILY SAGA *in the* SOUTH

GENERATIONS AND DESTINIES

Robert O. Stephens

LOUISIANA STATE UNIVERSITY PRESS

Baton Rouge and London

Designer: Rebecca Lloyd Lemna
Typeface: Galliard
Typesetter: Moran Printing, Inc.
Printer and binder: Thomson-Shore, Inc.

Library of Congress Cataloging-in-Publication Data:
Stephens, Robert O.
    The family saga in the South : generations and destinies / Robert
O. Stephens.
        p.   cm. — (Southern literary studies)
    Includes bibliographical references and index.
    ISBN 0-8071-1988-1 (alk. paper)
    1. Domestic fiction, American—Southern States—History and
criticism.   2. Historical fiction, American—Southern States—
History and criticism.   3. Southern States—In literature.
4. Family in literature.   I. Title.   II. Series.
PS261.S74   1995
813.009'355—dc20   95-853
                                                                          CIP

Portions of Chapter 1 appeared earlier as "Cable's Grandissime Saga" in *American Literary Realism, 1870–1910*. I gratefully acknowledge the permission of its publishers, McFarland and Company, Inc., to reuse much of this essay.

For
the Stephenses and Robertsons, the Joneses and Daughtreys,
the Joplings, Blakleys, Lawrences, Smiths, and Tadlocks,
and those extended families
from Virginia to Alabama to Texas
who supplied the background

CONTENTS

PREFACE

L ike many readers, I have found considerable pleasure in following stories of families through successive generations. As I read sagas of families in the South, the Northeast, the Far West, Britain, Russia, and Latin America, among others, I became aware that cultural differences shaped the identities and memories of families. But when my students and I in several classes on southern writers tried to find critical definitions and descriptions of family sagas, we found criticism and scholarship curiously silent on the genre. If no one else would supply answers, we had to find our own. Over several years in classes and seminars we puzzled over, sometimes refined, our insights, drew on related writings, and began to get glimpses of a coherent system of conventions.

This book is an early attempt to explore the long-practiced tradition of the family saga. Many have written these sagas, but few have analyzed them. Others, I hope, will extend and refine what is begun here, for the tradition is rich enough to reward many labors. To those who no doubt will say, "Why didn't you include [my favorite family saga]?," my answer is that I probably did but had to cut it. A book can bear only so much, and, unlike God, one can't love them all.

The sagas explored here, though, suggest major developments in the tradition of the family saga in the South. After identifying in the Introduction key saga elements found in the prototypal family saga of Genesis 12 through 50 and in family stories, I follow development of the genre from the appearance of its early incipient forms in country-house poems of the seventeenth century to its first full realization in the southern tradition, George Washington Cable's *The Grandissimes*.

In subsequent chapters I explore ways that different saga elements have dominated sagas, reflecting their times and circumstance. Chapter 2 shows how family sagas keyed to the Civil War deal with displacement of the inheritance. Chapter 3 examines the motif of family decline corresponding with decline of the agrarian tradition. Chapter 4, focusing on sagas written by women, explores implications of the patriarchal-matriarchal conflict resonating through generations. Chapter 5 looks at ways writers of black family sagas have redefined family in order to place the family story within the context of public history. Chapter 6 considers ways some of the latest generation of saga writers have modified, even stylized, conventions practiced by earlier writers. Chapter 7 analyzes relationships between sagas and their readers, particularly when authors act as readers.

In some ways this study has itself been something of a saga. I am grateful to many former students for pondering the problems with me; to Gaylor Callahan of the Interlibrary Loan Department of Walter Clinton Jackson Library for helping me to gain access to remote sources; to Kathleen Driskill, Julianna Baggot, Julie Funderburk, and Bob Langenfeld for help in preparing the manuscript; to Ginny Stephens for both encouragement and practical help in making revisions; to Christine N. Cowan for editing copy and saving me from embarrassing errors; and to Linda Webster for indexing the book.

The FAMILY SAGA *in the* SOUTH

Introduction

FAMILY SAGAS, SOUTHERN STYLE

Folklorist B. A. Botkin tells the story of a famous biblical scholar who gave a lecture on the Medes and Persians at a church in Virginia. After the lecture, a delicate old lady thanked him for his remarks and informed him that her mother was also a Mead.[1] More than an exemplum of the southern sense of family, the story reflects key elements behind the tradition of family sagas in southern writing: family lore exists within the framework of biblical reference and rivals it for authority. Further, in exchanges between these two poles of authority, the result is a large fund of imaginative reconstruction.

Shelby Foote and Eudora Welty illustrate the connection between continuous knowledge of families in southern communities and the work of southern writers in making narratives about that knowledge. Foote notes that knowledge of a long-term sense of community has its own implicit stories:

> But the glorious thing . . . about growing up in a Mississippi town, is what you got from it that you could use as a writer. . . . When you are thoroughly away from the ins and outs and vicissitudes of the family who lived two doors down the street, what their grandfather had done (and everybody knew perfectly well he had done it, and shame on him for doing it) and the tragedy that came on his children and then the glorious recovery of what the oldest boy managed to do when he opened the Buick agency, and so on—those things are of enormous value to the writer and I do not see anything that could take their place.

---

1. B. A. Botkin, *A Treasury of Southern Folklore* (New York, 1949), 8–9.

Welty similarly sees that such knowledge is "what gives you a sense of narrative and a sense of the drama of life," for "everything has consequences, and everything has a root."[2]

Such a sense of connection among family, community, and writer has made the family saga a principal feature of southern writing in the late nineteenth and twentieth centuries. The family—the extended family—has been the central and enduring institution in the South, and the community and the southern writer have been extensions of the kinship network of the family. More than in other sections of the country, though perhaps not more than in many non-American parts of the world, the southern family was the institution to fall back on when the public world changed, was convulsed by wars and depressions and poverty, when national policy ordained fundamental changes in public life. "In the South," writes Andrew Lytle, "family was the one institution common to all its parts. . . . It was family as institution which best expressed its culture. By family, I mean all the complex interrelationships of blood and kin, the large 'connections' which extended to the county lines and by sympathy overlapped states. . . . There are the geographical limits which allowed the family in this larger meaning (it was the community) to spread itself in a mild climate and over alluvial soils to give the institution its predominance as not just one but *the* institution of Southern life."[3]

But Lytle also saw that the family in the South "was called on to do more than its form allowed" and "should have been one among many institutional expressions of culture." For the southern family has had to function as the individual's link with the past, as the place where cultural values are learned at the mother's knee, as an extension of church and school, as a model for manners, and as a matrix for models of citizenship and leadership.[4] Indeed, the southern family has functioned primarily as

2. Louis D. Rubin, Jr., "Growing Up in the Deep South: A Conversation with Eudora Welty, Shelby Foote, and Louis D. Rubin, Jr.," in *The American South: Portrait of a Culture*, ed. Louis D. Rubin, Jr. (Baton Rouge, 1980), 75–76.

3. Andrew Lytle, "The Working Novelist and the Mythmaking Process," in *The Hero with the Private Parts* (Baton Rouge, 1966), 179; Andrew Lytle, "Foreword to *A Novel, a Novella and Four Stories*," ibid., 199.

4. Lytle, "The Working Novelist," in *Hero*, 179; Ellington White, "A View from the Window," in *The Lasting South: Fourteen Southerners Look at Their Home*, ed. Louis D. Rubin, Jr., and James J. Kilpatrick (Chicago, 1957), 169; John Shelton Reed, *One South: An Ethnic Approach to Regional Culture* (Baton Rouge, 1982), 31; John Shelton Reed, *The Enduring South: Subcultural Persistence in Mass Society* (Chapel Hill, 1974), 85–87.

families do in ethnic groups, by serving as a source for identification of the group, by allowing the family member to confine his social relationships to his own ethnic group during all stages of his life, and by adapting national patterns of behavior and values to its own cultural system.[5]

To a great extent, then, the family has become the image of the South to its members and its chroniclers. It has become "the enveloping action," not merely background, of individuals' stories that takes place simultaneously and interactively with the actions of individual members. Its hierarchies are the hierarchies of the South, with ranks of patriarchs, matriarchs, aunts, uncles, and cousins forming the outer circles of authority as well as of kinship. Its legends reflect the larger legendary of the region, with extended family members reenacting the fortunes of southern heroes and heroines. Its sense of place and of events associated with particular locations finally makes place an index of history more than of geography, so that place becomes "the present condition of a scene that is modified through its having been inhabited in time."[6] In the context of family sagas, this sense of place becomes associated with the family home and the life of the family, remembered as well as lived, around that center. Typically, the home place functions virtually as a family member through the generations and serves as an index of family values, often in contrast with the home place of a neighboring or associated family. Architecture becomes a family trait, so that a house with numerous wings and additions tells about the organic development and continued status of the family and stands in contrast with a grander and more architecturally proper nearby mansion that tells of late arrival to status with money gained elsewhere.

With place as the locus of family memory, writers of family sagas in the South turned to the family Bible as the mythic framework for interpreting remembered or re-created experience. The saga of Abraham and his descendants in Genesis 12 through 50 became the paradigm for analyzing the dynamics of family life. More than a record of births, marriages, and deaths, the family Bible also became the family's point of reference and its mythology. The historical or legendary acts of the patriarchs and prodigal children gained meaning when seen in the context of that commonly recognized lore. And out of that common fund developed a

5. Reed, *Enduring South*, 10–11.

6. Lytle, "Foreword to *A Novel*," in *Hero*, 197; Frederick J. Hoffman, *The Art of Southern Fiction: A Study of Some Modern Novelists* (Carbondale, 1967), 13–14.

set of narrative patterns that constitutes the systematic structure of the family saga. Elements in the system might vary, but the structure endures.[7]

As a structure told in narrative for contemplation and remembrance, the family saga provides a prototypal story with clearly recognized marking points and expectations. Among its principal features is the recognition that the saga shows a consanguine family through history measured in generations, at least three, and populous enough to serve as a microcosm of its times. Like the generational story of Abraham, Isaac, Jacob, and Joseph in Genesis, the saga accounts for lineal descent and for collateral descendants like Lot. In the scheme of descendants, the conjugal family of husband, wife, and children count for less than the extended family and serve instrumentally as units in a larger structure.[8]

The identity of the family is established by its removal from the former home of the ancestors to the home place of the descendants, as in the move by Abraham and Sarah from Mesopotamia to Canaan, and by the special attribute the family assumes for itself. Where for Abraham and his descendants the special attribute was his covenant with God, in later sagas the special attribute may be the memory of an original crime, vision, or sense of destiny of the ancestor, and the identity of descendants is related to preservation of the special attribute. Identity is further reflected in names given or denied to descendants as they show continued awareness of the special attribute.[9] In many southern sagas the act of naming then reflected the influence of family politics as well as of blood relations and was especially powerful in the case of former slaves related by blood to the master's family.

Shaping of the family story over the generations comes through such tropes as the lingering influence of a patriarchal-matriarchal conflict among the ancestors, displacement of the inheritance to a secondary or collateral descendant, and an awareness that later descendants lack the strength or nobility of earlier ancestors. As in the conflicts between Abraham and Sarah over the status of Hagar and Ishmael, between Isaac and Rebekah over the claims of Esau and Jacob, and among Jacob-Israel, Leah, and

---

7. Robert Alter, *The Art of Biblical Narrative* (New York, 1981), 47; Robert Scholes, *Structuralism in Literature: An Introduction* (New Haven, 1974), 10.

8. Nicholas Tavuchis and William J. Goode, *The Family in Literature* (New York, 1975), 3–4; Robert Boyers, "The Family Novel," in *Excursions: Selected Literary Essays* (Port Washington, N.Y., 1977), 6–7; E. A. Speiser, *The Anchor Bible Genesis* (Garden City, N.Y., 1964), 88.

9. Michael Ragussis, *Acts of Naming* (New York, 1987), 6–11.

Rachel over favored children, conflicts in later family sagas reflect clashing values between patriarchs and matriarchs that divide their descendants into rival clans. Displacement of the inheritance, as in Jacob's displacement of Esau, starts the family history in a direction different from that traditionally expected and prompts later descendants to see divine intervention in what may have been acts of chicanery and deceit. When later descendants realize their failure to maintain the family covenant, they enact the convention of family decline and show that in sagas dynasty and doom are related motifs.[10]

Narration of southern family sagas involves the key convention of the historian-narrator presiding over the collection and collation of narrative elements in a search for knowledge. Indeed, the process of the search becomes as important to the saga as is the accumulated recognition of forces at work in family history. Like the editor of the Yahwist, Elohist, and Priestly narratives in Genesis, the historian-narrator must set accounts side by side to evaluate them, even when they are partly or mutually contradictory. Whether the historian-narrator is an unnamed presence or a first-person participant in the narrative, he, or she, must also reckon with the effect of the research on the researcher. In the process, he must not only correlate family events with marking points in linear public history but also recognize cyclical time in the repetition of family events through linear time. By seeing actions of family members within their own historical contexts, the historian-narrator also sees ancestors and contemporaries limited to the knowledge and prejudices of their times.[11] He is then put in the position of puzzling over the values and motives of the ancestors, often because such values and motives come from the old homeland before removal to the new, as in the clash between Mesopotamian and Canaanite values in the Genesis narrative. Knowing the outcomes of earlier ancestral choices, the historian-narrator then becomes a kind of nemesis in presiding over the consequences of those choices. In the process the historian-narrator sees cyclical time at work in the repetition of type scenes in

10. Sven Armens, *Archetypes of the Family in Literature* (Seattle, 1966), 32–42, 222; Savina J. Teubal, *Sarah the Priestess: The First Matriarch of Genesis* (Athens, Ohio, 1984), 15, 54; Northrop Frye, *The Great Code: The Bible and Literature* (New York, 1982), 182; Speiser, *Anchor Bible Genesis,* lvii.

11. Patricia Tobin, *Time and the Novel: The Genealogical Imperative* (Princeton, 1978), 174; Speiser, *Anchor Bible Genesis,* xxiv–xxxviii; Robert Scholes and Robert Kellogg, *The Nature of Narrative* (New York, 1966), 241–43; Harry B. Henderson, *Versions of the Past: The Historical Imagination in American Fiction* (New York, 1974), 14.

family history—scenes at crucial points in family memory—such as the meetings of the future betrothed or testimonies of dying patriarchs in Genesis. He likewise becomes aware of the emergence of talismanic objects, actions, or places for the family, markers that condense abstract memory to concrete rituals of family value. Whether in Abraham's ritual of circumcision or in Israel's stelae of commemoration, Genesis furnishes multiple examples for recognition.[12]

Reaching beyond particular actions, the historian-narrator may finally recognize the significance of moments of vision, either the ancestors' or his own. Then insight goes beyond the debris and detritus of everyday life to see the work of destiny in family history and often beyond the apparent conflict between means and ends, as in Abraham's potential sacrifice of Isaac. At such times the narrator-historian may achieve a God-like clarity of vision and see destiny at work through flawed human agents as the ultimate purpose of the family history.[13]

Thus, in the systematic structure of the family saga southern writers could sense and use conventions derived from the Genesis narrative: continuity of the consanguine family through multiple generations; identity established at the time of removal to a new homeland; preservation of the family's special attribute; the lingering influence of patriarchal-matriarchal conflicts; displacement of the inheritance; decline in later generations when compared to the strength or nobility of the earlier; work of a historian-narrator to collect and evaluate evidence of the family past; correlation of family history with public history; puzzlement about actions and motives of the ancestors; recognition of type scenes; awareness of the significance of talismanic objects, places, or actions; and achievement of moments of vision.

Behind most family sagas in the South is the ghost of family stories. Like the oral tradition that informed the Yahwist, Elohist, and Priestly narrators in Genesis before they set their accounts into written form, the fund of family stories has supplied writers of sagas with initial sources, with key details, with imbedded narratives, and with insights that creative writers have used to develop their sagas into artistic structures. Reliance on an oral tradition is a kind of open secret between many writers of sagas and their readers. T. S. Stribling, for example, writes in his epigraph to *The Forge*, published in 1931, "In memory of/My Father and Mother/And

12. Alter, *Art of Biblical Narrative*, 51; Speiser, *Anchor Bible Genesis*, 53, 271.
13. Speiser, *Anchor Bible Genesis*, 162–66.

That Brave, Gay Group from Whom/These Memoirs Were Taken." In the dedication of her 1967 work, *Jubilee*, Margaret Walker remembers "my grandmothers: my maternal great-grandmother, Margaret Duggans Ware Brown, whose story this is; my maternal grandmother, Elvia Ware Dozier, who told me this story; and my paternal grandmother, Margaret Walker." Eudora Welty, perhaps the premier user of family stories, relates the practice to southern customs:

> As it happens, we in the South have grown up being narrators. We have lived in a place . . . where storytelling is a way of life. When we were children we listened a lot. We heard stories told by relatives and friends. A great many were family tales. . . . If we weren't around when something happened, way back, at least we think we know what it was like simply because we've heard it so long. We tend to understand what's tragic or comic, or both, because we know the whole story and have been part of the place.

For her, the source provides the authenticity: "Family stories are where you get your first notions of profound feelings, mysterious feelings that you might not understand till you grow into them. But you know they exist and that they have power." As she recognized, however, family stories are not artistic fiction, and writers have to condense, to point up traits, to reimagine, to place in a different context the family stories that become the bases of family sagas, including family stories told as part of the action of the family sagas.[14]

Many conventions and motifs of family sagas are already present in family stories. Apparently the same logic works in one as in the other, and though family stories are fragmentary and incomplete in comparison with sagas, they show the same narrative impulses at work, if on a more elemental level.[15] Together they show that the conventions of family conti-

14. Don Lee Keith, "Eudora Welty: 'I Worry Over My Stories,'" 142–43, Jan Nordby Gretlund, "An Interview with Eudora Welty," 212, and Bill Ferris, "A Visit with Eudora Welty," 161, all in *Conversations with Eudora Welty*, ed. Peggy Whitman Prenshaw (Jackson, 1984).

15. Recent studies have identified motifs in family stories that point to their use in larger works. Mody C. Boatright, "The Family Saga as a Form of Folklore," in *The Family Saga and Other Phases of Folklore*, ed. Mody C. Boatright, with Robert B. Down and John T. Flanagan (Urbana, 1958), 1–19, began the exploration, followed soon by Kim S. Garrett, "Family Stories and Sayings," *Publications of the Texas Folklore Society*, XXX (1961), 273–81. Then came the Smithsonian Institution study, *A Celebration of American Family Folklore*, ed.

nuity, removal as the beginning of family identity, search for a special attribute, displacement of the inheritance, the role of the family narrator, the attempted correlation of family events with historical events, the sense of dynastic decline, recognition of patriarchal-matriarchal conflict, use of type scenes, venerated talismans, and visions of destiny are recurring motifs in family stories. Central to all stories is the tendency to make them serve the family's needs: to provide a sense of social placement, to suggest paradigms for survival, to explain the present, to establish a sense of unity, and to supply clues to tacit understandings within the family. If the facts of history disagree, family stories imaginatively reshape the past to fit the family's vision of itself. Each generation has to reinvent the family past according to its own needs.[16]

Motifs of continuity in family stories, for example, help locate the family within a hierarchy of races, classes, or ethnic groups to advance presumed claims of superiority over other families or to locate the family within the network of kin so that admired ancestors or cousins in another branch become part of one's own family. In stories of black families, tales of endurance during times of trouble become celebrations of continuity. Stories of removal from the old homeland to the new often tell how an ancestor's name was changed by an ignorant or indifferent official, how former slaves changed their names, how the ancestor hid his former identity and provided speculation by the descendants on his reasons for doing so. Stories of family attributes account for peculiar traits and eccentricities of family members by giving them a genealogical explanation and rationalizing that they "come by it honestly." [17] The significance of the story of a family attribute is not in the story itself but in what the teller makes

---

Steven J. Zeitlin, Amy J. Kotkin, and Holly Cutting-Baker (New York, 1982), and within that collection Dennis W. Folly, "Getting Butter from the Duck: Proverbs and Proverbial Expressions in the Afro-American Family," 232–41; Amanda Dargan, "She Comes by It Honestly: Characterization in Family Folklore," 222–31; Margaret Yocum, "Blessing the Ties That Bind: Storytelling at Family Festivals," 250–59. Alex Shoumantoff, *Mountain of Names* (New York, 1985), details family practices and structures out of which genealogical studies come. Perhaps most comprehensive and insightful is Elizabeth Stone, *Black Sheep and Kissing Cousins: How Our Family Stories Shape Us* (New York, 1988).

16. Stone, *Black Sheep*, 40.

17. *Ibid.*, 69–70, 182–84, 20–23; Zeitlin, Kotkin, and Cutting-Baker, eds., *Celebration of Folklore*, 18; Dargan, "She Comes By It Honestly," in *Celebration of Folklore*, ed. Zeitlin, Kotkin, and Cutting-Baker, 225–31.

of it. The story may be a boast or a warning, but its effects are to persuade members that the family is special and different from other families and to say what the issues are for this family.[18]

Stories of displacement of the inheritance typically involve a missed assignment of roles in the family or the might-have-been of missed or lost fortunes. The issue in stories of missed roles often concerns the family's requirement that members stay close by or shows the family's tolerance in letting them wander and still return as members. Typically, sons are allowed greater range, especially for education, than are daughters, but they are more likely to be lost if they marry into strong matriarchal families. Stories of lost fortunes tell of an ancestor's prodigality or of his having been cheated or of fortunes lost by natural catastrophes.[19]

In family storytelling the teller of the tale corresponds to the narrator-historian of the saga. Usually the substance of the tale is known, in whole or in part, to the audience, so "the magic is in the telling, in the transformation of a daily history into story, of life into art." Thus, for a tale to be preserved in the oral tradition of the family, it must provide emotional satisfaction to the audience and reflect the skill of the teller in conveying mood and moral beyond content. Who may be the skilled and authoritative shaper of the family tradition varies according to age, sex, and closeness to the figures involved, as well as to narrative talent. The art of narration often depends on the ability of the teller to attribute stories to persons whose authority is already recognized by the audience or on the teller's plausibly presenting himself as the one most likely to know, so he can tell the story with himself as observer or participant.[20] Equally as often, women have become repositories of family lore both about women and men, especially when work took men away from the family. Apparently anticipating the transformation of family storyteller into narrator-historian of the saga, Lytle notes the emergence of a bardic voice: "Everybody in a country community knows something about a happening; but nobody knows it all. The bard, by hovering above the action to see it all, collects the segments. In the end, in the way he fits the parts together, the one story will finally get told."[21]

18. Stone, *Black Sheep*, 16–17, 7.

19. *Ibid.*, 28, 155–61, 207; Zeitlin, Kotkin, and Cutting-Baker, eds., *Celebration of Folklore*, 83.

20. Zeitlin, Kotkin, and Cutting-Baker, eds., *Celebration of Folklore*, 8; Boatright, "The Family Saga as a Form of Folklore," 19.

21. Stone, *Black Sheep*, 19; Lytle, "Foreword to *A Novel*," in *Hero*, 200–201.

Connections between family stories and historical events may be tenuous at best, and family stories may better reflect a later view of social conditions than of actual history. The story of a family's jewels being lost when hidden from the invading Yankee army, for example, may run into the problem that no Yankee army invaded that locale. But the story explains to later generations the absence of family jewels. Stories of illustrious ancestors are stories of decline only by implication. Usually a grandparent or great-grandparent is made the epitome of family identity and attributes, and though he or she may be dead, the ancestor is still a presence in family memory. The family believes its stories of the ancestor are true because it needs that version of the past, and older members tend to be believed even if they were thought unreliable when younger.[22]

As in sagas, the hint of matriarchal-patriarchal conflict exists in family stories, particularly those of survival in desperate times. In such stories the women hold the family together during long-term stress, whereas the men act mainly in emergency situations. Women's stories may also carry a subversive subtext that shows women must be taught to be strong even while they are trained for apparently submissive roles based on beauty and femininity.[23] The subversive theme of strong women in a family of conventional conformity then works with the motif of the special family attribute so as to define who is really a member of the family and perhaps to exclude someone like Cousin May because she is not emotionally kin to the women of the family.

Type scenes appear as type stories in family lore, with the courtship story as the type told most often. Such stories not only tell How the Family Began but also guide members on what to feel about love, warn them about passionate love as a danger to the family, instruct them about the importance of marrying for money rather than for love, and caution women to marry men who can be absorbed into their families. These stories tend to become stylized patterns of repeated family experience.[24]

Talismanic objects, places, and actions gain their value from family stories and without their attendant stories are soon forgotten. Such sto-

22. Boatright, "The Family Saga as a Form of Folklore," 3; Stone, *Black Sheep,* 35–36; Zeitlin, Kotkin, and Cutting-Baker, eds., *Celebration of Folklore,* 10.

23. Zeitlin, Kotkin, and Cutting-Baker, eds., *Celebration of Folklore,* 46; Stone, *Black Sheep,* 187–92, 200.

24. Stone, *Black Sheep,* 64, 51, 74; Zeitlin, Kotkin, and Cutting-Baker, eds., *Celebration of Folklore,* 14–16.

ries provide significance for heirlooms and, all too often, make them worth fighting over. Out of disputed oral bequests of heirlooms come family feuds, and one's family loyalties are tested by the view one takes of ancestral bequests.[25]

Visions of family destiny, though not so frequent in elemental family stories as in sagas, occur in courtship stories where later generations are encouraged to see the work of fate, or destiny, in initial sexual attraction that results in either disastrous or successful marriages. Stories of fortunes built on a moment of vision by the ancestor suppose a sense of destiny on the part of later tellers, whether or not the original ancestor had the vision.[26] As in southern family sagas, visions of the clan's past in family stories are construed to fit the needs of the present.

In form as well as content, the family saga in the South constitutes a tradition, much practiced but little analyzed, in southern writing. Supported by recognition of distinctive features in the southern family and community, by biblical prototypes and family stories, the tradition has largely taken the form of novelistic sagas but not entirely; short fictional forms and extended nonfictional treatments have also marked its development. Classifying the work as fiction or nonfiction is less important than recognizing how conventions of the family saga provide a system of communication and expectations for the readers whereby individual elements achieve significance through their placement in the framework. Each saga, with its implicit code inviting comparison with others in the genre, is subject to assimilation within the tradition even as the individual saga modifies the tradition.[27]

Forms of the southern family saga take their identities and meanings from their shifting cultural contexts. What may be considered nonliterary in one context becomes literary in another. Such is the case with Genesis 12 through 50, the matrix of religious law and tradition for a religious community but the prototypal family saga for a literary community. When he noted he read the Old Testament for "some of the most robust and most amusing folklore I know," William Faulkner demonstrated that process. "I read the Old Testament for the pleasure of watching what these amazing people did, and they behaved so exactly like people in the

25. Stone, *Black Sheep*, 243.

26. *Ibid.*, 67, 160–61.

27. Alastair Fowler, *Kinds of Literature: An Introduction to the Theory of Genres and Modes* (Cambridge, Mass., 1982), 112–14, 122, 151.

nineteenth century." [28] The same is true, say, for ostensible autobiographies, both fictional and nonfictional, which become family sagas as they include conventions of the form. Thus, William Alexander Percy's *Lanterns on the Levee* and Ernest Gaines' *The Autobiography of Miss Jane Pittman* come within the tradition, as does Lytle's memoir *A Wake for the Living*.

The family saga in the South has developed diachronically, through time, as well as synchronically, as a form with an essential identity from earliest times to latest. Conventions have varied in emphasis and meaning as the tradition developed. One convention that has been most open to further exploration and that has produced modifications in what characters and readers have been able to recognize as objective reality is manipulation of narrative point of view. After all the stories are told, in some sagas mystery still exists about what happened and why. Purposeful indeterminacy of knowledge has thus become one of the modifications within development of the family saga. That is, the convention functions by being warped out of its normally expected forms and thus introduces new expectations prompted by the convention.[29] Faulkner's 1936 novel *Absalom, Absalom!* is probably the prime example of this modified convention, but it recurs periodically, as in Shirley Ann Grau's *The Keepers of the House* in 1964 and Lee Smith's *Oral History* in 1983.

Development of the southern family saga has reflected understandings of a particular author and audience at a particular time within the tradition. Authors of sagas in the South by the late 1950s, for example, tended to see their work in light of Faulkner's achievement and responded in an anxiety of influence. Readers by that time tended to value new sagas for their differences from Faulkner's performance. Later works could thus take for granted conventions established earlier, and in still later works those accepted conventions would become stylized.[30] Correlation of family history with public history could, for example, abandon major reference points like the Civil War and turn to a kind of pastless, K-Mart recitation of popular culture, as Smith does in *Family Linen,* or it could convert the historical past into a timeless legend of Africa, as Toni Morrison does in *Song of Solomon.*

28. Steven Mailloux, *Interpretive Conventions: The Reader in the Study of Narrative Texts* (Ithaca, 1982), 150–51; James B. Meriwether and Michael Millgate, eds., *Lion in the Garden: Interviews with William Faulkner, 1926–1962* (New York, 1968), 112.

29. Thomas Kent, *Interpretation and Genre: The Role of Generic Perceptions in the Study of Narrative Texts* (Cranbury, N.J., 1986), 47–50.

30. Kent, *Interpretation and Genre,* 39; Fowler, *Kinds of Literature,* 170–88.

INTRODUCTION

Before the family saga began to flourish in twentieth-century southern writing, however, it went through a long ancestral development as did generations in the sagas. Those ancestral forms show how features begun with one intent accrued and shifted meanings until they became features of the southern family saga known to modern readers.

I

GENEALOGY OF A SOUTHERN
FAMILY SAGA

When George Washington Cable produced the first authentic southern family saga in 1879, his book had a long literary lineage. As a
family saga, *The Grandissimes* had early forebears such as the English
country-house poems and country-house sketches, as well as family-
centered novels of the eighteenth and nineteenth centuries. As in a family
genealogy, some of the early ancestors demonstrated latent qualities
that, combined with others, would become dominant through time and
generations. The development of the saga is analogous to development of
a family in which "the genetic make-up alters with slow time" and "the
genre's various historical states [are] very different from one another."
What matters more than external features is the "coding rules" that give
the genre its identity and integrity.[1]

Although they took a line of development different from the mimetic
tradition of the novel, the Norse sagas demonstrate a key distinction between socially oriented family sagas and warrior sagas. The ethic of warrior sagas emphasizes the individual aggressiveness of the heroes, often
at the cost of disrupting the social fabric. The family sagas, reflecting values of the whole society rather than those of only the warrior class, emphasize conciliation and restored social balance over personal grandeur.
English chivalric histories of the founders of noble families in the fourteenth century similarly illustrate a kind of legendary antecedent to family sagas within historic time. In accounts of Black Prince Edward Woodstock, Prince of Wales and of Aquitaine, and of the first Thomas Beauchamp,
who claimed descent from Guy of Warwick, exploits of the heroes are pre-

1. Fowler, *Kinds of Literature,* 43–44.

served for their posterity in chronicles redolent of romance. But they have their conventions. The chronicle of Woodstock by Sir John Chandos typically records seasons by formulaic phrases such as "when birds begin to sing" or "cease to sing," compares the prince's exploits to those of Arthur or Roland, presents the names of his companions in quasi-epic catalogs, dramatizes diplomatic exchanges between kings, gives his prayers and laments as direct addresses, berates Fortune, recounts his reception in England and Germany after great victories, and uses epithets suitable for a hero of romance. Chronicles of the first Thomas Beauchamp by Henry Knighton and Thomas Walsingham similarly recount his exploits as a hero of romance more than of history, and in the accounts through the later earls of Warwick, his fame depends more on the imagination of his chroniclers and descendants than on his successes in history. The descendants made of their ancestor model, "otherwise unattested in history," a hero in the manner of French and English romance.[2] What carries over into later sagas is the occasional tendency to treat protagonists as heroes of romance and include their trials and ordeals but within a realistic context.

During the Middle Ages and until early in the eighteenth century, the concept of family in English practice was based on the Latin concept *familia* as household or clan rather than on family in the sense of a conjugal group or even exclusively of a consanguine group. Family meant servants and retainers and all those living under the master's roof, though gradations of privilege obviously existed among retainers and within the master's kinship group. What was also part of the family was the house itself, which served as an index to the power and prestige of the family. Country houses were "power houses" where people lived who had power or who were reaching for power by taking on the accoutrements of power.[3] By the seventeenth century, the country house became the *topos* of several English poets who praised estates and their families and in the process admonished them to look to their heritage.

The genre of the country-house poem includes such works as "To Penshurst" and "To Sir Robert Wroth," by Ben Jonson, "A Panegerick to Sir Lewis Pemberton," by Robert Herrick, "To Saxham" and "To My

2. Theodore Andersson, "The Displacement of the Heroic Ideal in the Family Sagas," *Speculum*, XLV (1970), 593; Sumner Ferris, "Chronicle, Chivalric Biography, and Family Tradition in Fourteenth-Century England," *Studies in Medieval Culture*, XIV (1930), 29–36.

3. Mark Girouard, *Life in the English Country House* (New Haven, 1978), 312, 10, 2; Ian Watt, *Rise of the Novel* (Berkeley, 1957), 140.

Friend G. N. from Wrest," by Thomas Carew, and "Upon Appleton House," by Andrew Marvell. The conventions of these poems in many cases become protoconventions for southern family sagas and their immediate antecedents. Among them are (1) linkage of the country seat to the pastoral ideal, (2) a contrast between the natural architecture of the favored mansion and the architecture of a neighboring estate, seen as formal and artificial and indicative of the nonagrarian source of the neighboring master's wealth, (3) a call upon master and family of the estate to be responsible to their position as lord of the community, and (4) a vision of the continued fidelity and dignity of the family associated with the estate.[4]

In "To Penshurst" Ben Jonson invokes the good life of rural culture in contrast with the growing commercial economy of London and criticizes the outer society for its materialism and its departure from traditional agrarian virtues.[5] Among traditional virtues practiced at Penshurst, says Jonson, is hospitality, which once entertained a king hunting nearby but is also extended without reservation to lesser visitors like the poet himself. Thus he finds the master "whose liberal board doth flow/With all that hospitality doth know," this in contrast with the grudging hospitality of rich newcomers at "great men's tables"—men who compel guests "to sit . . . and yet dine away" on food different from what the host is eating. At Appleton House, as Marvell shows, Lord General Thomas Fairfax, retired from military service, enjoys the good life of lord of the manor and seclusion from the quarreling world outside.

The convention of contrasting the organically developed and natural country seat with its ostentatious neighbor grows out of the recognition that society has changed. Agriculture is no longer the basic source of wealth, and men who have made their fortunes elsewhere in commerce or coal mining or overseas trade now have their country gentry life.[6] Thus, Jonson contrasts the medieval English manor house with the Italianate architecture of the new rich. Penshurst is "an ancient pile" not "built to envious show,/Of touch [touchstone, expensive basalt], or marble; nor canst boast a row/Of polished pillars, or a roof of gold." At Appleton House Marvell similarly notes the house "was built upon the place/Only as for

4. William Alexander McClung, *The Country House in English Renaissance Poetry* (Berkeley, 1977), 18–19.

5. Richard Gill, *Happy Rural Seat: The English Country House and the Literary Imagination* (New Haven, 1972), 228.

6. McClung, *Country House,* 93, 19.

a mark of grace" and "all things are composed here / Like Nature, orderly and near." The modest house is filled with a great master in contrast with elaborate houses peopled with small men.

The duty of the denizens of these houses is not only to look after themselves and their retainers and lands but to furnish leadership for society—leadership that might fall by default to the nontraditional.[7] In "To Sir Robert Wroth" Jonson calls on Sir Robert to provide that guidance:

> To doe thy country service, thy self right;
> That neither want doe thee affright,
> Nor death; but when thy latest sand is spent,
> Thou maist thinke life, a thing but lent.

Marvell celebrates the Fairfax founder "Who, when retired here to peace, / His warlike studies could not cease" but planted gardens in the shape of his forts to extend order on the local level.

To writers of these country-house poems, the families themselves were extensions of the order and tradition associated with the houses, and the poets envision the continuity of generations in these places. At Penshurst Jonson sees that "His children thy great lord may call his own, / A fortune in this age but rarely known." In the generations of children he sees again the contrast between the enduring estate and the ostentatiously new:

> Now, Penshurst, they that will proportion [compare] thee
> With other edifices, when they see
> Those proud, ambitious heaps, and nothing else,
> May say their lords have built, but thy lord dwells.

At Appleton House Marvell sees the Fairfax daughter Maria as the appropriate heir and continuant of the line. At one with nature in the fields and garden, "Tis she that to these gardens gave / That wondrous beauty which they have," and she is trained in her role "Under the discipline severe / Of Fairfax, and the starry Vere" to supply "beyond her sex the line" of descendant Fairfaxes.

Country-estate poems of the eighteenth century, however, did not continue the genre in its pure form. In such pieces as Alexander Pope's "Epistle to Burlington" and "Epistle to Bathurst," Joseph Hall's Satire V, 2, and Charles Cotton's lines on Chatsworth in *The Wonders of Peake*, the contrast between the antique natural estate and the pretentious new

7. Girouard, *Life in the English Country House*, 5.

one was abandoned in favor of praising new mansions, and though in "Epistle to Bathurst" Pope scorns grudging hospitality, he sees country life as a "touchstone of moderation and the proper employment of resources." The country house rather became the subject as well as the setting of novels in the eighteenth century and early nineteenth century and, as setting and subject, was often treated symbolically. At Grandison Hall in Samuel Richardson's *Sir Charles Grandison*, the generous rooms and lawns reflect the character of Sir Charles; in *Tom Jones* Henry Fielding contrasts by absence of description Squire Western's place with Squire Allworthy's venerable and oak-sheltered home, more notable for nature than for art.[8] By the time of Jane Austen, the country home reflects a society in transition, where estates change owners by purchase as much as by succession and are supported by external wealth as much as by agriculture. In that time of flux, holders of country houses try to judge themselves by an inherited agrarian code while living according to a commercial ethic. In Austen's world, improving the estate means decorative development of the houses, parks, and landscapes more than improvement of the economy of the estate.[9] In *Mansfield Park*, for example, Henry Crawford's proposed improvement of Mr. Rushworth's gardens while Sir Thomas Bertram is away inspecting his properties in Antigua becomes a test of the good sense and fidelity of several characters at Mansfield Park. By the time of William Makepeace Thackeray's *Henry Esmond* at midcentury, its setting, Castlewood Hall, becomes the locus of changing relationships among the characters. His *Virginians* almost a decade later continues the chronicle of the family in a colonial Castlewood Hall at the time of the struggle for independence. Significantly, Thackeray consulted with southerner John Pendleton Kennedy as he prepared to write the second volume of the novel.[10]

For southern writers, though, the way to the family saga led through the country-house sketches on Sir Roger de Coverley by Joseph Addison and the romances of Sir Walter Scott. The Sir Roger sketches led to Washington Irving's *Sketch Book* and *Bracebridge Hall* and on to Kennedy's *Swallow Barn*. Scott's romances were the obvious and acknowledged models for William Alexander Caruthers' chivalric romances of early Virginia.

8. McClung, *Country House*, 175–78; Gill, *Happy Rural Seat*, 232–34.

9. Raymond Williams, *The Country and the City* (New York, 1973), 115–16.

10. Gill, *Happy Rural Seat*, 250; Jay B. Hubbell, *The South in American Literature, 1607–1900* (Durham, 1954), 459.

Kennedy and Caruthers were, as Francis Pendleton Gaines notes, beginners of the two principal traditions in nineteenth-century southern writing.[11] Although the chief descriptive or narrative interest in such works is in the present, the present activity occurs with knowledge of long family backgrounds as a dimension of the present, and protagonists typically refer to ancestors as guides, models, or warnings.

The *Spectator* papers on Sir Roger de Coverley incorporate from the beginning what is to become a convention of the family saga: appearing in Number 1 as chronicler and observer is Mr. Spectator, who speaks little, writes daily, and lives as a watcher of other people's lives rather than as an actor in them. In Number 2, the observed at his club is Sir Roger, baronet and gentleman of ancient descent in Worcestershire and now justice of the quorum at quarter sessions. During the month Spectator spends at Sir Roger's country estate, he observes and describes in Number 106 the good life of this country gentleman, including a tour through the portrait gallery. During this tour, recounted in Number 109, Sir Roger traces modifications in dress by his ancestors, contrasts his great-grandmother's petticoats to his grandmother's and later ancestresses' hoop skirts, points to the portrait of the ancestor who was the last man to win a prize in the Tiltyard, and tells the family story of this ancestor's delivering his fallen adversary to the adversary's mistress and finally the story of Sir Humphrey de Coverley, who missed death in the Civil War battle of Worcester because he "was sent out of the field upon a private message." The practice of collecting portraits became fashionable in the sixteenth century, and portrait galleries became status symbols as well as useful counters in the power game.[12]

Although it is derivative of English manner and subject, Irving's *Bracebridge Hall,* published in 1821, with the second edition appearing in 1826, makes the transatlantic leap and serves as a clear transition between English country-house writing and southern plantation lore. Now the spectator has become Geoffrey Crayon, Gent., who visits Bracebridge Hall in Yorkshire during the post-Napoleonic years to attend the wedding of Squire Frank Bracebridge's son Captain Guy to the squire's ward, Julia Templeton. During the season-long visit, Crayon savors the country life, learns the views of the squire and the history of the squire's family, and, like the country-house poets, sees the contrast between old families and new

11. Francis Pendleton Gaines, *The Southern Plantation* (New York, 1924), 18.
12. Girouard, *Life in the English Country House,* 101–102.

arrivals. Like its master, Bracebridge Hall is in the old style, "an irregular building of some magnitude" and of "the architecture of different periods." [13] As in the country-house poems, this natural house is contrasted with the house of neighboring, newly rich Mr. Faddy, who made his fortune in manufacturing, "retired from business, and set up for a country gentleman." He has refitted an old country place "until it looks not unlike his own manufactory," is jealous of trespassers, and practices inhospitality (166). As did Spectator, Crayon makes his tour of the family portrait gallery, guided here by the housekeeper, hears "a complete family chronicle," and detects changes in the ancestors from generation to generation (16, 26–27).

Drawing attention to the motif of family decline, Crayon sees the good life of country gentlemen like Frank Bracebridge doomed by the coming new rich. Too many such estates, he recognizes, are in the hands of creditors, and the estates' masters, the victims of political intrigues or their own extravagances. "A little while hence, and all these will probably have passed away. . . . The good squire, and all his peculiarities, will be buried in the neighbouring church. The old Hall will be modernized into a fashionable country-seat, or peradventure a manufactory. The park will be cut up into pretty farms and kitchen gardens . . . and all the other hearty merrymakings of the 'good old time' will be forgotten" (160–61, 307).

Despite Crayon's misgivings, country-house life did not so much disappear as transform itself in England into a link between the old order and the new commercial era, and in the American South it became the model for the plantation legend, of which Kennedy's 1832 *Swallow Barn* was both the first example and the model for those coming later. Prototypes for Kennedy's Frank Meriwether were Addison's Sir Roger de Coverley, Fielding's Squire Allworthy and Squire Western, and especially Irving's Squire Bracebridge. The English squire was "one of the few English traditions regarded affectionately by Americans." [14] More than that, the image of the country house and its squire continued the advance toward the family saga in the South, furnishing secondary motifs that would become primary conventions.

Kennedy's Swallow Barn plantation drew on *Bracebridge Hall,* and as his journals and early manuscripts indicate, his original plan was to write

13. Washington Irving, *Bracebridge Hall, or The Humourists,* ed. Herbert F. Smith (1821; rpr. Boston, 1978), 161.

14. William R. Taylor, *Cavalier and Yankee: The Old South and American National Character* (New York, 1961), 150.

a series of sketches on the country life of western Virginia with his narrator a Geoffrey Crayon-like painter. But his ideas changed as he wrote and his purpose became clearer. By 1829 it was evident to him that his subject was the tidewater plantation, with Frank Meriwether its squire, all seen by the visiting New York cousin Mark Littleton.[15]

As with narrators of later family sagas, Mark Littleton is conscious of his role as observer and chronicler. He reports on witnessed experiences at Swallow Barn, but as the love and legal complications thicken between Swallow Barn and The Brakes, where neighboring Isaac and Bel Tracy live, he is conscientious in accounting, in mock-serious fashion, for his sources on what went on beyond his observation: "I rely mainly on my contemporary Harvey [Riggs], as authority for such synchronous events as transpired at The Brakes. . . . In this I do but imitate and follow in the footsteps of all the illustrious chroniclers of the world, who have made it their business to speak primarily of what they themselves have seen and known, and secondarily, to take at second-hand, (judiciously perpending the force of testimony,) such things as have come to them by hearsay." [16] As he further suggests, such reports often reflect the teller as much as the tale.

Like the celebrators of seventeenth-century country houses, he contrasts his host's house with its neighbor; however, the contrast is not between the old and new but between two old mansions, one natural and informal, the other formal and rigid, both symbolic of their masters. Frank Meriwether, a relaxed, grayly handsome man at forty-five, genial husband and father of a growing brood, good manager of his affairs but reluctant to become harassed in public service, a Democrat full of newspaper opinions on political matters but fuzzy on religious questions, and easy master of his slaves, lives in a "time-honored mansion, more than a century old . . . an aristocratical old edifice" that is "built in defiance of all laws of congruity, just as convenience required" (27–28). At The Brakes lives Isaac Tracy, a seventy-year-old widower, a Tory once, and a tall and emaciated adherent of "the ancient costume," so formal that "his household is conducted with a degree of precision that throws a certain air of stateliness over the whole family" (77). His house is a "large plain building, with wings built in exact uniformity" of dark brick and with little embellish-

15. Joseph V. Ridgely, *John Pendleton Kennedy* (New York, 1966), 36–37.
16. John Pendleton Kennedy, *Swallow Barn, or A Sojourn in the Old Dominion* (Rev. ed.; New York, 1852), 375.

ment. The effect, says Littleton, is no more than that of a "sober, capacious and gentlemanlike mansion" (76–77).

The lawsuit that divides these opposite-tempered but congenial neighbors shows the force of the past on the present. A dispute dividing families and lands for generations, it began three-quarters of a century earlier, and its cause is signalized daily in the two portraits at Swallow Barn of old Edward Hazard, grandfather of Ned Hazard. One portrait shows him at twenty, conceited, in an embroidered waistcoat, cravat, and silk stockings. The other, taken at midlife, shows a waggish face, and together they sum up the career of a profligate and eccentric ancestor who left to his descendants the puzzle of undoing his errors. Having spent a considerable portion of his life in England, he returned to his patrimony Swallow Barn with enthusiastic but ill-considered schemes to increase his fortune. One such scheme was to dam Apple Pie Branch between Swallow Barn and The Brakes and build a grist mill. He agreed with Gilbert Tracy to purchase swampland that would be flooded by the pond, with the stated purpose of providing a pond for the mill. But the dammed pond held only enough water to run the mill for two hours: "It was like a profligate spendthrift whose prodigality exceeds his income." The mill was abandoned, the dam left to rot and be washed away by a storm. After Edward died and his successor Walter Hazard drained the swamp to provide pasture for his cattle, Isaac claimed that the land sold by Gilbert reverted to him because it was no longer used for the stipulated purpose of a mill pond. The case had gone through county court, superior court, court of appeals, and chancery court, each decision in favor of the Hazards, before Walter died and left the suit to his heirs. For Isaac, the worthless land involves "a question affecting family dignity," and winning the suit has become his aim in life (130–50).

The family dispute and lawsuit are further complicated by another protoconvention of the family saga: displacement of the inheritance. With his marriage to Lucretia Hazard, Frank Meriwether has become inheritor of the dispute. Having "lifted some gentlemanlike encumbrances which had been sleeping for years upon the domain," he has been "inducted into the proprietary rights" of Swallow Barn, and the "adjacency of his own estate gave a territorial feature to this alliance" (27). His Gordian plan is to surrender the disputed land by technical and confusing legal maneuvers without appearing to do so and thus give Isaac the illusion of having at last won his suit.

The families having been reconciled by comic manipulations of clever lawyers such as Philpot Wart, Kennedy could also follow the convention of relating the Hazard-Meriwether family to history. In the age of Andrew Jackson, he must ponder the relation of the local family holding to the debate between states' rights and national authority and also question the emancipation of slaves (164). Like the reconciliation of families in the comedy of manners, the resolution of the slavery question comes with the conversion of Mark Littleton, external challenger to the plantation code: "The contrast between my preconception of [the slaves'] condition and the reality which I have witnessed, has brought me to a most agreeable surprise." Under present conditions, he finds them "happier" than they would be under immediate emancipation (452–53). It was a conclusion with which writers of sagas later would have to come to terms.

The other line in the genealogy of southern family sagas, the historical romance in the tradition of Sir Walter Scott, came into southern writing with the cavalier romances of William Alexander Caruthers during the same decade Kennedy produced *Swallow Barn*. Caruthers' emphasis on family traditions in *The Cavaliers of Virginia,* in 1834, and *The Knights of the Golden Horseshoe,* published in 1841 and again in 1846, put his romances directly in line with the developing family sagas. After *Waverley* was published in 1814, Scott's romances brought the life and manners of ancient households into the main line of English fiction and soon into American fiction as well. Caruthers' own testimony in *The Knights of the Golden Horseshoe* confirms that he had learned to see with Scott's eyes: "We thank God that we have lived in the days when those tales of witchery and romance were sent forth from Abbotsford, to cheer the desponding hearts of thousands, and tens of thousands. He not only threw a romantic charm around the scenes of his stories, but he actually made the world we live in more lovely in our eyes. The visions which his magic wand created before our youthful eyes, rise up in every hill and vale in our own bright and favored land." [17]

As a writer of historical romances, Caruthers also had to deal with problems soon to confront writers of family sagas. He had to write of historical times so that the reader participates emotionally in historical scenes rather than knowing them only as intellectual constructs in the manner

17. Gill, *Happy Rural Seat,* 242–43; William Alexander Caruthers, *The Knights of the Golden Horseshoe: A Traditionary Tale of the Cocked Hat Gentry* (1845; rpr. Chapel Hill, 1970), 205; William Alexander Caruthers, *The Cavaliers of Virginia, or The Recluse of Jamestown* (1834; rpr. Ridgewood, N.J., 1968).

of the historian, and he had to interpret past life in light of his own time and knowledge. The contemporary pressures to which Caruthers responded included recognition in the 1830s that Virginia had been in decline since the Revolution because of depleted soil and anti-entailment laws and because many Virginia planters had removed to the opening Old Southwest for better land. Left behind were a number of new rich, former overseers, who, in changing the meaning of *cavalier* from political to social terms, began to look for distinguished ancestors and make claims to descent from the original two hundred Cavaliers. In the process they combined the plantation and cavalier traditions, rejected Revolutionary leaders as models, and turned to earlier and presumably better times as they cultivated the myth of the Cavaliers.[18]

In *The Cavaliers of Virginia* and *The Knights of the Golden Horseshoe,* Caruthers cultivates the mystique of the old families in pre-Revolutionary times and links that mystique with expansionist visions of the early nineteenth century. In *The Cavaliers* he relates in a mixture of history and fiction the episode of Bacon's Rebellion in the 1670s: Nathaniel Bacon's insurrection against the policies of Governor Sir William Berkeley to keep Jamestown settlers limited to coastal settlements to avoid conflicts with Indian tribes and to block colonists from their expansionist destinies. In Caruthers' myth, Bacon's service to the colony is linked with the revelation of his identity as a true cavalier. In *The Knights of the Golden Horseshoe,* Caruthers' purpose is to chronicle the first expedition to the Shenandoah Valley during the second decade of the eighteenth century as a first step to continental expansion and to make that venture the authentication of claims of the later first families of Virginia, whose ancestors were those semilegendary knights, among whom was his hero Henry Hall, known, after the revelation of his true identity, as Frank Lee.

In *The Cavaliers* Nathaniel Bacon is the ward of Gideon Fairfax, confidant of Governor Berkeley, and a man of uncertain ancestry. So clouded is his parentage that at the climax of volume one his marriage to Virginia Fairfax is forbidden by the mysterious Recluse, one of the regicides of Charles I, who claims that Nathaniel and Virginia have the same mother, Emily Fairfax. During the English Civil War, she, though a daughter of a royalist family, had eloped with a commonwealth officer, had a son by him,

18. Avrom Fleishman, *The English Historical Novel: Walter Scott to Virginia Woolf* (Baltimore, 1971), 13, 15; Curtis Carroll Davis, *Chronicler of the Cavaliers: A Life of the Virginia Novelist Dr. William A. Caruthers* (Richmond, 1953), 131–34.

lost him to the machinations of her family, and later married Gideon Fairfax when her husband was reported killed in battle. Not until later is it revealed that Nathaniel is the son not of the commonwealth officer but of
another, brought to the New World in secrecy with Emily's son and
saved when Emily's son died in a shipwreck. In effect, Nathaniel is the product of the best of both cavalier and commonwealth traditions, but a cavalier by training, as he shows when he leads the people in putting down the
uprising of a roundhead group at Jamestown.

During the confusion surrounding Nathaniel's ancestry and his being
prohibited by civil and canon law from marrying Virginia, Governor Berkeley insists that she marry Frank Beverly according to an agreement "settled
for years" between himself and her father and kept secret until Frank came
of age. In her appeal as a kinswoman of Sir William to set aside the
agreement, Virginia utters heresy in her objection to valuing the demands
of aristocratic families over the individuality of their members. In their
pride, she says, such families and their patriarchs act out of selfishness in
the name of the family, and marriages "are generally valued in propor-
tion to their ability to confer honour upon the common stock." In effect,
Caruthers here imposes nineteenth-century middle-class values on aristocratic families of the eighteenth century.

After he has led the campaign against the Indian confederation, defeated it at the falls of the James River, and been arrested by the governor's
party, at his trial for treason Nathaniel Bacon invokes history past and future in his defense. Echoing the sentiments that justified Indian removals
under Jackson in Caruthers' day, Bacon claims he has been "but an hum-
ble instrument in the hands of the Great Mover of these mighty currents"
and is among the first to point out "the importance of drawing a broad
line of separation between the European and the native, the first to show
the necessity of rolling to the west the savage hordes, as the swelling number of our own countrymen increase upon our hands" (II, 179–80). Death
for him as an individual will not "arrest the great movement," he says.

His success with *The Cavaliers* prompted Caruthers to exploit the cavalier myth further in *The Knights,* the project he first called *The Tramon-
tane Order.* Although the principal narrative of *The Knights* concerns Governor Alexander Spotswood's attempts to persuade the Crown and the
burgesses to support his proposed expedition "beyond the mountains,"
the expedition itself meant for his readers that the great names of Virginia
families had authenticated their distinction by participating in the expe-

dition. That they were serving purposes beyond themselves becomes clear in Spotswood's speech to the burgesses. Although it sounds as if they are going all the way to the Mississippi River or perhaps even the Pacific Ocean instead of just to the Shenandoah, Spotswood sounds the call to what would in a decade be called Manifest Destiny and to saving the continent for Americans:

> It is needless to disguise that from this time forward, there is to be a contest for supremacy on this continent. . . . Thus far, the race has been equal, or nearly so; now, however, Virginia holds in her hands the pass, the key, the gates of the mightiest empire ever conceived of by the most towering ambition. Is she to close this entrance of the world to the Far West—to suppress the energies of our race—to stifle the great onward enterprises, upon the threshold of which we have barely entered[?] (123)

Caruthers then presents the Cavaliers as the openers of empire, and in Spotswood's roll of honor after the expedition, the first names of Virginia stand foremost: Lee, Wormly, Page, Randolph, Peyton, Bland, Beverly, Harrison, Yelverton, Byrd, Fitzhugh, Fairfax, Dandridge, Carter, Washington, Taylor, Nott, Pendleton, Wythe, and Munroe, among others, an epic catalog for future generations (245). After the expedition, Spotswood presents golden horseshoes to the veterans in recognition of their exploit and as a memorial for their descendants. Made in recognition of their discovery that on the rocky terrain of the Blue Ridge Mountains their unshod tidewater horses, used to sandy soil, would need shoes, the golden horseshoes become talismanic objects during the governor's presentation: "You may wear them, gentlemen, through long and happy lives, and when you descend honored and lamented to your graves, may they descend as heirlooms to your children. . . . The simple words which form the inscription may some day reveal the history of a portion of our country and its honored founders, when the revolutions of empires and the passing away of generations, may have submerged every other record" (245). The inscription is "Sic juvat transcendere montes" (Thus does he rejoice to cross the mountains).[19]

The dynastic imperative prevails in motivations of the protagonist Henry Hall as well, for his chief concern is to establish himself as the true claimant of his heritage and name as Frank Lee. Although he enters

19. Curtis Carroll Davis, Introduction in Caruthers, *Knights,* xx.

the narrative tainted by involvement in the antiroyalist intrigue of General Sir Gilbert Elliot (half-brother to Governor Spotswood) in Scotland, Henry Hall must stand before his peers and cite his genealogy as Frank Lee, "to name the place of his family residence in Scotland, as well as to describe his living relations and their descent from the common stock of the Halls of ——— shire," and to trace "the collateral branch which had emigrated to America some fifty years before," all accompanied by his pardon from the new Hanoverian king (53, 163). He also has to deal with the problem of a displaced inheritance as he offers mercy and exile to the false claimant Henry Lee: if Henry will leave the colony, he will be forgiven the drafts he has made on Frank Lee's property and not be forced to sell his own to repay the debt (203). Thus, Frank Lee rejoices to establish the legend of generosity in the cavalier tradition.

As in his earlier novel, Caruthers treats history in *The Knights* in a high-handed manner. Not only is history the matrix of his dynastic narrative; it is reshaped as well to fit the narrative. His historical accuracy lies chiefly in matters of costume, in generic scenes of plantation life, and in the physical description of Williamsburg. But as with later writers of sagas, he can also impose contemporary concerns on earlier times. He reflects Virginia's much-debated interest in some form of emancipation when he has Frank Lee enjoin Henry Lee to free the slave Caesar upon his return to England (203), when he echoes the 1830s sentimental crusade against alcohol in Kate Spotswood's early eighteenth-century denunciations of wine and rum, and when he responds to the growing sentiment against dueling in Ellen Evylin's warning to Frank Lee that she "could never *accept that hand in marriage,* which has been previously stained by the blood of a fellow-being—shed in single combat, and in cold blood." [20] Although he maintains an omniscient authorial prerogative, like the narrators of later sagas, Caruthers also links himself with the narrative when he observes that among the Knights first settling the Shenandoah were "our own ancestors" (242).

When George Washington Cable's *The Grandissimes* was published in book form in 1880 after serial publication in *Scribner's Magazine* the preceding year, reviewers welcomed it as the saga of a Creole family reaching back to the earliest days of Louisiana. With the perspective that book publication allowed, the *Atlantic Monthly* saw that "the author has con-

20. Curtis Carroll Davis, *Chronicler of the Cavaliers,* 208–11, 332; Caruthers, *Knights of the Golden Horseshoe,* 217.

ceived, with a classic sense, the immense reach of a proud family," that "he has constructed a House of Grandissimes." In his review for *The Nation,* William Brownell similarly advised readers of the novel in serial form to reread it as a book in order to see perspectives missed earlier: "For one thing, the genealogies, which may have seemed confused heretofore, not only clear up but add an important element to the general effect; you feel the ancient and honorable character of the Grandissime and De Grapion ancestry, appreciate the strength of family feeling better, excuse its concomitant excesses more readily, and, perhaps more than all, through the appeal of this hazy past to the imagination, get a quicker sense of the reality of the different persons who have emerged from it." [21] In *The Grandissimes* Cable also faces up to that significant fact about many southern families that made them different: there is also a black line running with the white, and the family saga has to recognize them both.

The Grandissimes shows an author seized by history and capable of condensing history into a saga of a family. Cable began his fiction writing after exploring the Louisiana archives to find material on "the colonial history of Louisiana." [22] Out of that fund of history, he wrote the stories later to be collected in *Old Creole Days,* published in 1879. Most of those stories show incipient family sagas, reaching back to the earliest days of the colony. If the action of the story is in the present, the resonances come from a sense of a family past seen in the context of biblical family sagas.

In "Belles Demoiselles Plantation," for example, to understand the present actions of Colonel De Charleu and Injin Charlie, it is essential to know of the past of the De Charleu family, that the original Count De Charleu left behind a Choctaw wife when he was recalled to France to explain the loss of commissary records in a fire, that he conveniently forgot his Choctaw comptesse and half-caste orphan child and married a French gentlewoman, and that back in Louisiana he remembered the other branch of his family in time to recognize them in his will. Through the generations the *pur sang* branch rose "tall, branchless, slender, palm-like," while the "narrow, thread-like line of descent from the Indian wife, diminished to a mere strand" and the remaining survivor "was known to all, and known only, as Injin Charlie." [23] What endures in both branches is

21. Arlin Turner, ed., *Critical Essays on George W. Cable* (Boston, 1980), 15; William C. Brownell, "Cable's *The Grandissimes,*" in *Critical Essays on Cable,* ed. Turner, 18.

22. Arlin Turner, ed., *The Negro Question* (Garden City, N.Y., 1958), 12.

23. George Washington Cable, *Old Creole Days: A Story of Creole Life* (1879; rpr. New York, 1957), 123.

the sense of family. The colonel "will not utterly go back on the ties of blood, no matter what sort of knots those ties may be," and "he is never ashamed of his or his father's sins" (124). Charlie similarly feels that if he denies the claims of his "good blood," he will have lost his last shred of salvation. That "same ancestral nonsense" finally makes the colonel and Charlie act in the present according to their vision of family past.

Jean Poquelin similarly is recognized as "the last of his line" and inheritor of a past embodied in the heavy cypress Poquelin house, "grim, solid, and spiritless, its massive build a strong reminder of days still earlier, when every man had been his own peace officer and the insurrection of blacks a daily contingency" (179). That Poesque image of the past becomes important for Honoré Grandissime later, after he has restored the Fausse Rivière plantation to the Nancanou women, when he takes his desolate walk through the open plain beyond the city and contemplates the effects of his action on fortunes of the family. There he sees the sun setting ominously in the cypress and "the old house and willow-copse of Jean Poquelin." [24] In the context of these images of decay, he meditates on the possible dissolution of the Grandissimes. Like the Grandissimes and Don José Martinez, Jean and Jacques Poquelin pass through a transition period in the economic history of Louisiana, the time when indigo culture fails and "certain enterprising men . . . substitute[d] the culture of sugar" (181). The story is also useful later for *The Grandissimes* in focusing the present generation's conflict on differences between Anglo and Creole cultures and in evoking differences between the values of earlier and those of later generations. Not least, the story "Jean-ah Poquelin" introduces through the legends about Jean the issue of witchlore and voodoo, important to Palmyre, Dark Honoré, and Agricola in the novel.

When the editors at Scribner suggested to Cable in 1877 that it was time for him to write a novel if he expected to make his way as a writer, he turned to his former work as material he could develop into a full-sized novel. Among other materials, he returned to his earlier story "Bibi" to construct his story of Bras-Coupé, the centerpiece of *The Grandissimes*. The story of a semilegendary African rebel that he had been unable to publish in the early 1870s because editors thought it "too distressful" for their family magazines he made so essential a part of the novel that it could not be deleted. In particular, he tied it to the fortunes of the Grandissimes,

---

24. George Washington Cable, *The Grandissimes: A Story of Creole Life* (1880; rpr. New York, 1957), 263.

Fusiliers, and De Grapions as the explanation from the past for their present predicament.

In addition to his own earlier writings, Cable went back to Genesis for an older, more authoritative model for his account of the generations. His knowledge and use of the Bible are well documented. With the Genesis example and its conventions (continuity, removal, the special attribute, the displaced inheritance, the narrator-historian, the context of history, dynastic decline, perplexity over the actions of earlier generations, the patriarchal-matriarchal conflict, type scenes, talismanic objects and places and actions, and moments of vision), Cable planned and began writing his saga of the Grandissimes. That he began by writing of the earlier generations first is suggested by exchanges of memoranda with the Scribner offices. Robert Underwood Johnson, in whose hands the Cable project had been placed, decreed that the novel should begin in the present and called on Cable to shift the genealogical background chapters until later. After Cable had done so, Johnson wrote him on July 28, 1879, that the revision had been accepted and that "the first five chapters will make an excellent first installment, well rounded and leaving the interest where it should be—fixed on the meeting of Frowenfeld and the Nancanous." [25]

As is evident from the beginning of the novel, however, Cable did not entirely abandon family background as an introduction to present action. In his first chapter, on the September masquerade ball at the Theatre St. Philippe, he depicts characters in the present action in costumes suggesting the family past and hinting at identities and relationships from the past to be discovered and explained in the present: the Indian Queen, the Dragoon, the Monk, and the Fille a la Casette (or "casket girl" because the Huguenot refugee came to Louisiana with all her belongings in a small casket-trunk). In the process of Dr. Charles Keene's recounting the stories of the Indian queen, of the young dragoons who later became patriarchs of families, of the fille a la casette, all told to Joseph Frowenfeld as he recuperates from yellow fever—Cable also invoked the convention of the collector of the family tradition. As the reviewer for the *Atlantic Monthly* saw early, Joseph's role is that of chorus: "For though his action occa-

25. Arlin Turner, *George W. Cable: A Biography* (Baton Rouge, 1966), 30, 38, *passim;* Martha H. Morehead, "George W. Cable's Use of the Bible in His Fiction and Major Polemical Essays" (Ph.D. dissertation, University of North Carolina, Greensboro, 1980), 118–248; Kjell Ekström, *George W. Cable: A Study of His Early Life and Work* (Cambridge, Mass., 1950), 61.

sionally affects the story, his chief function is to ask questions and bring out prior conditions, and, especially, as we have hinted, to be the external conscience."[26] Dr. Keene's story to him, then, is one of family beginnings and family destiny, as Cable's persona-narrator observes: "For in the midst of the mist Frowenfeld encountered and grappled a problem of human life in Creole type, the possible correlations of whose quantities we shall presently find him revolving in a studious and sympathetic mind. . . . The quantities in that problem were the ancestral—the maternal-roots of those two rival and hostile families whose descendants—some brave, others fair— we find unwittingly thrown together at the ball" (14).

Dr. Keene's account is the story of the first generations—of the Indian queen Lufki-Huma and her meeting with the lost hunters Zephyr Grandissime and Epaminondas Fusilier, of the rivalry for her at Biloxi with Fusilier winning over Demosthenes De Grapion by a throw of the dice, of Georges De Grapion later marrying the fille a la casette and starting a line of single heirs in each generation, and of Grandissime marrying a woman of rank and starting a burgeoning lineage. In the process Keene establishes that the Grandissime, Fusilier, and De Grapion families as they exist in saga date from their removal to Louisiana in the 1670s.

Not until Chapter 18 and Dark Honoré's call on Frowenfeld is more of the explanatory past revealed. Here Dark Honoré tells of his father's career. Numa Grandissime supported law against chaotic revolt during the cession of Louisiana to Spain, took a quadroon mistress who had Dark Honoré by him, then submitted to family demands and married Agricola Fusilier's sister to keep peace and an earlier promise between families, begot both White Honoré and his twin sister, who was later to marry Don José Martinez, and educated both of his sons in France. To his older son he left the bulk of his property, and to his younger son, the duty "to right the wrongs which he had not quite dared to uproot" (108–109). Then Frowenfeld the discoverer has to wait until his call upon Aurora and Clotilde in Chapter 25 to learn the background of Palmyre and her relationship to Aurora and to White Honoré and of Aurora's relationship with the woman in the wall portrait, her ancestor, the fille a la casette.

Frowenfeld's discovery of the predicament of the present generation comes in his several talks with the two Honorés. His knowledge of the recent Nancanou-De Grapion past comes from Dr. Keene's story of the duel between Agricola and Aurora's husband (30–33). In any case, Frowenfeld

---

26. Turner, ed., *Critical Essays on Cable*, 14.

the discoverer, allied to the Grandissime-Fusilier-De Grapion families but not part of that line until his marriage to Clotilde, has, to himself and to the reader, accounted for the founding generations and, with a possible skip in generations among the Grandissimes and Fusiliers, the grandparental, the parental, and the present generations of the families.

In the process he also discovers the special attribute of the families: the paradoxical pride in family first, above all civil laws or ethical considerations, and the family's pride in purity of lineage despite their equal pride in Lufki-Huma as a maternal ancestor. It is completely in character, then, that Agricola can declare to Frowenfeld that family tradition is more authentic than history (19). After recounting Agricola's killing of Aurora's husband in the duel, Agricola's offer to return Fausse Rivière plantation to Aurora if she will concede the estate was won fairly in their wager, and her refusal to concede a point of honor, Keene reminds Frowenfeld that such Creoles are capable of "this same preposterous, apathetic, fantastic, suicidal pride . . . as lethargic and ferocious as an alligator" (32). That kind of pride manifests itself in Raoul's statement, after Frowenfeld has been hit on the head by Palmyre's Congo woman and seen by sneering Creoles as he comes from Palmyre's, that scars are part of being a gentleman (210) and in Agricola's observation that the man, not law, makes the crime (227). In his role as high priest of family pride, Agricola can offer Frowenfeld absolution for whatever peccadilloes he has committed: "If the different grades of race and society did not have corresponding moral and civil liberties, varying in degrees as they vary—h-why! *this* community at least would go to pieces!" In the name of instinct, "that guide of the nobly proud," he pronounces Frowenfeld "not guilty," and, like a priest, he says, "*absolvo te!*" (227). Honoré must similarly admit to Frowenfeld that claims of family pride prevent him from risking his position by questioning the system: "I am afraid to go deeply into anything, lest it should make ruin in my name, my family, my property" (154).

Part of Honoré's predicament comes from the displaced inheritance. The pride that insisted Numa Grandissime could not keep the quadroon mistress he loved also prompted him to leave his name as well as the bulk of his fortune to his illegitimate son Dark Honoré. The confusion of the two Honorés in the present action serves as a constant reminder of the displaced inheritance. Name, status, and fortune are all separated by the displacement, and not until the two brothers are reunited in recognition and fortune is the inheritance reclaimed.

That the family history is an index to the public history of its time is evident in Numa Grandissime's leadership of the peace party during the cession of Louisiana to Spain in the 1760s and in Honoré's leadership in the party of reconciliation during the cession to the United States in 1803 and 1804. In the present action of the novel, the scene at the Place d'Arms in Chapter 15 mixes members of the family with historical personages in a quasi-epic catalog of names: Sebastian de Casa Calvo of diplomatic fame, the intriguer for territory and trade Daniel Clark, "Julian Poydras, godfather of orphan girls," colonial prefect Laussat, conspirator James Wilkinson, former intendent Morales, and among them "Grandissimes simple and Grandissimes compound; Brahmins, Mandarins, and Fusiliers" (79–80). Also within the context of history are members of the divided family working at cross-purposes. Honoré advises Governor William Claiborne how to involve other Creoles in the new government (94), and Agricola harangues the Creoles with denunciations of the United States, of Governor Claiborne, of the English language, and of the fraudulent cession of French citizens to a claptrap Yankee government (48–51).

A part of history that is also part of local color in the novel is the family's surreptitious participation in voodoo practices. Voodoo lore becomes crucial in the family when Palmyre, through the agency of Clemence, leaves fetishes at Agricola's apartment to exact vengeance when bullets and knives have failed (307–309, 313). However specious its connection, voodoo is also linked with the larger economic life of the province. Whether because of or following Bras-Coupé's curse on Don José and his possessions, the indigo crops fail season after season and prompt a change in agriculture. "Providence raised up Etienne de Boré," who taught the planters to raise sugar cane instead of indigo (184–88), and the history of the province and the family takes a new direction.

The motif of greater nobility in past generations and the decline of later generations is closely linked in *The Grandissimes* with the inherited family attribute. Among the De Grapions, the young dragoon who married the fille a la casette began a long line of single heirs, "brilliant, gallant, much-loved, early-epauleted fellows" who married young and begot heirs quickly but whose pride made them "such inveterate duelists" that "the avowed name of De Grapion has become less and less frequent in the lists" of leading citizens (23). By Aurora's time she must recognize "we have no more men left to fight" for the family honor (121). Among the Fusiliers were "fierce-eyed, strong-beaked, dark, heavy-taloned birds, who, if they could not sing, were of such rich plumage, and could talk and bite, and strike, and keep up a ruffled crest and a self-exalting bad humor" (23). Agricola at the end of that line appears even to sympathetic Charles Keene as an atavistic regression from the intellectual to the physical: "Now, old Agricola shows the downward grade better. Seventy-five, if he is a day, with, maybe, one-fourth the attainments he pretends to have, and still less good sense; but strong—as an orang-outang" (101).

Only the Grandissimes, in selected instances, have maintained numbers and quality. From the rollicking Zephyr and his gentlewoman has come the "many-stranded family line so free from knots and kinks," with descendants "for the most part fine of stature, strong of limb and fair of face" (22). And though Numa suffered a failure of nerve in his decision not to defy the family and keep his much-loved quadroon mistress, in White Honoré Charles Keene can see the culmination of a long progressive development among the Grandissimes: "I have an idea that their greatness began, hundreds of years ago, in ponderosity of arm,—of frame, say, and developed from generation to generation, in a rising scale, first into power of mind, then into subtleties of genius. . . . Look at Honoré: he is high up on the scale, intellectual and sagacious. But look at him physically too. What an exquisite mould! . . . He is the flower of the family, and possibly the last one" (101).

As a member of the later generation, or an ally of the family, who recovers the accounts of earlier generations, Frowenfeld also has to confront and puzzle over the values and motives of the matriarchs and patriarchs. He is aided by Raoul Innerarity, whose explanations become "a key, a lamp, a lexicon, a microscope, a tabulated statement, a book of heraldry . . . a Creole *veritas*" and whose words "elucidate the mysteries," even though Frowenfeld soon learns to discount Raoul's statements about the antiquity of the families (118–19). In the process, Frowenfeld, Raoul, and the younger Grandissimes learn to doubt the values of their elders. When Frowenfeld asks Agricola to renounce his duel with Sylvestre, Raoul seconds the appeal (230). After Frowenfeld tries to take Agricola's apology and is slapped for his trouble, Raoul delivers the apology to Sylvestre and, contrary to the family code, demands that Sylvestre apologize to Frowenfeld as well (242). As Raoul learns the futility of family pride, he and his wife become reconciled with Aurora and Clotilde, especially after they help nurse Raoul's wife during her illness (303). When he takes Frowenfeld to the Grandissime family gathering and the guarded family talk concerns the prospective marriage of Honoré and Aurora, they also discover incipient sympathy among the younger members for love over family loyalty (305). It is likewise Raoul who rides to the site where Clemence is being lynched and tries to stop the lynching in the name of Honoré (323). Although Raoul does not know it, Sylvestre has already begun to doubt the code and has called on the others to let Clemence down (323). And when Agricola dies declaring his dedication to Louisiana forever and the words are inscribed on his tombstone, the younger members "felt, feebly at first, and more and more distinctly as years went by, that Forever was a trifle long for one to confine one's patriotic affection to a small fraction of a great country" (329).

In the history of the families, those dubious values associated with family pride have been the mark of the patriarchs for the most part. Despite Aurora's suicidal pride in refusing to consider Agricola's innocence in the card game and duel with her husband, the matriarchs have represented the moderating power of love and nurturing against patriarchal pride. Among the De Grapions, the women make their mark as nurturers of heirs after their proud husbands have died early in duels. By the time of Aurora and Clotilde, they are agents of healing, not vengeance, as is evident in Clotilde's nursing Frowenfeld during the yellow fever and after his wounding by Palmyre's Congo woman (12, 91, 209) and in Aurora's and Clotilde's nursing Raoul's sick wife. In their own situation Aurora and Clotilde demonstrate the matriarchal predicament of subjection to the patriarchal code. As unprotected, that is, unmarried, women, they must get a living without earning it, and they must be ladies first and survive second (255). The Fusilier women adhere more closely to the patriarchal code, if one judges by Dark Honoré's story that Numa was forced to marry Agricola's sister to keep peace in the family (108). However, even Madame Grandissime, née Fusilier, is willing to be reconciled with Aurora by the time of Agricola's death (325).

Among the Grandissimes, that matriarchal-patriarchal conflict flares at key moments to challenge family unity. When Honoré's sister is to be married to Don José and Agricola agrees to marry Palmyre to Bras-Coupé at the same time, Mademoiselle Grandissime resists patriarchal decree and demands that Palmyre not marry the African unless she wishes to do so (175). When the time for the wedding comes on that hurricane-struck evening, she again calls on Bras-Coupé to wait until she gives Palmyre in marriage (179). And when Bras-Coupé later pronounces a curse on Don José and his possessions, he exempts the women from his curse (187).

The Grandissime women's generosity can go only so far, however. As Raoul finishes his ritual recitation of the Bras-Coupé story at the Fête de Granpère, they agree that "it was a great pity to have ham-strung Bras-Coupé, a man who in his cursing had made an exemption in favor of the ladies," but undeniably "he had deserved his fate" (194).

The chronicle of the family similarly demonstrates use of talismanic objects and actions associated with its history. The stories of the fille a la casette and of Bras-Coupé are family heirlooms and are frequently retold. The story of the reluctant Huguenot is hinted first in Clotilde's costume at the masquerade ball, is told by Charles Keene to Frowenfeld in Chapter 5, and is alluded to by Aurora when Frowenfeld visits the Nancanou women and she shows him the wall portrait of the first Clotilde, the fille a la casette.

The story of Bras-Coupé serves even more as a talismanic reference point in the family's understanding of its role in destiny. Frowenfeld's encounters with the Bras-Coupé story become a repeated type scene in the narrative and run like a thread throughout the present action. Although not technically a family story in the sense that it is about one or more members of the family, it is based on actual New Orleans folklore, the story of a captive African prince who cut off his arm, hence the name, rather than submit to the humiliation of field labor. Told and retold in various versions by writers in New Orleans newspapers, by the Creole pianist and composer Louis Moreau Gottschalk and by Lafcadio Hearn in their books, and conflated with stories of other local insurrectionists, the Bras-Coupé story becomes in Cable's saga a symbolic account of the maiming effect of slavery and, within that context, an index of Creole family pride.[27]

Although Bras-Coupé in the saga keeps both arms, he demonstrates in his encounters with the family legend how the family code blinds itself to others' pride and how the family can use the Black Code to work its corporate will. Frowenfeld first hears hints of the story when it is told to his father as they approach New Orleans through the swamps where Bras-Coupé hid (10). Next, White Honoré tells him that Bras-Coupé is buried in the same cemetery where the Frowenfeld family lie, victims of yellow fever, and that Bras-Coupé changed the course of Honoré's convictions (38). Charles Keene sees a connection between Agricola's being stabbed

27. Turner, *George W. Cable,* 94–98; Robert O. Stephens, "Cable's Bras-Coupé and Mèrimée's Tamango: The Case of the Missing Arm," *Mississippi Quarterly,* XXXV (1982), 387–97; Barbara Ladd, "'An Atmosphere of Hints and Allusions': Bras Coupé and the Context of Black Insurrection in *The Grandissimes,*" *Southern Quarterly,* XXIX (1991), 63–76.

by a mysterious attacker and the Bras-Coupé story (101), and Raoul plans to paint Bras-Coupé as his second "masterpiece" (117). Aurora refuses to tell Frowenfeld the story because it would make her cry (145) but accounts for Palmyre's second change of heart by the Bras-Coupé episode (148). On the evening of the Fête de Granpère (169), Dark Honoré, White Honoré, and Raoul all tell the story: Dark Honoré cites it to explain why he will not work for the cause of the quadroons (196), and White Honoré tells Frowenfeld that the effect of the episode was to renew war between branches of the family when he had made peace (198). As noted earlier, the Grandissime women express their pity for Bras-Coupé (194). Aurora, before realizing that Honoré has come to return the title of Fausse Rivière to her and thinking he has come to insist on his rights for rent, taunts him with the rights denied Bras-Coupé (260). Finally, the ultimate voodoo fetish brought by Clemence to haunt Agricola is a small coffin in which lies the image of a cut-off arm with dagger (314). Clearly, the story of Bras-Coupé haunts family memory as the event which epitomizes its history.

Because of its pervasive influence as a reference point for the family, the story of Bras-Coupé also serves as a prime example of the moments of vision afforded by the generational perspective in *The Grandissimes*. Although the episode occurred only half a generation before, it has already achieved the status of family lore, as Raoul's recitation indicates, and has awakened animosities and rivalries between branches of the family dating from generations earlier. When Don José notifies the various kin of his prospective marriage to Honoré's sister and the coming marriage of Palmyre to Bras-Coupé, a return letter from the De Grapions assures him that "as sure as there [is] a God in Heaven, the writer [will] have the life of a man who knowingly [has] thus endeavored to dishonor one who *shared the blood of the De Grapions*" (176; Cable's italics). At that point, one recalls that Palmyre, during her willful childhood as Aurora's playmate and maid, was recognized as having come from "high Latin ancestry on the one side and . . . Jaloff African on the other" (60). That is to say, she was involved in ancient pride of blood as much as in her own "ruling spirit" as dark sister to Aurora. Aurora herself must similarly deal with the generational perspective when she realizes that the man she has learned to love is "a Montague to her Capulet" and that a Grandissime as her bridegroom may not be acceptable to Clotilde as a step-father (216).

Even more, White Honoré must face that generational perspective as he ponders restitution of the Fausse Rivière plantation to Aurora and

Clotilde. In the process he must look back to the passions of earlier generations, to present contingencies, and to possible future dissolution of family pride and fortune. The plantation is, in effect, a gift to him from the parental generation, as it was an inheritance to Nancanou from his fathers. His uncle Agricola had assigned it to Honoré, and he had kept it to avoid offending the family (221). Now it is the Grandissimes' only prosperous property in a time of insecure titles, uncertain appointments, and lack of ready capital (222). But it also represents property gained by the blood of another family, one both allied to and rivaling his through the generations. To keep the property is to save the family's fortune at the cost of its moral life, generating even more pride and defensiveness to justify keeping the plantation. To restore the property to those who own it by long familial possession is to jeopardize the future of his own family, and he can foresee desolation for the House of Grandissimes and his own fall to disgrace (244–45). The decision must be made, as he tells Frowenfeld earlier, within the context of "our dead father's mistakes," and he realizes that family honor can come at too high a price (223). Even after he returns the property, he can foresee the residual animosity of the family when he has Frowenfeld instead of himself named custodian of the Nancanous' estate, for if he dies, he says, "you might have trouble with my executors" (280).

Yet it is the vision of old family wrongs made right at last, of reconciling the black and white branches, that restores the family fortune. During that long evening, after the two Honorés take home the hemorrhaging Keene, White Honoré tells of returning Fausse Rivière and, recognizing "such mere justice" in acknowledging Dark Honoré as "the elder," restores the displaced inheritance in the firm known as Grandissime Brothers (268). The agreement is an echo of one reached earlier when the brothers were together in France and White Honoré had acknowledged the prior right of the elder brother. Back in Louisiana, however, he had "forgotten the unchampioned rights of his passive half-brother" until Frowenfeld and "the oft-encountered apparition of the dark sharer of his name" forced him to reaffirm that old recognition (279). In recognizing his elder brother, White Honoré comes to terms with the claims of the generations, though he cannot make full restitution. The longer view of the next twenty years, during which Palmyre in France receives a million dollars from the estate of Dark Honoré, shows that her exile and his thwarted life finally make full restitution for his "dead father's mistakes" impossible (331).

In *The Grandissimes* Cable brings into focus and full development that long study of the past begun during his explorations in the Louisiana archives. Even in "My Politics," written in the context of contemporaneous furor, he notes the following of himself at the earlier period: "Principles, especially principles of life, of conduct public and private, were everything to me; mere news was nothing. History, however, was a delight." [28] History personalized was the basis for his stories written in the 1870s and brought together in *Old Creole Days*. History personalized in a many-branched family became the basis for *The Grandissimes*, his depiction of the world of Louisiana and the South reverberating with its past in a time of fundamental transition. In the form of a family saga modeled on Genesis, he wrote of individuals caught in the grip of destiny.

With *The Grandissimes* Cable gave the family saga in the South its first full realization. His role as incipient critic of the code of the South, ahead of his time, provided a perspective enabling him to take the long view of the family saga. Not until the period after World War I, when other southern writers could also see the South critically rather than defensively, did the family saga come to full maturity.

28. Turner, ed., *Negro Question*, 2.

2

JANUS AT SHILOH
LOOKING BACK TO THE CIVIL WAR

When Caroline Gordon wrote in "Cock-Crow" about plans for her last novel, she wrote in memory of what she and her generation—the generation who had come to maturity in the 1920s—knew of their heritage: "I subscribed to the notion commonly held in my part of the country that we lived the way we lived and suffered certain privations as the immediate result of a general catastrophe—the Civil War, or as we called it, 'the war.' Things might have been different if we had 'won the war.' We had not won and they were as they were. An unfortunate state of affairs but one that could not be mended by complaints." Like other southern writers of her time, including fellow writers of family sagas, she knew that through her family she was an inheritor of the memory of the Civil War experience and could not, or would not be allowed to, forget it. "The examples of history are grim," she recalled. "In this world the right does not always triumph. It is dangerous to expect that it will." [1]

That Gordon identified her family with the grim trials of history is clear in her note that her ancestors "seem to have been cast in heroic mold" and that those heroes were "pitted against odds so desperate that only the continual exercise of heroic virtue" sustained them. Despite their heroic struggles, she knew, the family suffered the losses of war, and as a result the family's story was marked by a displacement of the inheritance—a legacy she shared with other saga writers of her generation. In the long view, she wondered, would it have been better "if our grandfathers had been carried off the field dead," for "the South that exists today has little of the Old South in it—we have sold out, certainly." [2]

1. Caroline Gordon, "Cock-Crow," *Southern Review,* n.s., I (1965), 557.
2. Ann Waldron, *Close Connections: Caroline Gordon and the Southern Renaissance* (New York, 1987), 97.

With others of her generation, she came to see that her agrarian in-heritance was as much legend as history but that it had its valuable parts—parts that were threatened by the successes as well as failures of the in-dustrial and commercial world outside. With the world of the grandfathers and grandmothers receding into the past, it came oddly into focus in a way it never had been when so close. How to render a critique of that world and to relate it to the world of their own time became Gordon's problem and that of her fellow southern writers. That several turned to the family saga as the appropriate form for this purpose made the period beginning in the late 1920s the great age of the family saga in the South. Such a re-sponse showed that history is hierarchical and that some periods or events keep their importance because of their "reverberation time": they retain meanings for the present when other times or events are closed out, their significance is known, and they become the true "past."[3]

Among southern writers of the 1920s and 1930s who critically exam-ined the war-haunted past, T. S. Stribling of Tennessee and Alabama was one of the earliest and most popular. His approach was that of critical re-alism, favored by H. L. Mencken and Sinclair Lewis. What Lewis did for mid-America in *Main Street* and *Babbitt,* Stribling did for the small town and city in the South, earlier in the 1922 novel *Birthright* and the 1926 *Teef-tallow* and more spaciously in his Vaiden trilogy, *The Forge* in 1931, *The Store* in 1932, and *Unfinished Cathedral* in 1934.[4] Greatly popular in their time, his works were seen as victories for Mencken's views of the South as the "Sahara of the Bozart" and gained critical acclaim and a Pulitzer Prize (for *The Store*).

Even while his popularity was soaring, however, soberer critics like Robert Penn Warren could see that Stribling followed literary fashions already becoming outmoded. Stribling's criticism, Warren thought, fol-lowed "the easy hick-baiting of a dead decade," his fiction was thesis-dom-inated, his characters and plots were "treated with an illustrative bias" in-stead of for their own dramatic possibilities, and his historical sense was "deficient" in substituting pseudosociological abstractions for historical complexities. In contrast with the works of William Faulkner, soon to eclipse him, his drama, said Warren, was that of "external circumstances, a con-flict drawn in the purely practical world," whereas "the drama that engrosses

3. Kent, *Interpretation and Genre,* 41.

4. T. S. Stribling, *The Forge* (Garden City, N.J., 1931), *The Store* (New York, 1932), and *Unfinished Cathedral* (New York, 1934).

Faulkner concerns a state of being, a conflict involving, to some degree at least, the spiritual integrity of a character." Warren was prescient. After his success with the Vaiden trilogy, Stribling wrote mainly detective fiction as his reputation declined and Faulkner's rose, and in the long view of literary history "he is now scarcely read except by a small group of readers in the South."[5]

Although publication of the Vaiden trilogy was spread over three years, Stribling insisted that the three novels be read as one continuous story.[6] Together they depict "one undivided social and spiritual movement" at three crucial times in the life of the Vaiden family: the Civil War and Reconstruction in *The Forge,* the 1880s and Henry Grady's New South in *The Store,* and the boom period of the 1920s in *Unfinished Cathedral.* Miltiades Vaiden, plantation operator in the first part, struggling storekeeper in the middle, and rich banker and patriarch by the end, is the dominating figure in relation to whose career other family members take their stance.

Written to reflect the temper of the twenties and early thirties, Stribling's saga depicts increasingly materialistic and business-oriented religion as well as southern fundamentalism at the time of the Scopes trial. In his portrayal of the Vaidens and their fellow citizens of Florence, Alabama, in their handling of a trial of six black men accused of raping a white woman, he commented on the furor surrounding another trial, the Scottsboro trial of 1931. Quite evidently, Stribling knew he had loaded the charge when he concentrated the ills of the South in Florence. In his "Apology to Florence," written shortly after completion of his trilogy, he acknowledged what he had done: "I have focused everything I found on Florence because that was the scene of my prolonged story. I am in the position of a very sad literary dog indeed which drags every bone to his kennel. . . . Naturally I need not say here that nowhere in the South exists such concentration of moral and financial quirks, twists, biases as I have depicted in Florence." His satirical trilogy, though notably different from the genteel tendencies of southern fiction, was within the larger tradition of family sagas and, like John Galsworthy's *Forsyte Saga,* could view sardonically the rending effect of money on human relationships. That he was probably influenced by

5. Robert Penn Warren, "T. S. Stribling: A Paragraph in the History of Critical Realism," *American Review,* II (1934), 463–86; Joseph M. Flora, "Fiction in the 1920s: Some New Voices," in *The History of Southern Literature,* ed. Louis D. Rubin, Jr., *et al.*(Baton Rouge, 1985), 284–85.

6. Edward J. Piacentino, *T. S. Stribling: Pioneer Realist in Modern Southern Literature* (New York, 1988), 15–16.

Galsworthy's example can be seen in his comment that *The Forsyte Saga* was one of the best novels he had ever read.[7]

In his saga Stribling reintroduced the recognition, silent since Cable, that southern families, in novels, at least, often had an unacknowledged parallel family of black relatives. In this respect he anticipated a major and frequent motif of family sagas in the South, one that distinguished the concept of family in southern sagas from those in other areas and cultures. Where earlier plantation-family novels like those of Kennedy acknowledged interdependence of master and slave or freedman but not their kinship, family sagas of the skeptical twentieth century saw household intimacy in sexual and kinship terms and abandoned the genteel pretension that white masters and sons were attracted to white ladies only. From Stribling on, the fact or suspicion of a parallel black branch of the family was a standard, if not invariable, element of the family saga in the South. What Cable and Stribling began, Faulkner and his successors made a major consideration.

For Stribling, discovery or acknowledgment of a black branch of the family was more a way of making the family a microcosm of the South than of presenting personal family history. Like most other southern writers of family sagas, Stribling drew on his own family past as framework for his trilogy. He acknowledged as much in his dedication of *The Forge* to the memory of "that brave, gay group from whom these memoirs were taken." Like the Vaidens in the trilogy, both the maternal and paternal sides of his family came to the Alabama-Tennessee border region from South Carolina in the late eighteenth century and demonstrated by their removal the beginning of their new identities as trans-Appalachian families. Stribling's mother Amelia came from the pro-Confederate Wait family of northern Alabama. Like old Jimmie Vaiden, his grandfather Wait ran a blacksmith forge until he developed a plantation large enough to support his family, defended slavery, and supported the Confederacy. The Catlins of the trilogy, by contrast, reflect the Stribling family history. Hill farmers in Tennessee, they kept no slaves, were loyal to the Union, and were Republicans where the Waits were Democrats. While he was preparing to write *The Forge*, Stribling spent a month at Shiloh reliving the battle and walking the terrain where his father and uncles had fought on opposing sides.[8]

7. T. S. Stribling, "Apology to Florence," *Wings*, VIII (1934), quoted in Piacentino, *T. S. Stribling*, 56; James E. Rocks, "T. S. Stribling's Burden of History: The Vaiden Trilogy," *Southern Humanities Review*, VI (1972), 221–23.

8. Wilton J. Eckley, *T. S. Stribling* (Boston, 1975), 11, 12–13, 69–70; Piacentino, *T. S. Stribling*, 50, 58–59, 152.

Stribling's ironic view of southern and family history seems to have had its basis in the divided views furnished by maternal and paternal sides of the family. Added to his own personal skepticism, these divided views interact uneasily in the Vaidens as Stribling's own ambiguous view of a southern family. Unlike the traditional southern kinship circle of close sympathies and loyalties, the Vaidens in his story constitute virtually an antifamily.[9] In *The Forge* particularly, the undercurrent of isolation and latent hostility runs through white Vaiden relationships. Although they are blood kin, each of them lives in his own secret world. Among the parents, old Jimmie Vaiden exists in his hard-shell Baptist preoccupations with predestination and biblical sanctions for slavery. Anticipating the matriarchal-patriarchal conflict that will echo through the generations, the mother Laura inhabits a world of clairvoyant realities and endures the scoffings of Jimmie's rationalism (19–20). Among the children, the oldest daughter, Cassandra, reads Thomas Paine on *The Rights of Man* while she denies the humanity of the slave girl Gracie sitting next to her (8, 14, 43). The other daughter, Marcia, longs for love but believes no dreams are possible around Vaidens and feels lonely in her knowledge that the Vaidens are not a close family (46, 140–41). Polycarp realizes he feels lonelier with his brother and sisters than he does around the slaves (107–108, 117–18). Miltiades recognizes that the family is a "hit-or-miss collection" of people who have nothing in common and senses a link between family nagging and their religious wrangling (154). Even when the brothers Polycarp and Augustus go off to join the Confederate army, they go in different directions to join separate units, and on the eve of Shiloh, when their units are finally brought together, Miltiades and Polycarp are unable to talk with each other (383). After Augustus is wounded, marries his nurse Rose MacClanahan, and brings her home, Marcia sees that Rose is the only one in the family who can speak about love without embarrassment.

In contrast, the black part of the family, though unacknowledged, finds greater identity with and shows greater loyalty to the Vaidens than the Vaidens themselves. Through the generations, Gracie is the focus of this ambiguous kinship. Daughter of old Jimmie Vaiden by the South Carolina slave woman Hannah, though unrecognized by him, she is closer as a sister to Marcia than is Cassandra, and throughout her life she identifies more with the white family than with the black community. She is the one who pleads successfully with the Yankee patrol to spare the Vaiden house, whereas

9. Rocks, "T. S. Stribling's Burden of History," 233.

the larger nearby Lacefield mansion, where Union officers have been entertained, is burned as they leave. She is an attendant figure, essential if unacknowledged, at the climax of each volume of the trilogy. At the end of *The Forge* old Jimmie dies in her arms as he wishes to die in the arms of his daughter Marcia. At the time of Miltiades' theft of the boatload of cotton from Handback in *The Store*, she is the one to whom he turns to hide the money from its sale, and at the end of the novel she tells Miltiades, too late, that Toussaint is his son by her, not General Beckman's son. Unfortunately, they arrive at the jail to find Toussaint already lynched by whites determined to teach blacks their place. At the end of *Unfinished Cathedral*, Gracie, now a withered shadow, rides in the first car of black mourners at the funeral of distinguished citizen Colonel Miltiades Vaiden. Throughout her life, though she urges her son Toussaint and her grandchildren to go north, where they can pass as white, she never lets them forget they are Vaidens.

Such irony is typical of Stribling's treatment of the Vaiden clan throughout the trilogy. As a satirist of southern pretensions in the manner of Sinclair Lewis, Stribling acts as his own narrator-historian so he can have distance and perspective enough to point out the ironies. Sometimes they are dramatic ironies made so pointedly the reader cannot miss them. On other occasions he halts his narrative to speak from his own omniscience about the discrepancy. The reader soon learns that his saga is constructed on the rhetoric of irony. Among the dramatic ironies, Miltiades instructs the slave George to look after the Vaidens while the white men are away at war, unaware that shortly before, George has symbolically killed Miltiades by firing a silver bullet at his picture (*Forge*, 166–68). In *The Store* Miltiades gains a reputation for honesty at Handback's store by giving blacks full measure for their purchases while at the same time he plans to steal a boatload of cotton from Handback (91–93, 115). In *Unfinished Cathedral* the high school student Red McLaughlin advocates lynching the six young black men as a way of protecting the purity of southern womanhood, then seduces Miltiades' daughter Marsan in the back seat of her father's car (70–72). Using his own voice, Stribling satirizes, for example, southern family genealogical pretensions when he shows Miltiades' wife Sydna poring over the genealogical charts of the Vaidens, Lacefields, and Crowninshields. On charts made by a genealogist ignorant about northern Alabama families, she has to "change the names about to some extent so that her family would fit into them," thus making Marsan eligible "to wear three stars in the Florence chapter of the D.A.R." and a fourth if Sydna changes enough entries (249). Among southern family sagas, Stribling's is especially notable for its ironic approach. Cable had been ironic enough in his deft way to outrage the Creoles, but fifty years later Stribling could depend on a readership instructed by Sinclair Lewis and H. L. Mencken to accept irony as the lens through which to see the whole of southern life reflected in the saga of the Vaidens.[10]

Irony then becomes the basis for the displacement of inheritance motif in the trilogy. Although Miltiades appears early in *The Forge* as a man who expects to make his way from overseer to plantation owner in traditional southern style, by marrying the plantation master's daughter Drusilla Lacefield, his career consists of a series of substitutions for the intended thing. As a southern gentleman and planter, he wants a son and a line of heirs, and he wants laws of entailment to preserve and protect what he finally accrues (*Cathedral,* 348). But his career and the career of his nephew, young Jerry Catlin, when Catlin emerges more prominently in *The Store* and *Unfinished Cathedral* as a compromised cleric, are marked by substitutions of mates and careers.[11] In effect, these substitutions serve as recurring type scenes in the saga as well as markers of the displacement of inheritance. When on the eve of her marriage to him Drusilla elopes instead with Emory Crowninshield, Miltiades carries his disappointment home with him, finds Gracie in the horse stable, sees her as "a kind of fluctuating impression of Drusilla," rapes her, and unknowingly begets his only son, Toussaint (*Forge,* 160–161). After the war, when Drusilla has been widowed and left with her daughter Sydna, named after General Albert Sidney Johnston, who fell at Shiloh, where Crowninshield was also killed, Miltiades expects again to return to the plantation and marry Drusilla, but combining career and family, he sees that running a store, not a plantation, is the way of the future and marries instead Ponny BeShears, daughter and heir of the operator of the crossroads store (*Forge,* 510).

The pattern of substitutionary scenes continues when both Miltiades' storekeeping expectations and his hopes for an heir fail to come true. While his business fortunes languish and Ponny fails to conceive, he becomes a bitter man of middle age. When Ponny finally becomes pregnant after twenty years, his hopes for an heir die with her and the baby at the same

10. Eckley, *T. S. Stribling,* 116.

11. Anne French Dalke, " 'Love ought to be like religion, Brother Milt': An Examination of the Civil War and Reconstruction Trilogy of T. S. Stribling," *Southern Literary Journal,* XIV (1981), 25–28.

time that he has been successful in getting the beginning of his fortune by stealing Handback's cotton. He realizes then that the price of his fortune is his heir (259). Later, as the precariously prosperous owner of Handback's store, he proposes to Drusilla again but, again rejected by her, marries instead her daughter Sydna and begets their daughter Marsan. Near the end of his life, when Marsan produces a son from her affair with Red McLaughlin and marries the schoolteacher J. Adlee Petrie, Miltiades is in the ironic situation of wishing his daughter had not married so the child could be a Vaiden in name as well as inheritance (*Cathedral*, 346). He finally hopes for a kind of immortality in the cathedral being built in Florence, where his sarcophagus will carry kingly inscriptions to the memory of Colonel Miltiades Vaiden. The cathedral left unfinished in the collapse of the real estate boom in Florence marks also the incompleteness of Miltiades' life and the collapse of the inheritance the colonel has lived for.[12]

The pattern of substitutions for Jerry Catlin confirms the type scenes as markers of the displaced inheritance for the rest of the family. When he enters the saga in *The Store,* Jerry is a spiritually aspiring young man, an agnostic about received religion in the manner of Robert Green Ingersoll but a believer in mystical benevolence. His quest to become an "Adept," a seeker of the good in the universe, is as theoretical as it is exalted, and when he has the chance to do practical good, he rejects the appeal for help by black Loob Snipes, dispossessed and hungry tenant farmer (*Store,* 264). By the time of *Unfinished Cathedral,* he is a thoroughly compromised assistant minister at the principal Methodist church in Florence and scorns the primitive Christian enthusiasm of the local Drownders sect. Instead, Jerry makes his reputation as a fundraiser for churches and as preacher of a bland and skeptical sermon at the Methodist conference, his topic: "If there be no God the Christian attitude is best" (372). His apotheosis is appointment to a large church in Birmingham where his talents as fundraiser and bland preacher will receive their reward. His amatory substitutions likewise follow Miltiades' example. Although he loves Sydna, he lies with black housemaid Pammy Lee as a substitute for Sydna, as Miltiades did with Gracie, and marries church organist Aurelia Swartout as the right move to advance his career. After Miltiades dies and Aurelia leaves him, Jerry turns again to Sydna as Miltiades had turned to Drusilla. But Sydna chooses previously rejected Lucius Handback and explains to Jerry why she did not choose him: "I think our two families were born to

12. Piacentino, *T. S. Stribling,* 111.

love each other . . . not to marry. Drusilla once told me that on the Vaiden and Lacefield lovers God had bestowed his cynical blessing of separation" (367).

The type scenes that provide architectural motifs also demonstrate talismans significant to the family. For Miltiades, the white Corinthian columns at Lacefield plantation embody the glamour of the Old South that he had hoped for as a young overseer. After Lacefield manor is burned, he spends the rest of his life trying to raise those pillars again.[13] When Sydna asks him why he wants a house that is more than a home, he tells her in a moment of confession that his obligation to the Old South is to "do some beautiful thing" with his money (*Store*, 387). When he marries Sydna and moves into the Crowninshield house with her and Drusilla, one of his first acts is to build granite columns on the front, though Drusilla manages to make the columns Ionic instead of Corinthian. When his hopes go beyond family and business to yearnings for perpetual remembrance, he pays to have granite columns on "his" cathedral. Ironically, he is killed by those falling columns when Eph Cady throws a bomb at him and the cathedral in protest at Miltiades' foreclosure and his use of black stoneworkers to build his monument.

Stretching over a seventy-year period of southern history, the Vaiden trilogy also provides ample opportunities for Stribling to reflect ironically on public events with which the family is associated. His narrative provides no speculations about the unknowability of history or recognitions that history is a function of the observer more than of the observed. Rather, for him history is a deterministic series of events and forces that families and individuals cannot control but must change in response to.[14] The Vaidens are present at public events throughout the trilogy not to shape them but to react to them and to put their hopes on what they see as trends of the times. After the war Miltiades, A. Gray Lacefield, and Handback join the Ku Klux Klan movement to help control the freed slaves, but in the process Miltiades learns from cynical General Beckman that political power is based on economic power, that the South will have to learn northern methods of dealing with blacks, and in particular that southerners must deal with, not force, blacks in order to get the products of their labor (*Forge*, 493). As a result of that recognition, he gives up his plantation hopes and begins operating a general store where blacks buy their provisions and mort-

13. Dalke, "Love ought to be like religion," 26.
14. Eckley, *T. S. Stribling*, 112.

gage their crops. In effect, his personal decision is made on a reading of history. In *Unfinished Cathedral* family and public history merge for old Miltiades in the Scottsboro-like trial of the six young black men when Gracie tells him that one of those men is his great-grandson, brought from Chicago to Florence by her stories of his Vaiden heritage (179–80).

That the Civil War looms as the commanding event of history for the Vaidens becomes evident as the family history grows longer. When in *The Store* Sydna begins to make legends of the family's heroism in the war and asks her husband to tell about her father's dying wish for him to look after his daughter, Miltiades astutely observes that she feels more of the tragedy of the war than do those who lived it (385). This tendency to participate deeply, intimately, and vicariously in an event is confirmed in *Unfinished Cathedral* when Miltiades, Drusilla, Sydna, and Jerry Catlin attend the United Daughters of the Confederacy convocation at Shiloh and Sydna contemplates the legend-making process: "Looking at the markers it was as if an astral army were maneuvering in a world where time stood charmed, and each division of the two contending forces occupied for eternity every successive position it had won, or lost, on that fateful Sunday and Monday in 'sixty-two.' . . . This common focusing of national history and their own dramatic family annals upon the scene gave it an overpowering sense of pathos and tragedy" (265–66).

In contrast with the legend of heroism, however, the Vaiden family has its own old crimes to live down. Although Miltiades has become a leading citizen of Florence by the time of *Unfinished Cathedral,* all the family and all the community know that his fortune was based on stolen cotton. The reader may be more sympathetic to his predicament than are the later generations of kinsmen and townsmen, for few seem to know that Handback cheated Miltiades first, by accepting his deposit of $2,500, proceeds from his first postwar cotton crop, when Handback knew he was going into bankruptcy the next day. In any case, Miltiades shows how usurious revenge can be when he steals nineteen times the worth of his loss. After his coup, he and the Vaidens have to live with the town's sometimes silent, sometimes taunting knowledge of his theft, a crime compounded by Handback's subsequent suicide. Out of this knowledge Stribling develops the saga motif of family decline, of the Vaidens' increasing moral compromise as they grow richer.

Throughout the second half of *The Store* and all of *Unfinished Cathedral,* knowledge of the old crime becomes a running theme, and responses to it by family and community members measure their moral integrity. While Miltiades waits to have the check cashed for the stolen cotton, he reflects on how he will have to learn to live with himself as a dishonored man, not the heroic colonel of Shiloh (197). When Marcia comes to Florence to see about her troubled son Jerry, she wonders where the flaw in the Vaiden heritage came from and fears for her son as a Vaiden. She cries for her brother's crime and senses the loss of a nobler past (267). The young lawyer Jake Sandusky explains to Jerry that he is shunned by the academy because people in Florence think in terms of families, not individuals, and Miltiades' crime carries over to him (275). In *Unfinished Cathedral* men who resent Miltiades' interference with their plans to lynch the six black men taunt his questionable morality with their knowledge of the cotton theft, but the vice-president of the bank admires Miltiades' earlier nerve in seizing his fortune and wonders if the old man has grown too cautious in his old age (59, 108). As he becomes more personally interested in Marsan, the schoolteacher Petrie speculates on what flaws lie hidden in her inherited character and ponders if there is still a potential thief in her genes (74). In a nice stroke of irony, though, Marsan thinks how complicated her life is and envies the clear-cut world of good and evil known to her ancestors (127–28). When he discovers Marsan is pregnant and unmarried, Miltiades wonders what flaw in the Vaiden heredity let her consent to be seduced, conveniently forgetting his rape of Gracie and his seduction of Drusilla (289).

More than in most family sagas, the omniscient perspective Stribling uses here provides moments of vision for his characters. At such moments the past is both linear and recurring as the Vaidens see themselves in the grip of forces they can barely comprehend and cannot control. In *The Store*, for example, while he is still an unsuccessful storekeeper, Miltiades muses on what his fate would have been if he had married Drusilla, daughter of the Old South, "the impossible one" (176). Drusilla, though, tells Miltiades that the ambitious Vaidens served "some interior purpose" that the pleasure-loving Lacefields lacked and "that is why all of us Lacefields had a tendency to lean on you Vaidens" (402–403). When Jerry falls into despair after Sydna marries Miltiades, Drusilla senses that "this was simply a recurrence of the fatal hopeless interplay of Vaiden and Lacefield blood" (502). A sense of recurring events comes to her more strongly in *Unfinished Cathedral*. When Marsan reveals she is pregnant and Sydna cries she cannot understand how someone brought up in the Lacefield and Vaiden

tradition "could have been so wayward," Drusilla, now the ironic matriarch, remembers "a moment between Miltiades and herself, and how their
distant uncandled giving had come home to both of them in Marsan," and
she thinks how "time did not go on, but that it was a vast wheel that turned
slowly round and round" (306). For Miltiades the severest moment of vision comes when Gracie tells him that one of the black men accused of
rape is his great-grandson. Then the old banker trembles at "the chain of
wrongs and violences around which his life had been molded," senses in
his life "the cold malevolent direction of Nemesis," and feels that "his
future lay under the shadow of the same unseen power which had shaped
the mein and horror of his past" (182). In his rendering of such moments,
Stribling abandons his role as satirist and becomes the brooding moralist
on the human condition.

In his afterword to the trilogy, Stribling recognizes that the family account was his own gesture toward perpetual remembrance. If the Waits
and Striblings were to continue in memory, they would have to do so in
the realm of imaginative fiction, not social history: "Each generation quickly
and completely forgets its forebears. I was filled with a profound sense of
tragedy that my own family, my neighbors, the whole South surrounding
me would be utterly lost in the onrushing flood of the years. History will
not rescue it from oblivion because history is too general to be human and
too remote to be real." In the long view Stribling probably got his wish.
In the tradition of the family saga in the South, he confirmed and advanced
the distinctive element in southern sagas of recognizing a frequently parallel black line of descent, lived with but seldom acknowledged. Unlike
others in the tradition, his saga emphasized a satirical view of the southern
family and southern mores, particularly in light of current or recent events.
The result was a saga of revelation more than of discovery, as the children
lived out the sins of the forefathers in a largely deterministic world.

In the technical development of the saga, Stribling made few advances;
his point of view was that of the traditional storyteller, knowing all and
telling all and leaving little for the reader to infer. Yet his was a performance
to build on. Faulkner bought all three volumes of the trilogy, inscribed
them, and kept them permanently in his library. Putting his name in a book
usually meant he had read and admired it, and if internal similarities are a
reliable indication, Faulkner saw in Stribling's saga numerous elements
of the southern family saga he could use in *Absalom, Absalom!* Both Vaiden
and Sutpen fail in their first marriages or intended marriages, both marry

plain, middle-class women in their second ventures toward starting a family line, both keep stores when their plantations fail, both refuse to acknowledge their part-Negro children and treat their families without feeling or compassion, both fail to perpetuate their family lines with white sons, and both are killed by avenging poor whites.[15] But Faulkner also showed what remarkable technical and epistemological advances could be achieved on a traditional form when he turned to *Absalom, Absalom!*

The great advances in family saga form in *Absalom, Absalom!*, published in 1936, derive from Faulkner's reinvention of the narrator-historian. No longer does the author as narrator-historian preside over the action, interpreting events and motives as did Cable or Stribling. Now the narrator-historian, multiplied several times, is a character in the narrative, limited in his perspective and knowledge as characters are when caught in the fury of events the outcome of which they cannot know. All the other elements of the family saga are adduced by them according to their needs. Recognition of type scenes may be appropriate to one and alien to another. Versions of special family attributes change from narrator to narrator, and puzzlements over the actions of ancestors are shaped by the amount of knowledge a narrator has or thinks he has. Even as the conventions are functions of the narrators rather than of the story itself, so the family has a subjective rather than an objective existence. As in family stories generically, the narrative serves the needs of the narrator, and what is "fact" is what the narrator wants to be significant fact. The narrative sense in the saga is not of a story that has happened and is being recounted but of a story in the process of evolving.

The principal reason for modifying the narrator-historian convention is that the Sutpen family is extinct, except for the ghostly Jim Bond howling in the ruins, and no family member remains to tell the story from inside. Rather, Faulkner depends on the convention of the community as an extension of the family, and what might have been the dynamics within the Sutpen family is left to conjecture, speculation, and inference by members of the community. For that community, particularly the Compsons and Coldfields, the story of the Sutpen family becomes their community possession to make and remake according to their own needs. The result is a saga of discovery, and finally of invention, rather than of revelation.

The process of discovery and invention by narrators in *Absalom, Ab-*

---

15. Piacentino, *T. S. Stribling*, 130–34.

salom! reflects the similar process Faulkner himself went through as he wrote the saga. The novel grew out of several published and unpublished stories Faulkner wrote during the late 1920s and early 1930s. In the stories, motifs that would reappear as contingent elements in the saga appear first as clear and established elements: Henry's objection to Charles Bon's marrying Judith Sutpen on grounds of bigamy, the octoroon's picture in Bon's locket, the imported French architect, Henry's hiding for years in the Sutpen mansion, dismissal of the youth from the door of the plantation house, Sutpen's seduction and dismissal of Wash Jones's granddaughter, Wash's killing of Sutpen, and storytellers telling their stories to potential narrators. But as Faulkner worked more on the book he first called *Dark House,* he revised to postpone information, to make stories contingent and ambiguous, and to keep Bon's Negro blood a matter of speculation, not knowledge.[16]

The result is that *Absalom, Absalom!* is a tale told so inferentially that the reader also becomes a narrator piecing old parts of the story together and emerging with a version as contingent as those of the other narrators. Indeed, the number of things in the saga not known by narrator or reader reaches to crucial questions of the narrative. Some are of incidental import but show the pattern of omission: how Sutpen got to the West Indies, how he put down the native insurrection, how he made his money, what the nature of his deal with Goodhue Coldfield was. Others are central, among them what Sutpen discovered about his Haitian wife; what he told Henry at Christmas, 1860; what he told Henry in the Confederate camp near the end of the war, what he meant when he told General Compson he had to make a choice and what he meant in saying he still had a trump card to play; what Quentin learned when he went with Rosa to Sutpen's Hundred; and, most critically, whether Bon was actually Sutpen's son and whether Bon was part Negro. After reviewing the facts cross-witnessed by narrators, the reader realizes that "the rest is pure conjecture."[17]

Conjecture, after all, is what Faulkner practices during his few autho-

---

16. Elisabeth Muhlenfeld, Introduction, in *William Faulkner's "Absalom, Absalom!": A Critical Casebook,* ed. Elisabeth Muhlenfeld (Jackson, 1984), xi-xxxii; Estella Schoenberg, *Old Times and Talking: Quentin Compson in Faulkner's "Absalom, Absalom!" and Related Works* (Jackson, 1977), 33-40, 76.

17. Duncan Aswell, "The Puzzling Design of *Absalom, Absalom!,*" 94-95, and Floyd C. Watkins, "What Happens in *Absalom, Absalom!?*, 86, both in *"Absalom, Absalom!" Critical Casebook,* ed. Muhlenfeld.

rial entries into the narrative. The best he can say about Shreve's and
Quentin's inventions is that they are "probably true" because the two young
men have effectively identified themselves with Bon and Henry. As they
imagine the lawyer in New Orleans, he recognizes that conjecture and
invention are all the narrators have to go on: "The two of them creating
between them, out of the rag-tag and bob-ends of old tales and talking,
people who perhaps had never existed at all anywhere, who, shadows, were
of what were (to one of them at least, to Shreve) shades too, quiet as the
visible murmur of their vaporizing breath." [18]

As primary narrator-historian in the saga, Quentin Compson is gath-
erer and hearer of the "rag-tag and bob-ends of old tales and talking."
Faulkner suggests that Quentin has often heard talk about or versions of
Thomas Sutpen's story. When Rosa Coldfield begins her tale, Quentin realizes that "the first part of it, [he] already knew," that "it was part of his
twenty years' heritage of breathing the same air and hearing his father talk
about the man Sutpen" (11), and when Mr. Compson begins his story that
evening, Faulkner says that for Quentin "it was a day of listening . . . the
hearing in 1909 mostly about that which he already knew, since he had been
born in and still breathed the same air" (31). That Quentin has talked about
Sutpen and the South at Harvard before that January evening in 1910 is evident in his response to Shreve's raillery that Rosa is "Aunt Rosa." Like numerous other young men from the South in northern schools, Quentin is
forced to act first as southerner, second as American. The call to explain
Quentin's region was "not Shreve's first time, nobody's first time in Cambridge since September," and "tell about the South" appears to be a generic
demand rather than Shreve's only (174).

The family saga that emerges from all the tellings is a function of the
narrators more than of the story itself, and the degree to which saga conventions are observed varies with the teller. That the Sutpens constitute a
multigenerational family of dynastic potential concerns Rosa Coldfield almost not at all. Besides asserting judgmentally that Sutpen was no gentleman and, worse, was a demon and an ogre, she is mainly concerned with
saving his cursed children from their father's sins. She is outraged, apparently without thinking of its dynastic implications, when Sutpen makes his
proposal, according to Shreve, that they marry only after she produces a
son (279, 284). Mr. Compson believes, if Rosa does not, that Clytie is
Sutpen's daughter by a slave woman brought with the wagonload of Ne-

18. William Faulkner, *Absalom, Absalom!* (1936; rpr. New York, 1951), 335–36.

groes into Jefferson and thus accounts for the black side of the Sutpen family (61). Upon Quentin's information about or reminder of Sutpen's Haitian marriage, Mr. Compson can also imagine Sutpen's return in 1866 with a sense of the short time he has to start a third line of sons (278). It is General Compson, Quentin's grandfather, who knows most about Sutpen's mountain Virginia background, his Haitian marriage and child, and, by 1864, with the sons of his first and second marriages alienated, his single-minded desire for a son to perpetuate the family name and line (292). Knowing how Sutpen was rejected at the door of the tidewater plantation house, he also understands something of the symbolic force in Sutpen's vision of a dynasty and remembers Sutpen explaining that "the boy-symbol at the door wasn't it because the boy-symbol was just the figment of the amazed and desperate child; that now he would take that boy in where he would never again need to stand on the outside of a white door" and that the boy would "look ahead along the still undivulged light rays in which his descendants who might not even ever hear his (the boy's) name, waited to be born" (262).

Identifying with Henry Sutpen and Charles Bon according to their own needs, Quentin and Shreve see Sutpen's dynastic design from the viewpoint of the sons and, in echo of the Old Testament, imagine Bon's recognition that Sutpen's sons will have to pay for his sins, like Abraham referring his creditors to his sons "to bear the burden of mine iniquities and persecutions" (325). With Bon, they can also imagine his not knowing why Sutpen rejected his mother (327, 329), and Shreve can envision Jim Bond and his descendants as the last of the Sutpens (378).

General Compson is source and shaper of the removal motif as the beginning identity of the Sutpen family. Their removal to America, probably as refugees from Old Bailey prison, is a matter of generalized speculation, but he can tell, by evidence directly from the source, of the Sutpens' removal from the Virginia mountains to the Tidewater and of Thomas' removal to Haiti and subsequently to Mississippi, where the baronial family takes shape (221, 224, 238).

Unlike families in other sagas, the Sutpens have as many special attributes as they have narrators. For Rosa, they are a cursed family haunted by a demon ancestor whose crimes spread their effects on other families, including her own, and whose crimes are so widespread they persuade God to let the South lose the Civil War (9, 11). For Mr. Compson, Thomas Sutpen is a heroic victim of fate (72–73) whose descendants also sense the role of fate in bringing them into love and conflict with each other, as Henry, Bon, and Judith are fatally drawn to each other and depend on fate to resolve their impasse. His appeal to fate, however, is a function of his own impotence as the lesser son of a greater father and of his need to make sacred what he cannot explain.[19] For General Compson, a resolute and ambitious man much like Sutpen, the special attribute is Sutpen's dynastic design, founded on his moral innocence that people should behave like units in a calculation and subject their individual aspirations to the founder's purpose (220, 263, 275). To the general, Sutpen is as blind to feeling when he asks Compson where he made his mistake in calculations as he was when he put aside his Haitian wife and son because they were not "adjunctive or incremental to the design" (240, 263). To Quentin, oriented to the predicament of the Sutpen sons, the Sutpens demonstrate the appeal and curse of the chivalric ideal in the Old and post–Civil War South (361–62), whereas Shreve, until he comes to share Quentin's view, sees Sutpen as a comic demon and the story of his children as comic horror theater, "better than Ben Hur" (217).

When they consider displacement of the inheritance, the narrators of *Absalom, Absalom!* emphasize the role of names in perpetuating or losing the family attribute. Mr. Compson speculates that when Sutpen saw his design threatened, he insisted on renaming his Haitian son so that the child would carry neither Sutpen's name nor that of the maternal grandfather (62, 265–66), in effect making him a pastless man. Quentin likewise recognizes displacement through naming when he thinks of Sutpen's futile despair in realizing that the alienated Henry in 1860 will go elsewhere and start a line of heirs with another name "among people who will never have heard the right one" (182). The pattern of misnaming continues in Quentin's reconstruction when Sutpen rejects Milly Jones's daughter and refuses to give her his name (292).

Mr. Compson and Quentin are likewise the two narrators who recognize the convention of decline. For the elder Compson the motif mirrors his sense of his own diminished role in a time when all heroic action is done and only a slow dying is left. His letter to Quentin on Rosa contrasts the "painless death . . . which takes the intelligence by violent surprise" with "a slow and gradual confronting with that which over a long period of bewilderment and dread it has been taught to regard as irrevo-

---

19. James Guetti, "*Absalom, Absalom!:* The Extended Simile," in "*Absalom, Absalom!*" *Critical Casebook*, ed. Muhlenfeld, 66.

cable and unplumbable finality" (173). In that light he can celebrate the heroic certainties of the earlier generation against the malaise of the later: people who were "larger, more heroic . . . who had the gift of dying once instead of being diffused and scattered creatures drawn blindly limb from limb from a grab-bag and assembled, author and victim too of a thousand homicides and a thousand copulations and divorcements" (89). Quentin, in contrast, measures decline among the Sutpens by their fall from godlike pride to the level of Wash Jones. Although with Rosa on that September evening he can still envision Sutpen riding over the land like a demigod and in legend still possessing the land with his descendants (363), with Shreve he measures Sutpen's decline after the war in his descent to storekeeper and in Wash Jones's gradual entry into the inner citadel of Sutpen's mansion. Where before the war Jones could approach no closer to the mansion than the hammock in the yard and was forced during the war by Judith and Clytie to go to the kitchen door, during Sutpen's decline he both drinks with the demigod, bringing him home drunk and helping him into the upper bedroom, and sleeps on the floor beside Sutpen's bed (183–84).

The Compson men are likewise the narrators who envision the matriarchal-patriarchal conflict in the Sutpen clan, an indication more of Compson than of Sutpen family dynamics. Mr. Compson is the source of information that in her childhood Rosa was taught to believe Sutpen was an ogre and a demon by her man-hating aunt (160). His other theme is women's unreality. "They lead beautiful lives—women," he tells Quentin. "Lives not only divorced, but irrevocably excommunicated from, all reality" (191). That is why, he says, they can endure pain "which would make the most spartan man resemble a puling boy," but they must have ceremonies and formalities and decorums (191–92). Out of that conviction he can relate how Judith went into her young womanhood in unreachable ethereality (67), how Ellen Coldfield Sutpen went into her butterfly summer of preparations for Judith's wedding, with Bon as a mere adjunctive acquisition (75), and how Rosa went to the Hundred in 1865, in southern woman fashion, to make over the household to her own taste and convenience, all "because that's what a Southern lady is" (86).

It is General Compson, though, who postulates the fundamental matriarchal-patriarchal conflict when Sutpen first tells him of the design and of his putting aside the Haitian wife. Morality is for women, the general thinks, and Sutpen should have known that mere justice is not payment enough for women's moral claims (265). For Quentin and Shreve that latent conflict is present in the sons as well. As they reconstruct the confrontation between Charles Bon and the octoroon woman at the time of his departure for the university at Oxford, Mississippi, they see Charles repeating the pattern. With difficult women, they think, one just leaves: "Because you can't beat them: you just flee" (312).

To the type scenes, however, all these narrators return obsessively as they try to rationalize what happened and explain how events fit into the family pattern. To a great extent the type scenes are dramatized expressions of the family attribute, however conceived. The key scene that all agree happened but cannot explain why is Henry's fatal confrontation with Charles at the gates of the Hundred. Although the scene is only tentatively reenacted in Quentin's narration (132–33), it is the reference point for everyone's comments. "Am I going to have to hear it all over again," Quentin wonders. "I shall have to never listen to anything else but this again forever" (277). The Henry-Charles confrontation, though, is the climactic but not the last of a series of rejections at the door that mark Sutpen family history. General Compson can tell of Sutpen's being rejected at the tidewater mansion door and Sutpen's rejection of the Haitian wife (232, 240, 264), Quentin can re-create Bon's dismissal from the front door at Sutpen's and Sutpen's recognition of Bon as his other self to be rejected (267, 333), and Shreve and Mr. Compson can reconstruct Sutpen's dismissal of Bon from his door in December, 1860 (265, 333–34). Quentin remembers Clytie's attempt to stop Rosa at the door in September, 1909, when Rosa enters to find what is hidden at the Hundred (351, 359). What the type scenes show is the struggle to define the family, who is included and who rejected and by what means.[20]

The talismanic objects in the Sutpen saga are Sutpen's big white house, Bon's letter to Judith, and the locket brought to Judith from Bon's body. Together, they are objects from the past whose meaning has to be deciphered in the present. Unlike mansions in the country-house poems and sketches and in later sagas, Sutpen's mansion has no counterpart in Yoknapatawpha memory. Hardly described, it is said only to be bigger and whiter than any others but remarkable for its grim and castlelike magnificence. Probably it is in the style of Corinthian-columned mansions of the Deep South; presumably it has some artistic integrity, if General Compson's memory of the French architect's amazement at his situation can be

20. George S. Lensing, "The Metaphor of Family in "*Absalom, Absalom!*," *Southern Review*, n.s., XI (1975), 109–14.

credited (256–57). In any case, Sutpen's house is significant psychologically in that it is a partial fulfillment of his design, for, as Quentin sees, Sutpen is like the tidewater Virginia planter lying in his hammock and being served drinks, by Wash Jones if not by a black slave (228, 233, 260). Because the plantation house exists more in the minds of narrators than in the public world of history, it becomes part of the interior landscape of the story. Its destruction by fire, the ultimate act of pride by Sutpen's children, suggests the end of the plantation myth.[21] It thus exists in the saga as a remembered reference point around which meanings gather and conflict.

Bon's letter to Judith, at least so identified in family tradition, acts as an even more enigmatic talisman. Reputedly written by Bon in the last days of the war and received by Judith shortly before or at about the same time Henry and Bon returned from the war, it was given by Judith a week after Bon's death to grandmother Compson, who received it in amazement, not at its content but at the manner of its presentation, and was kept in the Compson family, puzzled over by Mr. Compson and presented finally to Quentin before his trip to Sutpen's Hundred with Rosa. That it has a lingering effect on those who try to tell the Sutpen saga is indicated by the way it triggers Mr. Compson's narrative and, when it is recapitulated to Shreve, by the way it prompts him to imagine other letters. Besides Bon's gravemarker, it is the only documentary evidence in the saga that Bon existed. Written "without salutation or signature," it leaves unnamed the identities of author and intended audience, depending on contingent narratives by others for those identifications. As a message, it is also indeterminate: "We have waited long enough," it says, but who the "we" is, what the wait, and what the definition and purpose of "enough" remain unspecified. Whether the "we" means Bon and Judith, Bon and Henry, or more generally those whose lives have been suspended by the war is left to the reader to decide. That the letter was given by Judith to be read by others in other contexts suggests that its meanings are those more of a monument than of a message. Mr. Compson's and Quentin's attempts to read it historically rather than archaeologically fail to appreciate the conditions necessary for its decipherment.[22] It survives as a kind of monument in the family but keeps its secrets like the grave.

21. Thadious Davis, "'Be Sutpen's Hundred': Imaginative Projection of Landscape in *Absalom, Absalom!*," *Southern Literary Journal*, XIII (1981), 4, 12; F. Garvin Davenport, Jr., *The Myth of Southern History: Historical Consciousness in Twentieth-Century Southern Literature* (Nashville, 1970), 91.

22. David Krause, "Reading Bon's Letter and Faulkner's *Absalom, Absalom!*," *PMLA*,

If Bon's letter is cryptic, perhaps codeless, his locket, found by Judith after his death, is ambiguous but continuous in family memory. That it is probably not a ghost memory is attested by Rosa, who says she saw it in Judith's hand when she went to Sutpen's after Henry killed Bon (142). But whose picture was in the metal case and what the picture means vary with the teller. Rosa says the picture was of Judith but admits, "it's what I expected, knew . . . that I should find" (142) and does not distinguish between what she saw and what she expected to see, nor does she tell how closely she observed. This is the point at which she says, "there is a might-have-been which is more true than truth" (143). Mr. Compson, apparently speaking out of family tradition and deduction, tells Quentin that Judith found in Bon's coat "the picture of the octoroon mistress and the little boy" (95) and on the basis of that "fact" believes Judith did not know of the New Orleans woman in Bon's life until she found "the photograph which was not her face, not her child" (91). The locket question grew in ambiguity as Faulkner revised *Absalom, Absalom!* and took on meanings in the shifting contexts of the narrators' interpretations. By the time Shreve and Quentin ponder the problem, it has become the key to Bon's motives. Reasoning by what they believe had to be, they think the locket held the picture of "the octoroon and the kid" but not for the motives imagined by Mr. Compson. For them, enshrining that picture was the ultimate expression of chivalric love, a way of saying he was not worthy to be mourned (358–59). For other readers, the point is not what Bon intended to convey but how Judith and the family understood the implied message, as a "commission to care for Bon's quasi wife and son." [23] Disappeared but not forgotten, the locket and picture haunt family memory as a talismanic reference point and link the generations.

When Quentin and Shreve re-create the Sutpen saga by placing it within the context of history, they act out a paradox. While they treat the past as imaginative and speculative, they, especially Shreve, also attempt to reduce legend to norms of human behavior. Their co-creation begins with a droll and somewhat cynical acceptance of the mysterious and marvelous, but as they begin to "play," they become involved in what "had to be," in what

---

XCIX (1984), 225; Elisabeth Muhlenfeld, "Judith and Charles," in *"Absalom, Absalom!" Critical Casebook,* ed. Muhlenfeld, 176; Krause, "Reading Bon's Letter," 232, 230, 235–36, 238.

    23. Muhlenfeld, "Judith and Charles," in *"Absalom, Absalom!" Critical Casebook,* ed. Muhlenfeld, 185.

figures of the past had to think in their situations. They create people like Eulalia and the lawyer in New Orleans because, in the normal course of events, someone like them had to exist and act as they did.[24] When Quentin begins his recapitulation of the Sutpen story for Shreve, apparently told before in a less complete form, Shreve sardonically accepts the marvelous in his frequent interruptions with "the demon" (218, 223, 246, 267, 270, 274, 280, 296, 297) at the same time that he struggles to reduce motivation to the normal: "So he just wanted a grandson. That was all he was after" (271). When Quentin speculates about the French architect's motives in attempting to escape, Shreve appeals to motives understood by men his age: "Maybe he just wanted a girl" (218). Again, when Quentin first mentions the Haitian woman, Shreve appeals to the same norm, saying, "It's a girl" (247).

By the time Shreve arrives at the point of involvement where he can say, "Let me play a while now" (280), he is ready to place people of the story within the context of normalized expectations. In the process, he appeals to Rosa's thesis that "there are some things that just have to be whether they are or not" (322). Out of those things that "have to be," he can decide that Mr. Compson was wrong in saying Bon, not Henry, was wounded at Shiloh (344), that Sutpen finally told Henry about Bon's Negro blood in Carolina in 1865 (355), and that Bon's locket held the octoroon's picture, not Judith's (358–59). Implied in the reduction to what has to be is a theory of history in the family whereby events recur until they become the expected. That the approach is peculiarly southern is possible, for Quentin as a potential southern gentleman of the early twentieth century, and Shreve through Quentin, can imagine that racial feeling is the determining norm in Henry's decision to stop Bon.[25] As men of their own time, when conviction of white supremacy justified suppression of blacks in America and expanding of empires into lands of the colored races, they thought seeing Bon as a Negro was motive enough to explain Henry's action.

Despite Shreve's attempts, and to some extent Quentin's, to reduce legend to history, their moments of vision reach for the mythic beyond the actual. Although their visions may be as contingent as their "facts," they show the effects of research into the past on the researchers. Despite her forty-three years' hatred, at the gates of the Hundred Rosa shares with Quentin the sense that Sutpen is not dead but still rides "the Domain,"

---

24. Henderson, *Versions of the Past*, 261.
25. *Ibid.*, 265.

black stallion and rider galloping over the land possessed spiritually by him and his descendants, no matter how many have died or how much "they have taken it away" (363). Even as he realizes his first interpretation of the Henry-Bon-Judith predicament "does not explain" everything, Mr. Compson intuits the mystery of old heroisms, of passions beyond formula, of people of "heroic proportions, performing their acts of simple passion and simple violence, impervious to time and inexplicable . . . shadowy inscrutable and serene, against the turgid background of a horrible and bloody mischancing of human affairs" (100–101). Even though his sense of his own impotence may call for an inscrutable world, he can envision it as a world of larger-than-life people gaining grandeur despite the tricks of fate. So, too, is General Compson's vision of young Sutpen riding the rim of the human volcano in Haiti, a place not just where a shrewd and ambitious man could get rich quick but "where high mortality was concomitant with the money and the sheen on the dollars was not from gold but from blood . . . a theater for violence and injustice and bloodshed and all the satanic lusts of human greed and cruelty." This "lost little island," existing both out of time and as the climax of "ten thousand years of equatorial heritage," becomes General Compson's vision of the price men like him and Thomas Sutpen must pay for living a few years behind the columns of the great white mansion (250–51).

Quentin's most insightful visionary moment comes when, in imagining Wash Jones's instant of convulsive recognition that Sutpen will not "make it right" with Milly, he experiences the death of his belief in southern chivalry (288–90). With Wash, Quentin recognizes the betrayal of the South by its heroes and knows he, too, has no place to run to in this Götterdämmerung. Shreve's closing vision of the western hemisphere taken over by descendants of Thomas Sutpen through Jim Bond includes himself: "And so in a few thousand years, I who regard you will also have sprung from the loins of African kings" of a few thousand years before (378). His closing question about why Quentin hates the South emerges from this vision that all the distinctions they have labored over will "bleach out" in the end and the ordinary will win over the legendary. It is the countervision to the image of Sutpen still galloping over the land, still in spiritual possession through his descendants. As he suggests in the title of his saga, Faulkner saw that dynasties have a way of collapsing both in history and in fiction.[26]

26. Ralph Behrens, "Collapse of Dynasty: The Thematic Center of *Absalom, Absalom!*," *PMLA,* LXXXIX (1974), 31–32.

With *Go Down, Moses,* published in 1942, Faulkner introduced a new development in the southern family saga tradition by presenting the family chronicle in a mix of short and moderately long episodes rather than in sustained novel form. Phrases such as "annals of the family" and "family chronicle" throughout indicate his recognition of the form he worked with. Not until later in his interviews did he call it a novel. In reshaping his previously written stories to fit the needs of a family saga, he followed the practice of the redactor in the Genesis saga: combining individual legends within a new context, he found new significance for the parts in the larger scheme.[27] Displacement of the inheritance is by any measure the key motif of the saga, and he shows in Isaac McCaslin the fulfillment of his biblical prototype's name role in changing the line of succession as well as in being the late-born child of aging parents. As a chronicle of family episodes and family memory, *Go Down, Moses* functions as sagas are supposed to function, with members of the extended family, black and white branches, reconsidering and reshaping key stories to fit their needs and visions of who they are.

It is clear enough that when he first wrote the stories that would later be adapted to *Go Down, Moses,* Faulkner did not have in mind a saga of the McCaslin family, much less the key motif of displacement. In the published and unpublished stories Faulkner reworked to make his McCaslin saga, Isaac McCaslin is only a background figure in the great bear hunt, and he does have a son and grandson. Narrators of the stories come from the Compson and Sartoris clans, and no blood links are indicated between the white and black hunters. While Zack Edmonds and Henry Beauchamp still wait to be created, "Luke" Beauchamp is a comic rogue tenant farmer unrelated to his landlord Roth Edmonds, and no special link exists between Roth and Molly Beauchamp. For Sam Fathers, there is no indication of the burden of a part-black heritage, and in the first version of "Delta Autumn" the irascible young hunter is Don Boyd, not Roth, and he has no family link with the mulatto mistress he pays off.[28]

27. Herman Gunkel, *The Legend of Genesis: The Biblical Saga and History,* Trans. W. H. Carruth (New York, 1964), 44–46.

28. William Faulkner, *Go Down, Moses* (1942; rpr. New York, 1951). Faulkner's revisions have been catalogued and analyzed in Marvin Klotz, "Procrustean Revision in Faulkner's *Go Down, Moses,*" *American Literature,* XXXVII (1965), 1–16, and in Joanne V. Creighton, *Faulkner's Craft of Revision* (Detroit, 1977). Stories on which Faulkner drew for *Go Down, Moses* include the unpublished manuscript "Was"; an unpublished version of "A Point of Law" and "A Point of Law," *Collier's,* June 22, 1940; "Gold Is Not Always," *Atlantic Monthly*

In revising the unpublished and previously published stories for *Go Down, Moses*, Faulkner changed first-person narrative to the third-person viewpoint of a family bard, what Joanne Creighton calls "the incantatory Faulknerian voice that ranges over events past and future" and "operates both as a summary and a commentary" on the recording consciousnesses of participants in the saga action. That presiding bardic voice then reflects the minds of different family members as they live through their experiences and provides a large view of their thoughts and acts while they live minute by minute. "Was" is viewed from the perspective of nine-year-old Cass Edmonds but is conveyed through "another voice which represents a distillation of the story itself, a story whose purity and smoothness remind us of a legend, a family inheritance savored and no doubt elaborated during countless retellings," and it shows how that society has learned to see itself "uncritically but appreciatively" by a member of the family.[29] Viewpoint in "The Fire and the Hearth" shifts back and forth between Lucas Beauchamp and Roth Edmonds as they remember resonant portions of family history while they spar with each other, and the voice of the presiding family narrator-historian interprets their thoughts. When Roth, for example, draws on family memory of Lucas appearing on his twenty-first birthday to demand his legacy from Isaac, the hovering narrator takes over: "Only Zachary Edmonds and, in his time, his son Carothers knew that part of it. But what followed most of the town of Jefferson knew, so that the anecdote not only took its place in the Edmonds family annals, but in the minor annals of the town too:—how the white and the negro cousins went side by side to the bank that morning" (108–109).

Viewpoint remains consistently with Isaac in "The Old People," "The Bear," and "Delta Autumn" to show what the family member who displaced the inheritance saw and felt. If the observations are those of a boy and young man, aged ten to twenty-eight, and later of a man near eighty, the language in which those experiences are told is that, again, of the presiding family bard. When in "The Old People" Ike shoots his first buck

---

(November, 1940); the unpublished manuscript "An Absolution"; an unpublished version of "The Old People" and the *Harper's* story of the same name (September, 1940); "Lion," *Harper's* (December, 1935); "The Bear," minus part four, *Saturday Evening Post*, May 9, 1942; "Delta Autumn," *Story* (May–June, 1942); "Go Down, Moses," *Collier's*, January 25, 1941; and "Pantaloon in Black," *Harper's* (October, 1940).

29. Creighton, *Faulkner's Craft of Revision*, 127; Carl E. Rollyson, "Faulkner as Historian: The Commissary Books in *Go Down, Moses*," *Markham Review*, VII (1978), 31.

and is marked with blood by Sam Fathers, the language soars beyond the consciousness of the boy of twelve to describe the blood "joining him and the man forever, so that the man would continue to live past the boy's seventy years and then eighty years, long after the man himself had entered the earth as chiefs and kings entered it" (165). That what they bring to the experience shapes the meaning they draw from it is evident in Ike's and Cass's dialogue in the commissary: to Ike the ledger entries are moments in the family's history; to Cass they are records of business transactions, interpretations whose consequences differ markedly. As Ike interprets those ledger entries, though, like Quentin and Shreve in *Absalom, Absalom!* he must fill in the gaps with generalized knowledge of the family and its world and values and must supply the context for the ledger text.[30]

With such revisions and adaptations, Faulkner then presented *Go Down, Moses* as a new saga of the McCaslins, comparable to the saga of the Sutpens, though, as Cleanth Brooks has suggested, he would have made his intent clearer if he had named it *The McCaslins.* The less prosaic title, however, suggests biblical resonances commensurate with Isaac's vision and renunciation. In any case, Faulkner agreed that the McCaslin heritage was an ad hoc assemblage. When asked if the McCaslin genealogy was worked out before *Go Down, Moses* was written, he conceded that family continuity "came along as these people appeared" and explained further: "I would think of a character to write a story about and suddenly he would drag in a lot of people I never saw or heard of before, and so the genealogy developed itself."[31]

What he did not say was that the saga revolves around Isaac's renunciation and that the other saga conventions function as anticipations or reflections of that relinquishment. Indeed, episodes of the saga act as a running debate within the family, both black and white branches, and among family friends on the wisdom of that displacement of inheritance. In the anticipatory episode "Was," Cass Edmonds is introduced as Isaac McCaslin's "elder cousin" and "the inheritor, and in his time the bequestor, of that which some had thought then and some still thought should

---

30. Arthur F. Kinney, "'Topmost in the Pattern': Family Structure in Faulkner," in *New Directions in Faulkner Studies,* ed. Doreen Fowler and Ann J. Abadie (Jackson, 1984), 161; Carl E. Rollyson, *Uses of the Past in the Novels of William Faulkner* (Ann Arbor, 1984), 130.

31. Cleanth Brooks, *William Faulkner: The Yoknapatawpha Country* (New Haven, 1963), 244; Frederick L. Gwynn and Joseph Blotner, eds., *Faulkner in the University* (New York, 1965), 97.

have been Isaac's" (3). In "The Fire and the Hearth" Lucas doubts the Edmondses' rights to the land and remembers Isaac's better claim as the oldest McCaslin descendant in the male line as well as his own claim (36), and in his memory of his confrontation with Zack Edmonds over Molly, he recalls taunting Zack with trying to use old Carothers on him as Cass did with Ike (56). Roth similarly recalls the Edmondses' continued responsibility to black McCaslins after Ike relinquished his claim (106). That judging Ike's decision has passed down the generations in both branches of the family, black and white, becomes clear in "Delta Autumn" when the unnamed granddaughter of Tennie's Jim tells old Ike he was wrong in giving up the legacy to the Edmondses because it kept them from becoming men (360). Ike, as well, has his own inner debate on the enduring rightness of his decision, and during his ride to the late Delta hunt has to confront the consequences of giving up his own sons for the company of sons of men with whom he once hunted and of giving up the wilderness to exploitation by machines and profit-minded men (335–36).

In accounts of the McCaslin lineage developed during Faulkner's revisions, the sprawling branches of McCaslin descendants privilege the male line of descent that Ike abandons. Except for him, men in the male line act with authority and daring in knowledge of their derivation from old Lucius Quintus Carothers McCaslin, the original forebear whose removal from Carolina to Mississippi with the Carolina blacks Roskus, Fibby, and Thucydus marks the recorded beginning of the family (266). In "Was," Carothers' son-grandson Tomey's Turl, or Terrell, deals the cards that Hubert Beauchamp, looking at the likeness of Carothers in Turl's features, knows will beat him (29). Lucas Beauchamp likewise prides himself on being the oldest living McCaslin male descendant still living on McCaslin land, claims any gold he finds as his by right of male descent, scorns Roth as a descendant in the female line, and as a male McCaslin refuses to go to Roth's back door (36, 39, 44, 45). Their claims of male preeminence, though self-serving, celebrate the lingering authority of old Carothers McCaslin as progenitor of the line.

The family attribute that all acknowledge, even in relinquishment, is the peremptory authority of old Carothers, oblivious to others' judgments, self-created and self-justifying, primitive without appeal beyond himself. Unlike Thomas Sutpen, the new rich man who had to act in certain ways to acquire prestige, Carothers McCaslin was the true eighteenth-century-style aristocrat with the personal force, however cruel and ruthless, to make others imitate him, not he them.[32] For both Ike and Roth, Lucas is the true inheritor of the original Carothers McCaslin attribute. Ike remembers Lucas at the time he claimed his legacy of $1,000 at age twenty-one: "The face the color of a used saddle, the features Syriac, not in a racial sense but as the heir to ten centuries of desert horsemen. It was not at all the face of their grandfather, Carothers McCaslin. It was the face of the generation which had just preceded them: the composite type of ten thousand undefeated Confederate soldiers, almost indistinguishably caricatured, composed, cold colder than his, more ruthless than his, with more bottom than he had" (168). When he recalls the scene to Cass in the commissary, though, Ike remembers Lucas changing his name but not his nature, "not refusing to be called Lucius . . . but simply taking the name and changing it, altering it, making it no longer the white man's but his own, by himself composed, himself selfprogenitive and nominate, by himself ancestored, as, for all the old ledgers recorded to the contrary, old Carothers himself was" (281). As he realizes the significance of Lucas' victory over Zack in bringing Molly home, Roth senses Lucas' Carothers-like imperviousness to others' judgments: "He's more like old Carothers than all the rest of us put together, including old Carothers. He is both heir and prototype simultaneously . . . who fathered himself, intact and complete, contemptuous, as old Carothers must have been, of all black white yellow or red, including his own" (116, 118). Out of that recognition Roth can understand the basis of Molly's fears about the gold machine. She knows that Lucas can act as heedlessly as old Carothers in provoking God's curse on her children by exploiting the land for unearned money, in effect, by unburying the legacy left, she thinks, by old Carothers (123).

Except for Ike, Carothers' descendants, black and white, direct and collateral, accept the old man's spiritual legacy as a given of their lives. The basis of Ike's rejection of his McCaslin inheritance is his discovery of an alternate legacy taught by Sam Fathers. Instead of Carothers, he has the Old People as his spiritual ancestors. As Sam Fathers talks, Ike comes to recognize that what he is hearing is what he has known before hearing it, that the Old People ancestors precede the McCaslin ancestors, that he participates in the wilderness sense of Sam's Indian ancestors (171, 182), and that he has foreknowledge of the hunt within and beyond family tradition

---

32. Cleanth Brooks, "Thematic Problems in Southern Literature," in *Southern Literary Study: Problems and Possibilities,* ed. Louis D. Rubin, Jr., and C. Hugh Holman (Chapel Hill, 1975), 212.

(196). Even as Lucas, like Carothers, is self-created, Ike has the sense at ten that he is "witnessing his own birth," but it is "not even strange to him," for "he had experienced it all before, and not merely in dreams" (195–96). Cass seems to understand something of this alternate line of inheritance when he insists Ike inherited the land, if not from Carothers through Theophilus, then from Ikkemotubbe through Sam Fathers (300). Ike's repudiation of his inheritance at twenty-one is confirmation not only of his reading the commissary ledgers at sixteen but of his induction into the wilderness cult when he began to learn from Sam Fathers and vicariously from Jobaker.[33] If Sam had two fathers, Isaac has two sets of ancestors and chooses those of the timeless world of the imagination over those of history and farms and slaves or tenants.

For all the emphasis on patriarchal primacy, matriarchal power in the McCaslin saga challenges that primacy at key points, most often to discount claims of the men as they exploit their sense of possession. Where men act to exclude or to refuse to acknowledge, most women in the extended family act to sustain, nurture, and continue within the family covenant. In "Was," for example, Buck as the patriarchal representative shows his wariness of matriarchal claims in his evasions of Sophonsiba Beauchamp's wiles, and Hubert comically recognizes the wariness between patriarchal and matriarchal motives when he describes Sophonsiba's bed as "bear country" (22). Turl similarly recognizes matriarchal power when he tells Cass he is confident in his suit of Tennie because he has the women working for him (13). In "The Fire and the Hearth" Lucas recognizes that the woman is the key to the puzzle of relationships between black men, black women, and white men: "Women. I won't ever know. I don't want to. I ruther never to know than to find out later I have been fooled. . . . How to God . . . can a black man ask a white man to please not lay down with his black wife? And even if he could ask it, how to God can a white man promise he won't?" (59). In "The Bear" Ike similarly recognizes his wife's superior knowledge about the relationships of sex, family, land and legacies. During their conjugal embrace, he realizes the extent of her knowledge: "She already knows more than I with all the man-listening in camps. . . . They are born already bored with what a boy approaches only at fourteen and fifteen with blundering and aghast trembling. . . . She is lost. She was born lost" (314).

From the matriarchal point of view, men's exertions for money or mas-

---

33. T. H. Adamowski, "Isaac McCaslin and the Wilderness of the Imagination," *Centennial Review*, XVII (1973), 95–96, 99.

culine dignity are irrelevant to women's need to preserve. When Lucas is outraged at Zack for keeping Molly in his house and justifies his anger by his blood pride, Molly calls him "a fool" and cites the need to keep young Roth nourished, even if Aunt Thisbe has to "fix him a sugar-tit—" (50). When Lucas becomes obsessed with finding the buried gold, Molly says she has to be free of him because he is violating God's claim on the earth and endangering her child (102, 122). In "Go Down, Moses," Molly still affirms the claims of family over men's laws when she wants Butch Worsham brought home for a real funeral and burial. No matter that Butch has killed a policeman and been involved in the numbers racket, he is her "Benjamin" and must come home. In her claims, Gavin Stevens, one of the witnesses to the McCaslin saga, senses the "old, timeless female affinity for blood and grief " (376).

As Faulkner's presiding bard shows, the influence of matriarchs works at key points in the saga to shape the future destiny of the family. Despite temporary failure of her wiles in "Was," Sophonsiba shows the resolve beneath her simpers that will produce Isaac and will dismiss Hubert's mulatto mistress from Warwick Place to keep their mother's house from being defiled (303). Molly holds Lucas to his true place as man of the land instead of whiskey runner or gold hunter. Ike's unnamed wife shapes the childless future of his succession when she refuses to let their conjugal family extend into a consanguine one. For Ike, reading the ledgers, the vision of Eunice walking into the icy river at Christmas, 1833, epitomizes matriarchal dissent running through the patriarchal McCaslin legacy (268–71), a comment on the legacy that is a key part of his reason for renouncing it.

Although running family debate on the rightness of Isaac's renunciation of his inheritance implies a verdict of McCaslin decline through the generations, Lucas enhances the motif with his running comment on decline of the Edmondses as successors to the McCaslin legacy. His view of the diminishing Edmondses is, of course, biased by his view of himself as better claimant to the legacy. In his contest of wills with Roth, he contrasts the present holder of the land with Cass and Carothers "back in the old time when men black and white were men" (37). Developing that view as the contest continues, he constructs a scale of descending worth from Cass to Zack to Roth—a scale showing "that Zack Edmonds had been as much better a man than his son as old Cass Edmonds had been than both of them put together" (43). He sees Roth as an ineffectual grandson of Cass, who was "strong enough, ruthless enough, old Carothers Mc-

Caslin enough" to take the land from Ike (44). Ironically, though, Roth's one redeeming quality in Lucas' eyes is his temperamental kinship with Cass, "that almost choleric shortness of temper which Lucas remembered in old Cass Edmonds but which had skipped Zack" (59). Apparently, the Carothers-like temper of Cass, inherited by Roth, works on Lucas at last. In the divorce hearing, when Lucas submits to Molly's demand he give up the gold-finding machine, he also submits to the image of Carothers and Cass in Roth. Name usage measures shift in relationship at that point. Lucas, who resisted calling the father "Mister Zack" as the other blacks did and, as a McCaslin, insisted on calling him "Mr. Edmonds," now concedes to the son the compromise name "Mr. Roth Edmonds" (104, 129).

That the McCaslin family saga develops within the context of two contrasting versions of history is one of the key reasons for Isaac's displacement of the inheritance. In the human-centered view of history, the family participates in the life of Mississippi from the first decade of the nineteenth century to the fourth decade of the twentieth and knows the values of the old order, when men and women could be bought, worked, and bred like animals, through the hard times of Reconstruction, to old Ike's and Roth's time in the Delta, when machines and roads overwhelm the remaining wilderness and dictators in Europe and bureaucrats in Washington, D.C., impose new orders on the old. The McCaslin-Edmonds house stands as a measure of family development through history. When Lucas approaches Roth's house to report George Wilkins' whiskey still, he sees the house as a summation of family history, "the two log wings which Carothers McCaslin had built and which had sufficed old Buck and Buddy, connected by the open hallway which, as his pride's monument and epitaph, old Cass Edmonds had enclosed and superposed with a second storey of white clapboards faced with a portico" (44–45). For most actors in the saga, Cass embodies the human-centered version of history, a man with "one foot straddled into a farm and the other foot straddled into a bank," as General Compson says (250). As Cass tells Ike, his world is one of contingencies and complications and suffering endured, not absolutes: "And even suffering and grieving is better than nothing; there is only one thing worse than not being alive, and that's shame. But you can't be alive forever, and you always wear out life long before you have exhausted the possibilities for living" (186). His world stands in contrast with Ike's sacramental and God-centered version of history.[34]

34. Brooks, *Yoknapatawpha Country,* 263; Lucinda MacKethan, *The Dream of Arcady:*

For Ike, the human-centered version of history is epitomized in the commissary ledgers. As impromptu family historian, he sees the record as a tale of injustices done and unremedied despite attempts by his father and uncle to extend the legacy, if not recognition, to black McCaslins. But he puts away that version of history: "He would never need to look at the ledgers again nor did he" (271). Instead, Ike turns to history as the expression of the will of God. Within that divine will, possession of land takes the form of stewardship, and the fallen New World becomes a second chance for redemption through suffering (258–59). For Ike, his vision is truer than even the vision of the biblical writers, who he thinks were men much like Cass, caught up in the complexities of experience: "The heart already knows. . . . What they were trying to tell, what He wanted said, was too simple. Those for whom they transcribed His words could not have believed them. It had to be expounded in the everyday terms which they were familiar with and could comprehend, not only those who listened but those who told it too, because . . . [they] could comprehend truth only through the complexity of passion and lust and hatred and fear which drives the heart" (260). The issue then becomes whether Ike's vision of a purged and purified land can be realized in a world of "passion and lust and hatred and fear which drives the heart." [35] Although Isaac may live the rest of his life as a priest to that vision, in the McCaslin family the generations respect but do not believe it. To them he represents the alternate but unacceptable version of the family covenant.

Type scenes running through the McCaslin saga represent the three foci of action and decision by the McCaslin-Edmonds clan. The commissary, the hunting camp and stand, and the hearth at Lucas and Molly's cabin embody the conflicting forces at work in the family. The commissary is not only the proper scene for Isaac's relinquishment at twenty-one but as well the place of his reading the ledgers at sixteen (256). As the place of ledgers, it is also the place of the Books of Judgment: "To him it was as though the ledgers in their scarred cracked leather bindings were being lifted down one by one in their fading sequence and spread open on the desk or perhaps upon some apocryphal Bench or even altar or perhaps before the Throne Itself for a last perusal and contemplation of

Place and Time in Southern Literature (Baton Rouge, 1980), 175–76; Annette Benert, "The Four Fathers of Isaac McCaslin," *Southern Humanities Review*, IX (1975), 428.

35. MacKethan, *Dream of Arcady*, 175–79; Benert, "Four Fathers," 428.

the Allknowledgeable" (261). For later generations the commissary is an extension of the McCaslin legacy, which Lucas draws on without repaying (117). It is the place where Roth confronts Lucas on the folly of his hunt for gold and where Molly tells Roth she wants a divorce from Lucas (96, 101)—a place where fundamental decisions on the family's destiny are made.

The hearth and the campfire also represent two basic moral choices for the citizens of *Go Down, Moses.*[36] The fire on the hearth, lit when Lucas and Molly first marry and move into their cabin, continues throughout their long marriage, becoming the symbol of marriage itself among McCaslin blacks. In "Pantaloon in Black" Rider lights his hearth fire for Mannie in emulation of Lucas and Molly (46, 138). The cabin room in front of the hearth extends the scene for Roth as a part of family memory. In the cabin his friendship with Henry Beauchamp develops as their fathers' had (110). After that fateful day when "haughty ancestral pride" comes to Roth and he rejects Lucas' cabin for Zack's house, he discovers he can no longer return to the intimacy of Molly's fire or table. When he goes back to eat there, he finds himself eating alone as Lucas and Henry leave. "So he entered his heritage. He ate its bitter fruit" (114). In effect, Lucas' cabin with its hearth fire becomes the citadel of black McCaslins as the commissary with its ledgers does of the white McCaslins and Edmondses.

As Ike renounces the commissary and what it stands for, the hunting camp and stand become his type scenes, indicative of his alternate heritage. "The Old People," all but part four of "The Bear," and "Delta Autumn" constitute a series of graduated scenes as Ike is inducted into the mystique and mystery of the wilderness and into his vision of history as the expression of divine will. Significantly, by the time of "Delta Autumn," he sees the hunting tent as his true home (351) and acts as priest of the sacred fire at the camp. There he has his ritual glass of whiskey and water, tells the young hunters to "Eat it all up," and recites events of former hunts and exploits of former great hunters (344).

As priest of the hunt, Isaac also acts as keeper of talismanic objects and actions associated with the hunt. Near eighty, he still keeps the shotgun given him by Cass at Christmas, 1878, and the compass and silver-mounted horn given by General Compson (205, 300). Passing on the sacred object, he gives the horn to Roth's mistress for Roth's son (363). The whiskey Ike serves and drinks in the delta camp carries over meanings from for-

---

36. David Mickelson, "The Campfire and the Hearth in *Go Down, Moses,*" *Mississippi Quarterly,* XXXVIII (1985), 312–15.

mer times when, in the camps of his boyhood, hunters drank, "drinking not of the blood they spilled but some condensation of the wild immortal spirit, drinking it moderately, humbly even, not with the pagans' base and baseless hope of acquiring thereby virtues of cunning and strength and speed but in salute to them" (192).

Ike's silver cup legacy from Hubert Beauchamp, kept only in memory rather than possession, shows how talismanic objects have their value in story and memory, by enhancement through thought rather than through actualities of living.[37] As the silver cup of gold coins, wrapped in burlap and sealed with the Beauchamp stamp, changes mysteriously into a tin coffee pot filled with copper coins and liens on Isaac's legacy, the process parallels Hubert's decline and the destruction of Warwick Place and with it the loss of an alternate and presumably untainted legacy, one unmarked by the acts of old Carothers. With failure of the Beauchamp legacy, which he did not have a chance to renounce, Ike can only hold the memory of it for the remaining fifty or more years of his life. As Cass notes, that legacy had become only a pile of coppers "still not old enough yet to be either rarities or heirlooms" (308).

If writing the past in *Go Down, Moses* was for Faulkner an act of creation, not discovery, learning the past, for the McCaslin family he created, was an act of discovery, and the effect of researching the past was to change the researchers. If Isaac's was the extreme response, Roth retrieves the past only to repeat it. Lucas acknowledges his link with the family past by accepting his place as a man of the land on the land taken by the ancestor for whom he refused to be named. As Faulkner saw in *Go Down, Moses,* the family past is dangerous country where one can be ambushed by knowledge.

Displacement of the inheritance, then, became the crucial convention of family sagas keyed to the Civil War. Around that central occurrence other conventions took supporting roles. Because of the catastrophe of the war, family history and expectations, formerly baronial in vision, took new turns toward diminished destinies. The past on the other side of the fault line took on legendary dimensions that descendants had to reimagine for their austere purposes, and their speculations turned from what might have been to what had to be.

37. Stephen Barker, "From Old Gold to I.O.U.'s: Ike McCaslin's Debased Genealogical Coin," *Faulkner Journal,* III (1987), 23.

3

AGRARIANS' LAMENT
THE LONG DECLINE

Despite their generalized confidence that life on the farm close to nature was the answer to threats of industrial imperialism, the Nashville Agrarians showed their misgivings when they descended to particulars. Their doubts emerged especially when they spoke in terms of southern families. Although in *I'll Take My Stand,* the Agrarians' manifesto published in 1930, John Crowe Ransom could proclaim that "Southerners have a filial duty to discharge to their own section" and Andrew Lytle could describe in loving detail a typical day on a traditional but hypothetical family farm, they could also see that the lure of urban and industrial benefits tempted sons and daughters to commercialize family farms or to leave them for the city. With "threats of an early departure from his hearth and board," children of the agrarian would urge him to save the farm by mechanizing it.[1] In the long view of family sagas, this shift of values from old to new introduced displacement of the inheritance and began a long decline in family history, in which later generations lacked the vision and endurance of the earlier.

In the minds of the Agrarians, this invasion by industrial and commercial operators was a further result of the catastrophic Civil War. In Ransom's view "the carpet-baggers are again in [our] midst," trying to remake the southern economy in the image of the nation's. For families, this mechanization meant displacement of the inheritance by breaking up the family as a socioeconomic unit and dispersing the younger generation to work away from the homeplace. "This [dispersal] begins the home breaking,"

---

1. *I'll Take My Stand: The South and the Agrarian Tradition* (1930; rpr. New York, 1962), xix, 205, 217–33.

Lytle saw. "Time is money now, not property, and the boys can't hang around the place. . . . They must go out somewhere and get a job." [2] In exemplary family sagas by Caroline Gordon, Allen Tate, and Andrew Lytle, this process over the generations demonstrates how clans on plantations lost their hold on the old style of living and either lost the homeplace or saved it in a new form by converting it to industrial or commercial uses. As they did so, they provided critiques of the agrarian tradition and its successors.

In choosing to make her first novel, *Penhally*, a family saga, Gordon turned to her own family history and the larger world of the family in the South. A product of the Meriwether clan in Kentucky, she knew the history of the family from constant exposure in family talk. Not needing to look into old letters and Bibles, she knew from the lore virtually in the air she breathed that the first Meriwether came to Kentucky from Virginia in 1809, bought 10,000 acres at a dollar an acre in southern Kentucky, and built the house he called Meriville; that his son, Gordon's great-great-grandfather, influenced by Sir Walter Scott, built the brick house Woodstock, with a deer park and race track, and began breeding Woodstock horses, later favored by Confederate officers; that her grandmother Caroline grew up at Woodstock, inherited nearby land, married her cousin Douglas Meriwether, who rode with Nathan Bedford Forrest during the war, and, influenced by Nathaniel Hawthorne, built the house called Merry Mount; that her mother Caroline Meriwether married at seventeen her Virginia-born tutor James Maury Morris Gordon and followed him into western Kentucky, Arkansas, and Missouri before returning to the family lands. As Caroline Ferguson Gordon, born at Merry Mount, she knew that there was much intermarrying between the Fergusons and Meriwethers and that the family was so close it called its various kinships "the Connection." She was thinking in the same vein when, shortly after *Penhally* was published, she told Josephine Herbst that out of family stories "your imagination picks up, unbeknownst to you, all sorts of things." So, she continued, "I picked up material for one chapter which I know will be the best in my book from a chance remark of my uncle's." The dedication of the saga is to the memory of her ancestor Charles Nicholas Meriwether of Woodstock and to her uncle Rob, Robert Emmet Meriwether, and the family recognized both themselves and their stories in the book. [3]

2. *Ibid.*, 23, 236.
3. Waldron, *Close Connections*, 33–35, 90, 96–97.

A second strain to enter the novel was the family tradition of classically trained scholars, especially exemplified for Caroline Gordon by her father. James Gordon ran academies to train Kentucky youths in the classics and trained his daughter in the classics before she studied more Latin and Greek at Bethany College.[4] Out of that classical training, she learned to see the family in terms of heroes, myths, and tragic flaws.

Penhally is a rich example of the family saga of revelation. Like a Greek tragedy, it proceeds inexorably according to its premise, and conventions of the family saga are instrumental in working out implications of that premise. The issue of primogeniture and entail functions as the tragic flaw of the family, reflecting the family's, and the South's, frozen loyalty to a condition whose time has passed but whose reasons for existing have endured. The premise came from Gordon's own family tradition. She wrote later: "In my childhood I heard a good deal of talk about [Thomas] Jefferson's abolition of the laws of primogeniture and entail. The Meriwethers who had made a practice of entailing land, as the only way they knew of keeping it in the family, now had to content themselves with entailment which could last only two generations. It was felt that 'Mr. Jefferson . . . had made *quite* a mistake.' My uncle Rob, it seems to me now, spent a lifetime protesting against 'Mister Jefferson's mistake.' "[5] If the issue could be so clear in Meriwether family councils, it is not necessarily so in the Llewellyns' tradition in her novel. If old Nicholas Llewellyn's insistence on entailment as responsibility to one's successors on the land is part of the agrarian position, Caroline Gordon, the novelist and heir of such a family tradition, could take a more critical view of Jefferson versus Llewellyn. Indeed, *Penhally* poses a running debate between entailment and pastless opportunity represented by Nicholas and Ralph Llewellyn and their heirs, and the verdict is mixed.

The break-up of old living patterns in Virginia in the late eighteenth century, including Jefferson's abolition of primogeniture and entailment, Nicholas remembers, had been the reason for the family's removal to Kentucky, and the family's trek along the Wilderness Road to its new beginnings becomes the epic memory from his boyhood for his middle age as it is his dream when he is dying during Reconstruction.[6] "A man could not, actually, entail his property on his own children's children! That was

4. *Ibid.*, 35–36.
5. Caroline Gordon, "Always Summer," *Southern Review*, n.s., VII (1971), 433–34.
6. Caroline Gordon, *Penhally* (1931; rpr. New York, 1971), 9, 192.

one reason why his grandfather, Robert Llewellyn, had approved of his son's coming west" (37). He has to remember, though, that his father Francis, like his grandfather Robert, was trying to live by a European view of family and property—a view measured in his memory by his father's four wives: sent to "Edinboro" for a classical, old-world, gentlemanly education, Francis had married the Scotswoman Ellen Laurie, who died at sea; then his own mother Nancy Allard of Virginia; third, Lucinda Crenfrew of Virginia, mother of his half-brother Ralph; and finally Mary Barnhart of Kentucky. That Ralph takes a view against entailment is a measure of his link with the western and later development of family (21).

Whether "Mister Jefferson's mistake" means doom or salvation for the family in Kentucky becomes the issue in all three parts of the novel, and Gordon chooses the variation on the family saga that takes the reader directly into the life of each generation without agency or perspective of a later family narrator. As she takes the reader inside the minds of family members, history and memory are one. Allowed to know thoughts of the principal characters, the reader is privy to their motives and values but knows no more than those characters know and in the end must puzzle over why some family members make their crucial and fatal choices.

In Part One, the prewar and wartime episodes of family history, the emphasis is on the minds of Nicholas and his heir John, and the family debate appears to run in favor of entailment. As in the English country-house poems and sketches, the contrast favors Nicholas' Penhally, with its natural evolution of wings and additions, its stone structure, and its grove like the grove back in Virginia, over Ralph's Mayfield, a richly furnished, red brick mansion with Corinthian columns and a racetrack for fast horses in the manner of the new rich of the Old South (1–2, 12, 26). And Penhally's ritualized hospitality contrasts with the prodigal music and dancing at Mayfield (21). Nicholas' view of Jefferson's mistake rests on his conviction that the head of the family puts his obligation to family over self-interest. He has thought of the land as the family's, not his as the right of the oldest son. A family lives together in mingled generations as a household, he believes, and Ralph's wish to separate and live with his conjugal family brings the notion of family and property into new perspective. Like Chance's later love for the land, the concept does not become conscious until it is threatened.[7] On the eve of war, Nicholas confirms his view of

7. Andrew Lytle, "Caroline Gordon and the Historic Image," *Sewanee Review,* LVII (1949), 577.

entailment by willing Penhally to John and his eldest heirs. Although he acts in accordance with established custom according to prewar views, his act is that unrecognized fatal flaw with harsh consequences for later generations. As in a tragedy, though, at first what he did seems right. While Nicholas preserves Penhally during the war, declares himself against a war brought on by nonlandowning politicians, and hides gold when he sees Confederate money becoming worthless, Ralph embraces the war, spends his wealth to outfit a cavalry regiment, and is ruined by war's end, with Mayfield mortgaged to Nicholas.

During Part Two, the postwar period, the running debate begins to turn against Nicholas' faith in the old-style family. He rejects Alice Blair as a suitable wife for John because of "her blood" (181) and approves John's marriage to his cousin, Ralph's daughter Lucy, as a way of reuniting the separated family. Whereas Lucy becomes a matriarchal preserver of family memory, Alice marries a tobacco merchant from Louisville, moves abroad, becomes rich in nonagrarian commerce, and prepares her heir Douglas Parrish to repossess Penhally as a country place supported by outside money. As a woman who, old style, married for property, Lucy begins to show the consequences of her choice when she alienates her son Frank, who marries, unwisely as it turns out, for personal love and self-interest and ends up a suicide. At this point the locus of power in the family shifts to the matriarchs, and the men, weakened by war and disenfranchisement, become as impotent within the workings of the family as in the world outside.

In the modern period Chance, Nicholas' great-grandnephew and the younger son of Frank, recognizes that entailment had its value in regarding land and estate as a trusteeship ("It made a man feel that he was not really the owner, or at least that he had heavy obligations to his successors"), but for his brother Nick, heir to Penhally, it is an outgrown concept (233). As a banker, he thinks of land as money. Although Penhally may have been saved through hard times by primogeniture and entail, to the later generation the estate is a property, not a style of life, and he sells it for a good price so it can become a Virginia-style hunt club. Even though Chance may hold true to the founding vision, the running debate over "Mister Jefferson's mistake" shows the motif of family decline. The personal strength of patriarchs and matriarchs makes it an issue of family destiny more than a sign of the times.[8]

8. *Ibid.*, 576.

Her long evenings of talk at Benfolly, Gordon and Tate's home, with Allen Tate and Andrew Lytle about the Civil War, as Lytle wrote his biography of Nathan Bedford Forrest and Tate worked on his never-finished biography of Robert E. Lee, gave Caroline Gordon a sure grasp of the effect of history in her family saga. The Civil War as a public event parallels and modifies the fracture in the Llewellyn family and represents what Lytle sees as the enveloping action beyond the family. The forces leading to war are anticipated in the family as Nicholas recognizes the growing power of the New England manufacturers and their Tariff of Abominations (7) and as the Llewellyns and Crenfrews at dinner in 1861 discuss what effects John Brown's raid on Harpers Ferry in Virginia will have on them and their kin (61). The issues of abolition and emancipation come home to them when they talk of Dr. Crenfrew's freeing his slaves three years earlier. With no one willing to hire them, the freedmen are left on his hands, as in Virginia the Llewellyns were left with worn-out land and slaves to feed (63–66). The war becomes the breaking point for the family, as for the South, at Shiloh, where John is wounded, and at Gettysburg, where Charles, the hope of the Llewellyns of Mayfield, is killed with Morgan's Raiders while trying to reach the site in time for the turning-point battle (98–100, 159–60). John remembers also that General Albert Sidney Johnston, on whose daring the battle at Shiloh depended, was killed riding Ralph's warhorse Fire Eater (107). As Chance notes of his grandmother Lucy, life stopped for most of them with the war, and all they had left was family legend.

With displacement of the family inheritance both by family action and by the Civil War, family fortunes take a new turn. Ralph's values, based on a distributed inheritance, though apparently defeated by Nicholas and the war, reappear with Douglas Parrish, Alice Blair's grandson. Rich from tobacco processed and marketed, not grown, he and his Maryland-born wife Joan reclaim Penhally, he for its family associations, she for its use as a hunt club. Her motives are not wholly those of a woman of fashion, though. Echoing Nicholas' earlier contrast, she values Penhally for its natural evolvement as a family home, "a wing added here to meet the needs of a growing family, an L stuck on there, merely because it was the most convenient place to put it," and thinks "the whole thing had a line and character that the more pretentious houses did not have"—houses she found "tiresome . . . with their Corinthian columns and double parlors and fantastic balconies of wrought iron" (260). More clearly than those with more emotional ties to Penhally, as a collateral descendant she sees that it can endure in a nonagrarian time only as a country seat supported by outside money and is ready to preserve the old in terms of the new.

Her decision echoes the matriarchal-patriarchal conflict that has run through the family since the time of Nicholas' successors, and her decision, like those of her matriarchal predecessors, reflects the puzzling element in family history. Just as Nicholas could never understand why his double first cousin Charlotte Llewellyn chose his cousin Jeems Llewellyn over him, the later family men cannot understand the motives of the matriarchs. John never knows why Lucy turned against her son Frank even as a child and wonders what she means as she says, "I knew it," when news of Frank's death comes, but "he had not thought then to ask her what she meant by that" (203). Neither can Chance fathom why his grandfather John defers to Lucy's demands when he is a strong man otherwise: "There was a sort of compulsion on him that made him do her least bidding. . . . It was almost . . . as if she had something on the man!"(230).[9] Nor, ignorant of rumors about his mother Faneuil, can Chance understand why his father shot himself when he had more advantages than his exhausted and disenfranchised grandfather had (239).

In her use of family saga conventions, Gordon employs type scenes, talismanic objects, and moments of vision to link later generations with the earlier. In his generation Nicholas sits at the flat millstone under the poplar tree and thinks of it as the place of the fathers as he reviews his father's life as a classical scholar and husband of four wives (20–22). By the time of later generations, the paintings of that first wife, the Scotswoman, and of old Nicholas, now family talismans, look down from the hall at Penhally as judges on the family's apostasy from the family covenant (245, 270). When Chance shows Douglas Parrish the gravemarker of the first Francis Llewellyn, he thinks of his ancestor's picture in the hall as that of a younger son whose sense of purpose had endured beyond the accidents of history: "A younger son, with no patrimony, he had gone off into the wilderness in search of the land he had not inherited, and all the people who had lived and died and been buried on this hill had come into being through the stirrings of this one man's pride" (256). The similar scenes opening and closing the novel also round out the sense of family destiny. In 1826 Nicholas

9. Rose Anne C. Freistat, *Caroline Gordon as Novelist and Woman of Letters* (Baton Rouge, 1984), 56–58, attributes his acquiescence to guilt over marrying Lucy for convenience rather than for love. See also Lytle, "Gordon and Historic Image," 577.

walks in the grove beside Penhally and thinks of his quarrel with his brother (1–3). In the twentieth century, as Penhally is opened as a hunt club, Chance walks through the grove area, sees the changes made, and thinks of his quarrel with his brother for selling the family home (279).

That was the ending Gordon first planned. As she told Ford Madox Ford, she envisioned that "the young man went out on the porch and looked around and the land which he had known seemed to have been obliterated—I believe the last words were 'as if by a wave of the hand.' " [10] But on Tate's urging, she changed to the more violent ending of Chance shooting his brother and telling Parrish to call the sheriff. Why Chance put a pistol in his pocket when he let his fiancée Emily Kinloe persuade him to attend the opening of the hunt club is unexplained (273). If the scene suggests anything about family history, it is that Chance, like his grandfather, defers too readily to matriarchal wishes, for "he had not even asked Emily why she had decided at the last minute that they must come." Gordon's last-minute decision was less in keeping with her plan for a family saga than was her first intention.

Despite the overdramatic ending, Gordon contributed to development of the family saga in the South a classic example of the genre. In traditional fashion, *Penhally* begins the narrative in the past, shows the tragic flaw established in the beginning generation, and works out the implications into the present. Her example shows kinship of the family saga with the historical novel as the reader is taken emotionally and sympathetically back into early generations without intermediary action of narrators in the present. The result is a family saga of revelation rather than discovery. In Gordon's view, history, including the family past, is knowable and thus available for critique and evaluation. For her at the beginning of her writing career, the family saga was the right vehicle for such an examination.

With *The Fathers* in 1938 Allen Tate introduced a new dimension in the family saga in the South with his first-person narrator and historian of fallen family fortunes. The narration by Lacy Buchan, retired physician and puzzled descendant, provided Tate with new possibilities for assessing a family past. Childless bachelor and end of his line, Lacy puzzles over displacement of his inheritance as the major motif of his family history and sees in himself the embodiment of family decline. In writing *The Fathers*, his first and only novel, Tate confronted in complex and personal terms implications of the large themes he had announced polemically in his earlier essays.

10. Waldron, *Close Connections,* 97.

The way to *The Fathers* came through Tate's earlier agrarian and tra-
ditionalist thought conjoined with issues precipitated by Tate's own unresolved family puzzles. As late as 1936 Tate summed up his agrarian views
in his address "What Is a Traditional Society?" to the Phi Beta Kappa chapter at the University of Virginia with his assertion that the key to traditional society is the unity of economic and moral functions. Further, he
insisted, that unity is necessary for the transmission of values through generations: "Ante-bellum man, insofar as he achieved a unity between his
moral nature and his livelihood was a traditional man. . . . In order to make
a livelihood men do not have to put aside their moral natures. . . . The kind
of property that sustains the traditional society is not only *not* hostile to
a unified moral code; it is positively the basis of it. Moreover it is the
medium, just as canvas is the medium of the painter, through which that
code is passed on to the next generation." *The Fathers* brought to conclusion Tate's "involvement in the programmatic side of Agrarian-
ism."[11] Before he reached that point, however, he had already made major decisions of closure about his earlier thought and opened new veins of
exploration.

Among his acts of closure was his decision to abandon his biography of Lee, a long-contemplated project after his biographies of Stonewall
Jackson and Jefferson Davis. Not only was he discouraged by the success
of Douglas Southall Freeman's biography of Lee, but he had also become
ambivalent about his subject. To him, Lee was so perfectly the embodiment of impersonal, formal, and uncomplicated southern convention that
the general offered little range for exploration of the complexities of personal motives in conflict with public values. Moreover, he began to feel
Lee was a cynical man without the will to subject his personal convictions to scrutiny in the context of public issues.[12] Instead, then, Tate turned
to his own family history as the embodiment of a more complex version
of the traditional South.

From his father's side he knew family stories of the four Tate brothers who removed from County Antrim, Ireland, to Virginia in the eighteenth century and moved on to North Carolina, South Carolina, Tennessee, and Kentucky. The Allen branch had begun in America with Robert
Allen's arrival in Port Tobacco, Maryland, in 1690 as indentured servant

11. Allen Tate, *Essays of Four Decades* (Chicago, 1968), 556; John L. Stewart, *The Burden
of Time: The Fugitives and Agrarians* (Princeton, 1965), 191.

12. Stewart, *Burden of Time*, 344; Michael Kreyling, *Figures of the Hero in Southern Narrative* (Baton Rouge, 1986), 121.

to a cabinetmaker. His grandson Rhodam Allen migrated to Tennessee in 1794 and to Shelby County, Kentucky, in 1795. Allen Tate recapitulated much of this family past in the early 1930s when he wrote "The Migration" to prove to himself he could master details of the pioneer life of a family.[13] Narrated by Rhodam Elwin, seventy-two in 1851 and a twenty-five-year resident of Saint Joseph, Missouri, after living earlier in Tennessee, "The Migration" tells of his father's life and times "for the instruction of his posterity" (317). Like the Tates, Elwin came from County Antrim and, like Robert Allen, arrived in Port Tobacco. After brief stays in Annapolis and Fredericksburg, Virginia, he served in the Continental Army, moved to North Carolina after the war, and then traveled by the Wilderness Road to Tennessee to claim the land payable to a Revolutionary War officer. Remembering depletion of the soil in the older colonies and states, the elder Elwin, near the time of his death, gives the narrator's son John Robert the kind of advice that passes through generations in family stories: "Chew tobacco if you will but never grow it" (347).

On his mother's side Tate heard even more stories of the Varnalls who arrived in Saint Mary's County, Maryland, late in the seventeenth century and settled in Charles County. From that background came the novelist's mother, born at Chesnut Grove, Fairfax County, Virginia, in a house built on the site of Pleasant Hill, burned during the Civil War. Part of his mother's childhood was spent with the family of her uncle John Stewart Bogan, who became the model for Major Lewis Buchan in *The Fathers*.[14] Although they lived in Kentucky, Tate's mother thought of Virginia as the "family's true home" and took her younger son to visit the ruins at Pleasant Hill. So important was the Virginia connection in family memory that Tate believed he had been born in Fairfax County, "for that was where my mother said I was born, and she always bent reality to her wishes." Not until after his mother's death, when Tate was driving his father around Winchester, Kentucky, and his father pointed out the house where Allen was born, did he know he had not come from Virginia. After his brother Ben told him that the rest of the family knew his true birthplace, Tate felt as if family lore had made him the victim of a shell game.[15]

That family memory had not only the power to reconstruct but as well the power to haunt is seen in Tate's poems "A Dream" and "A Vision,"

13. Radcliffe Squires, *Allen Tate: A Literary Biography* (New York, 1971), 14–15; Allen Tate, *The Fathers and Other Fiction*, ed. Thomas Daniel Young (Baton Rouge, 1977), 311 n.

14. Squires, *Tate Literary Biography*, 14.

15. *Ibid.*, 18; Allen Tate, *Memoirs and Opinions, 1926-1974* (Chicago, 1975), 7–8.

both written in 1932. In the first an ill nine-year-old boy dreams of walking with his mother's grandfather, a figure in eighteenth-century clothes, down a red clay road until they meet a tall, greasy man with stringy hair who speaks "from the deep coherence of hell" and the great-grandfather shudders as the world falls. In the second a young man of twenty walks alone in a park at midnight, hears "some old forgotten talk," and sees a tall man with stringy hair and hears him say with relentless eyes and voice, "I'm growing old [and] . . . you have no choice." In his correspondence with Tate, Donald Davidson noted "the close correspondence" between these dream and vision poems and Lacy Buchan's vision in Part III of the novel.[16]

The puzzle about his great-grandfather also had connotations of a breach of family trust for Tate. In answer to a question once asked about the source of the plot of *The Fathers,* he recorded its partial source in a note to the 1977 edition of the novel: "Once I thought I had found it in the court records of Fairfax County, in a deed-of-trust from my great-grandfather to one of his sons for the benefit of his daughter, my grandmother: this deed proved by inference that my great-grandfather did not wholly trust his son-in-law. There was a conflict in the family. But there are conflicts in all families. The discovery of the deed-of-trust at most actualized, gave a sort of historical reality to, a plot already forming in my mind" (313).

That plot is suggested by the "Sonnets of Blood" sequence written in 1931. The sequence poses an alienation between two brothers based on their opposing temperaments and accomplishments and on characteristics inherited from a line of ancestors in Virginia. The speaking brother is much like Allen Tate himself, studious and contemplative and prototypal of Lacy Buchan in *The Fathers;* the brother addressed is much like his elder brother Benjamin, an active and successful businessman and prototype of George Posey in the novel.[17] In Sonnet X the two brothers are characterized as one Attican and the other Thracian, and the speaker in Sonnet IX sees the two warring brothers evoking Atreus and his brother Thyestes.

From the Varnall strain of the family, those who removed from Maryland to Georgetown, Tate drew materials for his first piece of fiction, "The Immortal Woman," published in 1933. The story of an old woman who

16. Allen Tate, *Collected Poems, 1919–1976* (New York, 1977), 61-62; Donald Davidson to Allen Tate, January 1, 1963, in John Tyree Fain and Thomas Daniel Young, eds., *The Literary Correspondence of Donald Davidson and Allen Tate* (Athens, Ga., 1974), 388.

17. Squires, *Tate Literary Biography,* 22, 110.

sits outside a forlorn house in Georgetown and distractedly wraps into balls strings of twine until mysterious gentlemen come to take her away, "The Immortal Woman" is the presumptive aftermath of events later to be chronicled in *The Fathers*. Tate acknowledged the connection later in his "Note on 'The Migration' and 'The Immortal Woman,' with a Glance at Two Scenes in *The Fathers*," following the conclusion of the 1977 edition of the novel (311–14). The old lady on the bench, he said, "is like 'little Jane' in *The Fathers*, and Dr. Beckitt, who came for her once in his 'muddy Victoria,' is Dr. Buchan, narrator of *The Fathers*." Tate identified Old Major Beckitt as Major Lewis Buchan in *The Fathers* and added that "in this story he has not, fortunately for me, hanged himself," so "I will use him as a character-in-the-round in my novel." The prosperous-looking young man who comes at the end to take away the old woman "could be George Posey's son or grandson, or my brother Benjamin" (312). The Maryland connection is also source for the critical scene in *The Fathers* when Yellow Jim attacks, perhaps rapes, Jane Posey. To Donald Davidson's objection about "the (to me) unnecessary blood-kinship of Yellow Jim & his own white folks," Tate assured him the episode was based on a family story of "actual circumstances pertaining to a negro in my grandfather's family," but one occurring after the Civil War, and the relationship was one of first cousin rather than of half-brother. His grandfather had gotten the man paroled from prison after he had killed another Negro, and the man "had tried to assault one of the ladies after he had heard her say she was afraid of him." Tate admitted, "I wouldn't have felt so secure with an invented incident." His comment on his security with actual events of family history was consonant with his note to Davidson a year earlier on his unease with writing fiction: "The inventions of poetry are credible, but the inventions of fiction seem to me to be monstrous and unbelievable. You can believe in a figure of speech, but how can you believe in circumstances of your own invention?" [18]

The way to achieve conviction, Tate discovered, was to let Lacy Buchan tell the story of the fathers. Through Lacy he could have fiction filtered through figures of speech. He told Lytle six months after the novel was published that he had found the key was to "get a tone and point of view in the first sentence, have a final objective, and then let the point of view discover what lies between beginning and end." The saga that Lacy

18. Tate to Davidson, October 3, 6, 1938, and October 7, 1937, in Fain and Young, eds., *Literary Correspondence*, 318–19, 306.

chronicles, however, is not so much one he remembers or discovers as one he invents. His narration is formed by his need to understand rather than to tell what happened, and what is told is a function of his need to justify that "final objective" of Lacy's love for George Posey despite all the pain George causes. As several commentators have noted, there are enough ominous silences and confusions in Lacy's account to suggest he is not an altogether reliable narrator.[19] Lacy gives no reasons or sometimes too many for matters included, fails to note such apparent contradictions as George's selling Yellow Jim for "liquid capital" when he has ready money to pay for Semmes's indiscreet letters to the Stacy woman and to buy arms for the National Rifles in Georgetown, and neglects to explain what side George chose for his ultimate allegiance.[20] Lacy himself notes, "You remember what you cannot understand" (272), and puts that possible understanding in the context of dynastic vision or madness, saying, "Only grandfather Buchan, who was dead, and Susan, who was mad, knew everything" (272). For what he states as his basic perplex at the beginning of his narrative is the question of moral costs of change: "Why cannot life change without tangling the lives of innocent persons? Why do innocent persons cease their innocence and become violent and evil in themselves that such great changes may take place?" (5). Even he may be involved in the complicity of those costs.

Of the matters Lacy finds pertinent to recall, one of the first is his family background. Besides the Buchans and Lewises of Pleasant Hill and the Gores from the Valley of Virginia, he remembers in a premonitory way his great-grandfather Benjamin Buchan, the Scots immigrant adventurer who married Mary Armistead the year he landed, despite the displeasure of her father, and "the name of Buchan, obscure in origin, became assimilated

19. Allen Tate to Andrew Lytle, March 22, 1939, in Thomas Daniel Young and Elizabeth Sarcone, eds., *The Lytle-Tate Letters: The Correspondence of Andrew Lytle and Allen Tate* (Jackson, 1987), 135; Robert S. Dupree, *Allen Tate and the Augustan Imagination* (Baton Rouge, 1983), 127; Daniel B. Ahlport, "Tate's *The Fathers* and the Problem of Tradition," *Southern Studies,* XIX (1980), 364; Richard Law, "'Active Faith' and Ritual in *The Fathers,*" *American Literature,* LV (1983), 359; C. Hugh Holman, "*The Fathers* and the Historical Imagination," in *Literary Romanticism in America,* ed. William L. Andrews (Baton Rouge, 1981), 89–90; Patricia Kane, "An Irrepressible Conflict: Allen Tate's *The Fathers,*" *Critique,* X (1968), 13; George Dekker, *The American Historical Romance* (New York, 1987), 329–30; Stewart, *Burden of Time,* 337-38; Squires, *Tate Literary Biography,* 136; Freeman Bishop, *Allen Tate* (New York, 1967), 113; Lynette Carpenter, "The Battle Within: The Beleaguered Consciousness in Allen Tate's *The Fathers,*" *Southern Literary Journal,* VIII (1976), 4–13.

20. Carpenter, "The Battle Within," 13.

to that unique order of society known latterly as the Virginian aristocracy" (4). In other words, from the family past he knows of previous displacements of inheritance like the one he is about to tell concerning George Posey. Despite the family tradition of continuity and its connections with the linear history of the colony and state, within the family events repeat themselves. In Lacy's mind the displacement that comes with George Posey has its justification in previous cycles of family history. The pattern he is concerned with is not so much a dialectic of Buchan versus Posey as a repetition of displacement when George marries Susan despite the displeasure of Major Buchan and takes the family's history in a new direction.

At the same time, Lacy also shows a strong sense of family continuity, though oddly that sense is associated with death. At his mother's burial, the last time the clan is assembled to the fifth and sixth degrees of kinship and a ritual occasion of community, he sees his uncle Armistead kneel and lean on his father's gravestone, and Lacy thinks how he and a man old enough to be his great-grandfather "should be held in *religion* as I should say it now, to the long message of the dead" (104). Later when he is recuperating from his fever at Pleasant Hill, he visits the family graveyard and thinks "how many processions of how many slow feet had followed the path by the garden into the brick wall" and "how many more would follow it, I among them, and then they would follow me" and the "processions would go to the end of time" (281). Knowing of George's displacement of the inheritance, Lacy can still put that displacement within the context of family continuity.

That Tate came to realize even more strongly the link between displacement and continuity can be seen in his revised conclusion to *The Fathers* in 1977. Admitting he had written the original conclusion in haste, he later has Lacy stand at another cemetery fifty years later and remember how George "restored his wife and small daughter and what he did for me" (314, 306–307).

The special family attribute displaced by George is for Lacy embodied in his father, Major Buchan. A man of eighteenth-century sensibilities and formal manners, Major Buchan is the man of "a Traditional Society," so ingrained with social awareness that he has no life separate from that of his public manners. His grief at his wife's death is communal grief, and his view of the government in Washington, D.C., is that it is "our" government, set up by Virginians, and one can no more secede from it than one can secede from one's family (129). When at the time of the secession crisis the major reads morning prayers for the family in time of calamity, Lacy senses the mingling of private and public sorrows, "as in all highly developed societies the line marking off the domestic from the public life was indistinct" (125). The trouble with such unity of public and private life, he remembers his cousin John Semmes say, is that men like Major Buchan derive from days of the early republic, still believe in men's rational behavior, and cannot comprehend less rational motives of men serving their own interests at the expense of the community: "Your pa is still living before he was born—in 1789. . . . They can't understand that reason and moderation haven't anything to do with the crisis. They won't let themselves see what's going on" (124).

As the Jacob-like displacer, George Posey is a different breed, seen as different by the Buchan family but not understood. Lacy recalls that the family explains George's actions as town behavior in light of George's grandfather's removal from Anne Arundel County, Maryland, to Georgetown (5, 16, 20). Blind to niceties of scrupulous behavior, George outrages Major Buchan by giving Lacy a gun without first consulting the major, in effect, usurping the traditional privilege of the father, and enters the family circle without first asking about Mrs. Buchan (25). Blind to nuances of ceremony, George is unaware of Major Buchan's icy snub when the major fails to ask about his family during their conference about his marrying Susan, and Lacy realizes his father is telling George he has "no claim upon any other member of the family" (34). If he is oblivious to ceremonial nuances, George is nevertheless aware of the myths guiding the world of the Buchans and their kind. At the Gentlemen's Association Tournament, he mocks the myth of chivalry by playing to excess his Ivanhoe role, wearing a mask, flaunting his orange and black ribbons, using a curb bit on his mare when others do not, putting the victor's wreath in Susan's lap rather than on her head, and hitting John Langton rather than duelling with pistols when they dispute over his victory (63–75).

For George is capable of direct, efficient action in place of ceremonial indirection, and Lacy comes to recognize that form of behavior as the way of the future. He admires George's ability to make people do his will (10), he approves George's selling a family of slaves when George takes over Pleasant Hill and then applies the money to the major's gentlemanly debts at the bank in Alexandria (131), and he appreciates George's putting the plantation on a paying basis and "protecting me from the consequences of our situation" (133). As Lacy comes to see, George is protecting the family estate by converting it into a business rather than a home "for the enjoyment of the heirs forever" (134). George's displacement of the inheritance is complete when he buys out the shares of Lacy's brothers, Charles and Semmes, by lending money to the estate for the transaction. Like an old and confused Isaac, Major Buchan, "upon representations from Brother Charles, as the eldest son," in summer, 1860, conveys "some sort of deed of trust" to George Posey "for all the landed property" and fulfills the ominous clue Tate found in those Fairfax County court records of his own family. Again the agrarian enterprise is rescued by the intervention of commercial or industrial money.

As Lacy comes to understand, however, George's strength is also his weakness. Personal rather than communal in his motives, he lacks the insulations of communal ceremony against the insults of life.[21] He "received the shock of the world at the end of his nerves," Lacy recognizes, and faces death "in its aspect of greatest horror—the corrupt body" (185). Lacy keeps a vision of George riding on the edge of the abyss of things unknowable and unconfrontable whereas the Buchans in their ceremonial lives have tacitly agreed to ignore that abyss (179). For all his naturalistic energy, George embodies the darkly romantic, Poesque alienation and will to power beyond ordinary human feeling explored in Tate's "The Angelic Imagination."[22] Like the other Poseys who have withdrawn from communal living into their Poesque private selves, George cannot accept the impersonal and ceremonial supports shown in Mrs. Buchan's funeral and tells Lacy he wants to be thrown to the hogs (107). Lacy translates this wish into the insight that the Poseys would throw their dead into the river if not for their church (256) and sees its application soon afterward when George allows Semmes to fall into the Potomac after he shoots him and throws Yellow Jim in the river (258). The urge to such direct, unceremonial action prompts George to break the sword of the Federal captain and slap him at Pleasant Hill before First Manassas and results in the burning of Pleasant Hill, emblem of the communal life, the next day (303).

21. Arthur Mizener, Introduction to *The Fathers,* by Allen Tate (Chicago, 1960), xiv; Richard J. Gray, *The Literature of Memory* (Baltimore, 1977), 87, 92; Walter Sullivan, "The Fading Memory of the Civil War," in *The American South,* ed. Rubin, 247; Robert Brinkmeyer, *Three Catholic Writers of the Modern South* (Jackson, 1985), 4–46; Dekker, *American Historical Romance,* 298–99; Thomas Daniel Young, Introduction to *The Fathers and Other Fiction,* by Allen Tate (Baton Rouge 1977), xvi–xvii.

22. Fred Chappell, "A Choice of Romantics: Allen Tate's *The Fathers,*" *Shenandoah,* XL (1990), 38–40.

In his meditation on what happened during the displacement, Lacy recognizes the significance of talismanic objects and actions in the process. An old man, he thinks, "can only bring back the objects around which, secretly, the emotions have ordered themselves in memory," and those objects become the few "symbols that will preserve only so much of the old life as they may, in their mysterious history, consent to bear" (22). Those things kept in memory and in hand include the brass shot-pouch given him by his father after he received the gun from George Posey. The pouch had belonged to his great-uncle Ben, killed at Cowpens in 1781, and had been passed from his grandfather Dr. John Buchan to the major to Lacy (22). Its connection with the family's tie to Revolutionary War values can be seen in Lacy's response of playing "soldier in the Revolution" that day, but the pouch is with him and George's gun when he serves on the battle line at Manassas (299), and it becomes part of the continuing tradition. The portrait of his grandfather, though, is Lacy's most symbolic talismanic object. He remembers the portrait of Dr. John Buchan in eighteenth-century dress, presiding over the parlor at Pleasant Hill, judging from his position the actions of George Posey in leaving the funeral of Lacy's mother, and "staring into the distance with dropsical eyes" over her coffin (22, 90). Transported out of Tate's "A Dream," the grandfather walks with Lacy on his passage through the depleted fields and tells him that George Posey does evil without intending to because he acts alone like a tornado (267–68). Out of this talismanic memory, Lacy comes to his moment of vision. George, says the grandfather, is like Jason in search of the Golden Fleece and is unaware he involves himself "with the humanity of others" like Medea or Susan and desecrates his fathers' graves. "He was a noble fellow in whom the patriarchal and familial loyalties had become meaningless but his human nature necessarily haunted him, and he made a heroic effort to combine his love of the extraordinary and the human with the ancient domestic virtues" (269).

Judging by the old virtues, the phantom grandfather rejects the displacement George represents, but the grandfather and his values are "dead as herring" to Lacy, who rejects the vision and thinks, "I have nobody to guide me now" (269). Yet he does have a guide in the grandfather's example, if not his classical scholarship, for Lacy takes over the precedent of the physician in the family after Semmes's death and shows in his childless decline the dead end of that family tradition. At last he is left to tell his story and puzzle over events without the old guidelines.

Like other puzzled narrators, Lacy is left with the mystery behind events. In the parlor before his mother's funeral, he sees but does not understand "the fury of Susan's glance, the astonished mask-like trance of Semmes' gaze" as he realizes with Semmes that Jane is now a woman rather than a playmate: "There are scenes that last a lifetime and remain like keys to the mystery of life: this was one of them but it survives for me through no act of understanding on my part, no judgment of motives" (93). Lacy especially puzzles about his sister Susan's motives as she becomes the meeting point between the traditional Buchans and the mystery of George's new behavior. After their mother's burial, she instructs Lacy, "Tell Papa, I can't help it. I have to go." Lacy wonders afterward, "What did she want me to tell papa? What was there to tell?" (111–13). Later he tries to fathom Susan's motives in putting him with Jane and keeping her away from Semmes (201), wonders at Susan's strange smile when Jane agrees to marry Semmes (215), a frightening "smile of satisfaction," he thinks (217), and feels doubts start in his mind at Susan's "decisive glare" after she examines Jane following the attack by Yellow Jim (227). Fifty years later, Lacy can still ponder the meaning of and the blame for events that followed the attack and concludes that, in light of all men's capacity for evil, it is possible only to say that some men acted better than others but that even those who acted out of honor could become pathetic victims of circumstance and bring "untold sorrows and troubles" on their families (218–19). Eventually, he includes himself in that company when he thinks how his lie that he did not love Jane "may have hastened the enveloping destiny of all these people" (213). When he says, "You remember what you cannot understand" (272), Lacy admits finally his own failure of self-knowledge as well as his failure to understand the representatives of the older tradition.

Whether he understands so or not, it becomes clearer as he tells his story that Lacy is alien to his own tradition and is readier than others to accept George's displacement of that tradition. His confusion about meanings is shown in his failure to comprehend such cryptic terms as *it, that, they,* and *this thing* in his father's and sister's speech. The *it* in his memory of kissing Jane may mask more intimate knowledge than a man of traditional honor can tell: "[in the dark of the hall] I took her hand and drew her to me and kissed her. When it was over I could see because my eyes had got used to the dark" (198). His inability to understand may reflect instead an unwillingness to understand. That Tate recognized the problem appears in his later note on the closing scene of *The Fathers*. To critics who wonder how Lacy can love a man who inflicted such sorrow on his family, Tate answers that Lacy "has the instinct of survival, regardless of principle" and that he at the same time "affirms the principles George scorns, and in a scene, and in a sense, as his surrogate attributes them to George." [23] Turning to George helps Lacy "survive in a new world" where, if those traditions are not active, they are still remembered. His story of them celebrates both their former existence and their displacement.

Andrew Nelson Lytle's *A Wake for the Living: A Family Chronicle*, published in 1975, shows how the family saga in the South takes on additional dimensions from a nonfictional account of a family's range through generations. Written as a virtual last testament, *Wake for the Living* was prepared for by his previous essay comments on the southern family and such stories as "Jericho, Jericho, Jericho," essentially a truncated family saga in short-fiction form. In this respect, Lytle reversed the usual pattern of converting the actual into the apocryphal. For him, his own family had legendary dimensions that fiction could not enhance. He wrote his chronicle, he told Tate, as a fable for "instructing the three girls [his daughters Pamela, Katherine, and Lillie] as to who they are." In doing so, he followed a family tradition handed on to him from his father Robert Lytle, a "celebrated raconteur and repository of family lore," so expert that Caroline Gordon posited some ancestral storytelling artist in the family past with talents rooted "beneath the level of his own consciousness." [24] Out of that tradition Lytle recognized the presence of storytelling talents at family gatherings: "There would always be one voice more capable than another of dominating the conversation. It was a kind of bardic voice. . . . The bard, by hovering above the action, to see it all, collects the segments. In the end, in the way he fits the parts together, the one story will finally get told." [25] As son of the father, Andrew Lytle set that task for himself.

Well before he began his own family chronicle, Lytle had pondered

23. Bruce Pirie, "The Grammar of the Abyss: A Reading of *The Fathers*," *Southern Literary Journal*, XVI (1984), 81–83; Law, "Active Faith," 361; Carpenter, "The Battle Within," 20; Tate, *The Fathers and Other Fiction*, 314.

24. Lytle to Tate, January 31, 1960, in Young and Sarcone, eds., *Lytle-Tate Letters*, 296; Caroline Gordon to Andrew Lytle, March 15, 1943, in Mark Lucas, *The Southern Vision of Andrew Lytle* (Baton Rouge, 1986), xii, 136.

25. Andrew Lytle, "Foreword to *A Novel, A Novella, and Four Stories*," in *Hero*, 200–201. Later retitled "The Subject of Southern Fiction," the essay appears in Lytle's *Southerners and Europeans: Essays in a Time of Disorder* (Baton Rouge, 1988), 55–63.

the role of family in his 1957 "Foreword to *A Novel, A Novella, and Four Stories*" and anticipated as themes for fiction the matters he would develop in his nonfictional chronicle. First, the family acts as an enveloping action for the southern story, that dynamic force shown concretely in the "action proper" of the narrative (59). Second, the family functions as a private microcosm, combining diversity in the whole, where people live "fairly close together without losing their privacy or their family distinctions" (62). Third, the family as a microcosm lives in the concrete world of its own rituals and ceremonies, its own place, its own manner of dealing with the quotidian details of living, not as an abstraction. He explains: "People do not live in a vacuum. They live somewhere. The natural man is an abstraction. He has never been seen, but what is natural to men always shows itself shaped by the manners and mores, the institutional restraints of a given time and place" (60). In *Wake for the Living* he sums up the effect of his family as a concrete Christian response to the trials and demands of life, a hierarchical setting for knowing "who you are" in contrast with the abstractions of state power, democracy, and equality.[26] Fourth, in the world of the southern family, "the matriarch becomes the defining image," and matriarchs act as monitors of "family integrity, with the very practical aim of keeping the bloodlines sure and the inheritance meaningful." In the endless talk of women visiting, the truly important things emerge: "Every human possibility was involved, including politics, but the bloodlines were the measure of behavior. There was never any doubt about the argument between environment and heredity. Environment was what heredity inherited" (61–62). Fifth, the family acts as a counterbalance to the Faustian view of the public world, which sees "material ends as the only proper reward for action." The family, even amid the decline of other institutions, sees "the City of God as the end of the drama" (63) and proposes that natural actions of its members have supernatural implications. In *Wake for the Living* he begins his chronicle with recognition that "the sense of eternity gives a perspective on things and events which makes for a refreshing clarity" and that the family "by its habits and customs discovers the identity between the natural and supernatural, that mystery which becomes ceremony to people who make their living by the land and the sea" (3). In effect, for Lytle, family life is sacramental.

In "Mister McGregor" in 1935 and "Jericho, Jericho, Jericho" in 1936, Lytle drew on family stories for fictional characters, the extent of which

26. Andrew Lytle, *A Wake for the Living: A Family Chronicle* (New York, 1975), 269.

would not become clear until almost forty years later in *Wake for the Living*.[27] He saw early the fictional possibilities of family types and sublimated the historical into the apocryphal, perceiving the potential powers in what he knew of the actual, or at least of the actual as filtered through family stories. Where in his essays on the southern family he saw matriarchs as potent preservers of family integrity, in the fiction they overwhelmingly become figures of authority who dwarf their men and make them impotent in will if not in sexual capacity. The nameless McGregor heir in "Mister McGregor" has become, because of the example of his strong mother, a talkative alcoholic unwilling to fight, except when someone puts salt in his whiskey, and unwilling to marry. "She'd rather manage folks than eat," he remembers, and she becomes for him the epitome of all women: "Most of 'm enjoy fighten . . . can get fat on it. When they win out, they put the man down amongst the chillun and give him a whuppen when he forgets his manners or sasses back. . . . That's how come I never married." She finds her surrogate in the slave coachman Rhears, who challenges the narrator's genteel father with the defiant words "Mister McGregor," not "master." "It was a question of authority," the son and narrator sees, and in his fight with Rhears the issue for Mister McGregor is husband versus wife as well as master versus slave. Rhears acts not only as the agent of her will to power but as the expression of her dominating spirit. He is the only one on the place who can manage the horses she likes, the ones "that wanted to run away all the time." The family sources for the fictional confrontation on the cost of matriarchy become clear in *Wake for the Living* as Lytle remembers Sophia Ridgely DeShields Lytle, who had a zest for spirited horses and a black coachman named Caesar capable of "holding them in" (148).

Drawing on family lore, Lytle made "Jericho, Jericho, Jericho" into a brief saga dominated by the matriarch of Long Gourd plantation, Kate McCowan, who is clearly like "Grandma," his great-grandmother Julia Searcy Lytle. Although Kate is like Julia in dominating her husband and in successfully running the plantation after his death, the fictional matriarch shows in a way the ancestral one does not that the cost of matriarchy is the dwarfing of the heirs. Thinking of herself as an austere Joshua ready to use savage means to take and keep the promised land of Long Gourd plantation, by the end of the day she will die she recognizes that

27. Andrew Lytle, "Mister McGregor," *Virginia Quarterly Review,* XI (1935), 218–27; Andrew Lytle, "Jericho, Jericho, Jericho," *Southern Review,* 1st ser., I (1936), 753–64.

her grandson and heir Dick McCowan is ready to abandon his agrarian heritage and move to town with a wife "too small in the waist" to bear children and match the fertility of Long Gourd. Then she knows she is like Jericho, not Joshua, and the walls come tumbling down. If the motif of decline is dominant in the fictional saga, Kate, like Julia, fights and works and schemes in heroic manner along the way. Both make the plantation succeed with the aid of black Uncle Ike as overseer (199), both send cleft-palated Jack, brother in the story and son in the chronicle, off to school to get him away from liquor and bad companions (200), and whereas Kate remembers Iva Louise and her charges of land stealing from her weak husband, Julia has the dilemma of her daughter Lizzie asking her to rent her place to raise money for Lizzie and Harry to get married (207). Where Kate remembers old Mrs. Matchem, who drove her daughters with a buggy whip into wasp-waist corsets, Julia records for family memory her scorn for the Rutherford woman "who used to tie her daughters' corset strings to the bedpost and whip them with a buggy whip, until their belly bands were so tight they barely drew a hearty breath" (138). Where in *Wake for the Living* Julia's husband Ephraim, long an invalid with a heart condition, falls dead across the foot of her bed, in "Jericho" Kate feels death creeping up, almost erotically, from the foot of her bed. In story and chronicle the details are similar but their purposes different. For Kate they point to the failure of fertility for the long-cherished plantation; for Lytle they are part of family history under the eye of eternity.

When he came to write *Wake for the Living*, Lytle already knew the direction his story would take. As he wrote it, the conventions of the fictional family saga found their place in his own family's chronicle. His sense of continuity in the family over the generations found its complementary statement in the family's special attribute. The Lytles and the Nelsons on the maternal side were "all kin or connected in some fashion" by intermarriages, he noted (109), so much so that he sensed a kind of "spiritual incest, far more insistent than its physical inbreeding" (131), and as in the most complexly related family sagas, he had to supply genealogical charts for both Lytles and Nelsons to show the tangled lines of descent. He was, he realized, related to the Lytles through the Nelsons as well as directly through the Lytle line, and through the Lytle connection he was "three times kin or connected" with the Mortons (130–31). He was similarly related to the Smiths and Graveses by an "intertwining of kinship" (113). The result was that conjugal families were a minor part of the connection. He lived in a network of cousins and aunts and uncles and saw that "old maids and old bachelors were the strength of the family," for "they were the visible sign that man and woman and child are not enough" (13). Living up to his observation that family exists not in the abstraction but in a specific time and place, he tells how the Lytles settled on their chosen spot on a branch of the Stone River in middle Tennessee in 1798 and began "living in one physical place through successive generations" as they took on the "illusion of ownership, whose traditions recall the first glance and the growing enlargements and modifications of what the family call ours" (105). For the Lytles the family genius meant to stay in middle Tennessee and to develop the rituals of country living, of realizing self-sufficiency, and of learning to respect food managed well to the end of the season (139, 141–43, 147).

The linked families' sense of identity came with their removal across the Appalachians to Tennessee from North Carolina and Virginia, and their reasons for removal put the family within the context of public history. The Lytles of North Carolina had fought as officers of the Continental Army during the Revolution, had been charter members of the Society of Cincinnati (the order of Revolutionary War officers and their eldest male descendants who proposed to become the landed aristocracy of the new republic), and had been paid for their army service in grants of land in middle Tennessee. At first, Robert Lytle had been a pro-Crown supporter in the Regulator troubles of the early 1770s, but his sons Archibald and William opted for the colony when war came (61–64). By the end of the war, Archibald held the rank of lieutenant-colonel, William that of captain, and they received land grants commensurate with their ranks. They moved together from Hillsborough, North Carolina, William with his new wife Nancy, Archibald still a bachelor, along the Wilderness Road to middle Tennessee, looking, as Lytle says, for uncursed land. The Nelsons had come to middle Tennessee from Augusta County, Virginia, first to the Holston area of east Tennessee, then to the Nashville area by 1816. Some had been caught in public history; Lytle's ancestor Alexander Nelson, for example, had the dubious distinction of being one of thirteen Americans killed at the Battle of New Orleans in 1815 (108–109, 122).

As narrator-historian of this complex chronicle, Lytle is careful to present his family documents or to refer to them in specific terms. As the "facts" of the family past, supplemented by family stories, they furnish the basis for his interpretations but also for the mysteries they evoke. As he looked at the papers granting 7,200 acres to Lieutenant-Colonel Archibald Lytle, he recognized that "it was the beginning of my education, that ancestral riddle of the past, the name for the moving present, for nobody lives in the past" (45). Lytle could produce the will of still-bachelor Archibald, giving his estate to his brother William, and thereby authenticate the legitimacy of the land's passing through William's line (95). He could reproduce the tombstone inscription of Nancy Taylor Lytle, wife of William, lauded as an esteemed lady despite rumors of indiscretions when she was a social leader of early Nashville (124, 106). In William Franklin Pitt Lytle's will, he saw evidence of the ancestor's belief that he held his estate as a stewardship by divine appointment, leaving it to the "care and keep" of "God's Son" but also to the trusteeship of two nephews, one for the benefit of his sons, the other for his daughters (158). The arrangement, which provided trusts for his family and provided for his slaves to be kept together, depended on a sense of place to sustain kinship and came "as close to primogeniture as times allowed" (159–61). What William Franklin Pitt Lytle could not know, as the brooding family historian observes, is that the coming Civil War would invalidate those arrangements made in confidence of heaven's authority (159). He could also con the letters written by his ancestor Ephraim Lytle, then a prisoner of war, to his wife Julia and therein detect loss of confidence as Ephraim sat separated from his land (176). He could cite the journal of another collateral ancestor, General William Lytle, who had made his way across the mountains to the Ohio River and had settled in Cincinnati. The branches came together during the Civil War when the Ohio Lytle's son, now General William Haynes Lytle, U.S.A., was present to protect the Lytle property in Murfreesboro (178–79). The significance of such a search by the family narrator-historian is that it was all preparation for his becoming an artist at the end of the line, and he could trace his moments of insight as an artist within the context of family memory (14).[28]

Part of the process, though, is narrator Lytle's puzzling over reasons why Ephraim did not want his wife Julia to visit him in prison. As he pores over actions and motives of the ancestor, he feels the need to apologize to "this ancestral ghost for this effort at understanding." He wonders, "Who can read the thought of the dead," but recognizes, "We must fumble at trying, else communion is at the mercy of instinct" (176). There is

28. Lucas, *Southern Vision*, 141.

also the mystery of Sophia DeShields Lytle's actions during the Federal occupation of Murfreesboro: Why did she betray her stepson, Uncle Frank, to General Lytle and cause Frank to spend the rest of the war in prison? Why did she marry a Yankee captain? What were the family's motives in ostracizing her and letting the town dump garbage at her gate? Nor could Lytle ask her these questions when the family's former houseboy, John Greer, introduced him to her in 1927, for by then she was a Sibylline figure over a century old (179–80, 252). From her and all the other ancestral ghosts, he asks forgiveness for spying into their lives and "a compassionate sympathy for [his] ignorance in recalling them to mind" (270).

Among those ghosts in the moving present called the past, he senses the development of matriarchal power in the family as a consequence of the Civil War, that watershed in family history, when matriarchs like Julia Searcy Lytle rose to new authority. She had become more dominant than her demoralized husband Ephraim, and more was known about her in family memory than about her husband or sons. As guardian of the family covenant, she had resisted a move to the west and had kept to middle Tennessee as the locus of family kin (132). After the war she endured, holding the inheritance intact, and embodied the reality and authority of living completely in a specific time and place. That was her legacy to all the later women in the family. Their participation in the rituals and ceremonies of living becomes the substance, philosophically considered, of family life: "The woman is neither worldly nor spiritual. She is the vessel of life. Hence substance is a familiar mystery to her, its loss damaging. . . . She may do and may be many things. One thing she will not do: accept an abstraction as having anything to do with the business of living. Whatever life is, she knows it manifests itself in and through substance" (4). Despite the Lytle family genius of staying in one place through generations, Andrew's father Robert was known in the family and community for his restlessness and readiness to move to new opportunities for business success. It was the matriarchal, Nelson side of the family that showed the instinct to stay settled in towns (29).

From the Nelson side also came the talismanic story, often told, that linked family fortunes with the crisis of the Civil War. Lytle's grandmother Molly Nelson, "Mama" in family memory, as a girl was shot in the neck by a Yankee soldier. Before he would allow her father to call a doctor, a Yankee lieutenant forced the father to take the loyalty oath (23). Family memory then centered on her later neck coverings as an index to suffering by survivors of the war.

If Lytle found no renunciations or displacements in his family record, he nevertheless saw the long pattern of decline. As with others of his generation, he saw the Civil War as that time when family fortunes, parallel with the fortunes of the region, began their slippage. In the family record he could find presentiments of that decline in the account of the great party given by Katherine Wells Lytle Carney and Legrand Carney in 1853 when their son married Marie Butler. Their house, called The Crest, had the memorial value of representing the crest of middle Tennessee society before the war. As William Franklin Pitt Lytle and his wife attended the festive occasion, he had his premonitions of personal, family, and social mortality and made his will out in light of that evening's insights and as secession loomed (144–51). That vision was confirmed as secession came and the war signaled destruction of the South's initial sense of a federal republic (164). Ephraim Lytle's Tennessee regiment faltered at the Hornet's Nest at Shiloh, and Ephraim was captured and lost his confidence (169–76). In later generations the agrarian life of the Lytles gave way to the powers of commerce and social planning. Sophia DeShields Lytle Harrison's crumbling plantation house became the site of a Carnation Milk Company plant, with a shopping center across the pike, and Robert Lytle's plantation Cornsilk in northern Alabama was flooded by a Tennessee Valley Authority project during the Depression (255, 259).

In writing his chronicle "to tell my girls who they are," Lytle writes from the enlarged vision of having "come to live in the sense of eternity" (3). The clarity afforded by that perspective could let him see the family documents, the towering matriarchs, the family stories, and their parallel public events all as examples of individual struggles within the long view of the family caught in the grip of destiny. If it was the family's genius to gain and hold the chosen land of middle Tennessee, it was the family's destiny finally to lose the land and a sense of coherence as the world changed. Even at the end, though, with the terrestrial basis for the family dissipated in an urbanized and commerce-oriented society, Lytle invokes the family's "inheritance in the Life Everlasting." The shades of the ancestors now live in memory beyond change, and "who they are" is now measured for posterity by spiritual rather than social identities.

The first generation of family saga writers, haunted by memory of the Civil War in the lives of their family communities but energized by challenges of the post–world war years, produced a landmark era in the developing tradition of the family saga in the South. Besides their works, written within the main tradition, other works with different emphases also drew on the tradition. Robert Penn Warren's *All the King's Men,* for example, turns at last on what Jack Burden learns from Cass Mastern, his Civil War ancestor, and Jack acts as family narrator-historian in his struggle with the Cass Mastern story. Whereas most of the first-generation sagas presume a patriarchal inheritance, though, a related line of sagas, written by women and discussed in the next chapter, explore the matriarchal inheritance and develop a further modification of the tradition in the South.

4

THE MATRIARCHS ON THE PORCH
WOMEN ON THE FAMILY SAGA

In Harper Lee's *To Kill a Mockingbird,* Atticus Finch comes to that time when, at the urging of his sister Alexandra, he has to deliver to his motherless children Jem and Jean Louise, nicknamed Scout, the obligatory lecture on their debt to their "gentle breeding." Aunt Alexandra, he says "at a gallop," wants "to talk to you about the family and what it's meant to Maycomb County through the years, so you'll have some idea of who you are, so you might be moved to behave accordingly." Astounded, Scout later realizes his difficulty: "I know now what he was trying to do, but Atticus was only a man. It takes a woman to do that kind of work." [1]

Scout's realization says in short form what a line of women writers of family sagas in the South has been saying since the 1930s. Out of the prototypal pattern of Sarah's alternate vision to that of Abraham in Genesis, women writers have shown how the strengths, and sometimes the flaws, of families have emerged from the growing power of matriarchs in southern families. Although men writers such as Faulkner and Lytle have celebrated the legendary influence of women like Molly Beauchamp and Julia Searcy Lytle, their sagas are largely patriarchal in emphasis, concerned with dynastic energy and masculine concepts of honor. With the rise of writers such as Katherine Anne Porter and Eudora Welty, however, the family saga shifts the burden of meaning to the matriarchal vision. Reasons for emergence of the matriarchal vision, and through vision, power, might vary from family to family, but the effect is the same. Whether the matriarchs took charge when the men died from war wounds or when they lost their morale after the great defeat of the Civil War, these women

---

1. Harper Lee, *To Kill a Mockingbird* (Philadelphia, 1960), 136–37.

shifted the locus from public politics to the enduring strength of the private family and its extended kinships. They determined who should marry whom, made their private sense of decorum and propriety a matter of family rule, maintained rituals and occasions that held one generation to another, and kept talismanic objects that embodied family memory. When southern men knew disappointment after defeat in a decades-long cycle of poverty, the matriarchs showed the enduring and nurturing power of care that survived economic shambles. Indeed, the chief characteristic of the southern family from the post–Civil War period until well into the twentieth century was change in the status of women. They learned to work outside their homes, often in fields formerly worked by slaves and tenants. They married maimed veterans of the region's and nation's wars, often earlier than did women in the North or West, turned to education, often working to put their daughters through schools, usually as teachers, and became matriarchs instead of belles.[2]

Beyond their families, matriarchs institutionalized themselves in southern life in the United Daughters of the Confederacy and in women's groups or auxiliaries of local churches. In heroizing the veterans of a lost cause and of later wars, they also marginalized their men: in making heroes of them, the matriarchs also made their men victims of their expectations. In the process the women became preservers and defenders of the old order, for in the sagas matriarchs are purveyors of family stories of former glories and better times. In effect, men exist in the matriarchal vision as subjects of stories told by women in the family; their purpose is to become the lore told by the matriarchs. In stories told by women on the porch, the past is preserved in a form often better than it was in actuality, often clearer and simpler in retrospect in order to allow morals to be drawn or attributes to be identified. The hands of destiny or consequences of old flaws become evident and teachable to the young. And out of the stories a collective memory emerges.

Katherine Anne Porter's Miranda stories in "The Old Order" group from *The Leaning Tower and Other Stories,* published in 1944, in "Old Mortality" and "Pale Horse, Pale Rider" from the 1939 *Pale Horse, Pale Rider,* and in "The Fig Tree," brought together with the other stories in 1965 in *The Collected Stories* of Katherine Anne Porter, show one form of the family saga that developed from collective family memory. Never collected

2. Arthur W. Calhoun, *A Social History of the American Family from Colonial Times to the Present* (3 vols., 1917; rpr. New York, 1977), III, 11–17.

into a coherent single saga, never rewritten to fit a single context as Faulkner did for *Go Down, Moses,* the Miranda stories nevertheless imply each other and leave the reader to act as redactor beyond Miranda to order and clarify the saga. That at least in Porter's mind the stories were connected can be seen in her frequently repeated comment that they are all parts of a larger work. When "The Grave" was accepted by *Virginia Quarterly Review* in 1935, she professed amazement that the story could be read as an independent work. By 1937 she foresaw inclusion of the Miranda tales in a larger work to be called *Many Redeemers.*[3]

The stories were never integrated into a single work but appeared individually in popular and literary magazines.[4] Part of the reason for their scattered publication lies in Porter's method of composition. She recorded in her journal in 1936 notes about the "exercise of memory" as "the chief occupation" of her mind: "All my experience seems to be simply memory, with continuity, marginal notes, constant revision and comparison of one thing with another. Now and again thousands of memories converge, harmonize, arrange themselves around a central idea in a coherent form, and I write a story." She insisted to numerous interviewers that the stories were written in single sittings or during sustained periods of writing after long gestation, that they were written with little or no revision, and that no editor was allowed to change them.[5]

3. Joan Givner, *Katherine Anne Porter: A Life* (New York, 1982), 288; Archer Winston, "Presenting the Portrait of an Artist," in *Katherine Anne Porter: Conversations,* ed. Joan Givner (Jackson, 1987), 10.

4. Katherine Anne Porter, "The Circus," *Southern Review,* 1st ser., I (1935), 36–41; "The Grave," *Virginia Quarterly Review,* XI (1935), 177–83; "Old Mortality," *Southern Review,* 1st. ser., II (1937), 686–735; the story "The Old Order" (later renamed "The Journey"), *Southern Review,* 1st ser., I (1936), 495–509; "The Source," *Accent* (Spring, 1941), 144–47; "The Witness" (then titled "Uncle Jimbilly") and "The Last Leaf" under the joint title "Two Plantation Portraits," *Virginia Quarterly Review,* XI (1935), 85–92; and "Pale Horse, Pale Rider" in the collection of three short novels *Pale Horse, Pale Rider* (New York, 1939). The unsystematic writing and publication of the stories are further evident in the case of "The Fig Tree." Written in Bermuda in 1929 and intended for publication in *The Leaning Tower and Other Stories,* "The Fig Tree" was misplaced in Porter's papers for years, was rediscovered and published in *Harper's* in June, 1960, pp. 55–59, and finally was included in the "Old Order" stories in *Collected Stories* in 1965. Darlene Unrue, *Truth and Vision in Katherine Anne Porter's Fiction* (Athens, Ga., 1985), 245–46; Willene Hendrick and George Hendrick, *Katherine Anne Porter* (Rev. ed; Boston, 1988), 47; William L. Nance, s.m., *Katherine Anne Porter and the Art of Rejection* (Chapel Hill, 1964), 84.

5. Katherine Anne Porter, "Notes on Writing," in *The Collected Essays and Occasional Writings of Katherine Anne Porter* (New York, 1970), 449; Givner, *Porter Conversations,* xvi.

The key word in her description is "memory," and for Porter that meant a collective family memory or observation. In some instances memory was personal. Closer to the truth is her statement that events in her stories have their basis in experience not necessarily her own: "I have never written a story in my life that didn't have a very firm foundation in actual human experience—somebody else's experience quite often, but an experience that became my own by hearing the story, by witnessing the thing, by hearing just a word perhaps. It doesn't matter, it just takes a little—a tiny seed. Then it takes root, and it grows." Her grandmother Catherine Porter was a primary source of family stories. Living her last years on a dirt farm in central Texas, she remembered and told about the better times of her youth in Kentucky, and Porter heard the stories she would reimagine in her family chronicle. During her adolescent years in San Antonio, she also looked up descendants of her great-aunt Eliza, the other link with the Kentucky years of the family, and heard from them stories of the family's past to supplement her grandmother's tales.[6]

What she heard was a legend of the Old South. From that fund of collective memory, she learned the basis for her Miranda stories, the Rhea family saga. That the stories transformed history into an acceptable family legend can be seen in her "Portrait: Old South" from 1944: "We had been a good old family of solid wealth and property in Kentucky, Louisiana and Virginia, and we remained that in Texas, even though due to a temporary decline for the most honorable reasons, appearances were to the contrary." If in her autobiographical comments she remembered family status and wealth as greater than the records show, her "memory" is a tribute to the power of family stories as well as to the authorial tendency to merge creative imagination with the source of the imagined event. In the process of editing family memory to fit her saga episodes, for example, she combined the story of her own early marriage at sixteen with that of her aunt Ione Funchess, a reputedly beautiful orphan from Mississippi who eloped from a New Orleans convent with Porter's Uncle Newell. With the help of a legendizing imagination, Ione's elopement from the convent became not only Miranda's in "Old Mortality" but Porter's as well, and the Methodist day school she attended in San Antonio became a New Orleans convent.[7]

---

6. Givner, *Porter Conversations,* 89–90; Givner, *Porter Life,* 81.

7. Katherine Anne Porter, *The Days Before* (New York, 1952), 158; Givner, *Porter Life,* 20, 57–58; Hendrick, and Hendrick, *Katherine Anne Porter,* 1–2.

Clearly, Porter rejected the immediate circumstances of her youth, including her birth name Callie Russell, which she changed to Katherine Anne, and had to gain perspective on them before they could be transformed into a fictional vision. It took distance as well as time to achieve that perspective. Although she left home in 1916, she needed nearly twenty years to realize their possibilities for an incipient family chronicle. Her residences in Mexico, Bermuda, Spain, Germany, Switzerland, and France were necessary, she said, to "give me back my past and my own house and my own people—the native land of my heart." [8]

The central idea around which the "thousands of memories converge, harmonize, and arrange themselves" in Porter's vision is the power of the matriarchy in the family. Her grandmother Catherine Porter was source of the matriarchal vision as well as of the family stories. After Harrison Porter's wife died in childbirth when Callie Russell was two years old, Catherine Porter, then sixty-five, took the grandchildren to raise and in the process to indoctrinate them with her vision. All stories agree "she was strong-willed, uncompromising, and firmly convinced of her own infallibility." Extremely pious, she had a "domineering presence" and a "paralyzing effect on the men about her, including the grandchildren's father, whom she treated as if he were one of the children." That the grandmother's contempt for men passed to the granddaughter can be seen in the writer's depictions of weak men through the generations. Willene and George Hendrick note that "for personal and artistic reasons Porter emphasized the matriarchal aspects of her fictional family." [9]

In her saga of the Rhea family, Porter shows the generations dominated by the legacy of the matriarch Sophia Jane. Embodying values carried over from pre–Civil War years to the later nineteenth century, the matriarch figure has a stunting as well as an enduring effect on her children's generation and a smothering and authoritative force on the grandchildren—the force against which they will eventually need to rebel. To a great degree, Sophia Jane's assumption of matriarchal power resulted from her own secret rebellion against traditional restraints imposed on her during her girlhood and early marriage. In the process she showed the conflict inherent in predicaments of Porter's strong women: the forms and claims of the genteel tradition brought forward into times when the genteel tradition has to give way to new forms and claims of the "new

8. Givner, *Porter Life*, 212.
9. *Ibid.*, 53, 54; Hendrick and Hendrick, *Katherine Anne Porter*, 44.

woman." [10] By her assumed authority she made her personal decorum the rule of the family.

In the saga account, Miranda serves as the observing consciousness, the focus of awareness of the matriarch's legacy. Her role is to assemble the pieces of family lore, to sift them for credibility, and to record them into a coherent view. In Part I of "Old Mortality," Miranda and her sister Maria, then eight and twelve, accompany their grandmother on her semiannual inspection of family mementoes in the attic and listen to stories associated with them. "They listened, all ears and eager minds, picking here and there among floating ends of narrative, patching together as well as they could fragments of tales that were like bits of poetry or music, indeed were associated with poetry they had heard or read, with music, with the theater." [11]

Not a narrator but a recording consciousness, Miranda gains her knowledge from three perspectives. She is first a participant in family memory as part of a communal act. In "The Grave" she has "her powerful social sense, which was like a fine set of antennae radiating from every pore of her skin" as she feels the force of old women, peers of her grandmother, telling her to act the role of a future matriarch. She also knows, "though she could not say how," that her father is in disgrace after the grandmother's death (365). In "Old Mortality" Miranda and Maria participate in family memory beyond their years: "[They] knew they were young, though they felt they had lived a long time. They had lived not only their own years; but their memories, it seemed to them, began years before they were born, in the lives of grown-ups around them" (174). Second, she is a minor figure on the periphery of others' portraits in the family. In "The Witness" and "The Last Leaf," portraits of Uncle Jimbilly and Nannie Gay, respectively, she is one of the child auditors of Uncle Jimbilly's dubious tales about the beatings and burning of slaves in the old days and one of the amazed family observers of Nannie Gay's transformation from alternative grandmother to "aged Bantu woman of independent means" (349). In their father's deference to Nannie Gay they see "the smothering matri-

10. Nance, *Porter and the Art of Rejection*, 94; Jane Flanders, "Katherine Anne Porter and the Ordeal of Southern Womanhood," *Southern Literary Journal*, IX (1976), 47–60; Barbara Harrell Carson, "Winning: Katherine Anne Porter's Women," in *The Authority of Experience: Essays in Feminist Criticism*, ed. Arlyn Diamond and Lee R. Edwards (Amherst, 1977), 239-56; Jane Krause DeMouy, *Katherine Anne Porter's Women: The Eye of Her Fiction* (Austin, 1983), 6, 15–16.

11. Katherine Anne Porter, *The Collected Stories* (New York, 1965), 176.

archal tyranny to which he had been delivered by the death of his father," and they note that "still he submitted, being of that latest generation of sons who acknowledged, however reluctantly, however bitterly, their mystical never to be forgiven debt to the womb that bore them, and the breast that suckled them" (351).

The third perspective for Miranda is that of direct participation and experience in events. In "Old Mortality" she and Maria are evaluators of the legends of Amy and Gabriel in Parts I and II, and in Part III Miranda alone hears and judges Eva Parrington's alternate version of Amy's legend. As in the Spanish version of her name, Miranda acts as the seeing one in the family chronicle, just as she is, like Prospero's daughter, the marveling one. Significantly, however, Miranda's recording consciousness is more often internal than dramatic. On most occasions her responses to experience are unspoken and kept for further reflection or exchanged silently with Maria. On the few occasions when she speaks out, she is scoffed at or hushed by less reflective family members. Her rhetoric becomes more and more that of reticence.[12]

The knowledge Miranda gains of the family's three generations spans a century, from approximately 1820 to 1920. The grandparents' generation is marked by conflict between patriarchal and matriarchal authority, with the failure of the patriarchs coming in the Civil War, "when to be a man wounded and ruined in the war was merely to have proved oneself, perhaps, more heroic than wise" (337). Sophia Jane's view of men before the war, at least in retrospect and embodied in her husband, was that they lacked aim, failed to act in crises, tended to start projects on which they failed to follow through, and expected others to be happy to serve them. In contrast with women as keepers of domestic security, men lived "a dashing life full of manly indulgences, the sweet dark life of the knowledge of evil . . . the delicious, the free, the wonderful, the mysterious and terrible life of men!" (335). In compensation for her disappointments in marriage, Sophia Jane turns to her children and learns the satisfactions of nurturing them and shaping them according to her sense of decorum and destiny: "The Grandmother's role was authority, she knew that; it was her duty to portion out activities, to urge or restrain where necessary, to teach morals, manners and religion, to punish and reward her own household according to a fixed code" (328). How Miranda knows the

---

12. Janis P. Stout, "Miranda's Guarded Speech: Porter and the Problem of Truth-Telling," *Philological Quarterly*, LXVI (1987), 266–68.

sorrows of the grandmother's secret life Porter does not say. As a child of the family, she may be able to infer unsaid things from their context in family stories, and causes of the matriarch's secret sorrows may be as much the product of reconstruction through imaginative application of general behavior as is Miranda's understanding of the social conditions of the family before her birth.

In any case, to the family of children and grandchildren Sophia Jane is the matriarch in several legendary, near-mythic dimensions. As the Source, she "creates" Nannie Gay by assigning her a place in the family when she enters her name and birth date, both arbitrarily decided, in the family Bible (328), makes Nannie Gay her double throughout life, and promises to meet her in the hereafter (348). To the two matriarchs, their joined lives seem "almost mystical events" (330). As the Nurturer, she presides like a fertility figure over fields and gardens during her annual returns to the farm, takes pride in the orchards she has planted (322), and learns the mystique of nursing ("something holy, God-sent, amends from heaven for what she suffered in childbed") when she nurses both her children and those of Nannie Gay when Nannie is sick of puerperal fever (334). As Keeper of the talismanic family treasures, she preserves the rolling pin, razors and case, and portrait of the patriarchs but domesticates them by making patchwork cases for the razors, a velvet and satin envelope for the portrait, and a complicated patchwork cover for the rolling pin (326). Keeper of her husband's bones as well, she expresses her matriarchal will by having them removed from one location to another in Kentucky, Louisiana, and Texas and eventually buried beside her "as she had planned" (362). As Bringer of Order, she carries out the yearly ritual of inspecting tenants' houses and pantries, presides over their housecleaning, adjudicates their complaints and pleas, provides "that restoring touch" to house and garden, and takes her ritual ride on Fiddler and her ritual walk through the orchards, followed by her retinue of grandchildren (322–24). As Authority Figure, she never relaxes "her firm hold on family affairs" and, as a benevolent tyrant, provides "the only reality" to grandchildren "in a world that seemed otherwise without fixed authority or refuge" (324). At the summer house with Nannie Gay, she establishes her command post in the side garden where they can see, hear, and interpret the sounds of family life. During winter in the city they shift to the grandmother's room to continue the same supervision (326–27).

But Sophia Jane's version of matriarchy is traditional Old South in values, baronial in its vision, with expectations of making advantageous marriages for sons and daughters. The limitations of her vision show when she encounters the "new woman" her youngest son marries, one "altogether too Western, too modern . . . who was beginning to run wild, asking for the vote, leaving her home and going out in the world to earn her own living." Imprisoned in her sense of nineteenth-century decorum, she shudders "at the thought of women so unsexing themselves" (333) but recognizes that, though forms change, the matriarchy continues: the new daughter-in-law looks at her own husband "as if she had already got him sized up."

In her parents' generation Miranda discovers in "Old Mortality" the family romance, the legend of Amy, which incorporates the genteel fictions the matriarchy lives by. Although much of the lore about Amy has been absorbed as though Miranda and Maria "lived not only their own years" but "their memories" of what went before, they are also present to hear new installments on the legend as they listen to Sophia Jane talk with Cousin Isobel about Amy's wedding, as they meet Uncle Gabriel at the Crescent City racetrack, and as they visit Gabriel's second wife Miss Honey at the shabby Elysian Fields hotel (182, 197, 201). Miranda completes her encounter with the legend when she meets Eva Parrington on the train to Gabriel's funeral and witnesses the meeting between her father and Eva. Only then does she realize her generation is the one excluded from the family romance.

What Miranda discovers is that the legend of Amy the beloved exists as a myth of the Old South matriarchy, extended to the next generation. Although Amy appears to be a rebel against expectations and restrictions of the grandparents' generation, she too lives in the twilight romance of life taken from books and theater. The family, Miranda comes to realize, believes in "a life beyond this world, as well as in the next," in "the nobility of human feeling, the divinity of man's vision of the unseen, the importance of life and death, the depths of the human heart, the romantic value of tragedy" (179). If such phrases seem like clichés of romance, they are nevertheless the "truths" her parents' generation lives by. For their world is the world of the masquerade at the Mardi Gras ball in New Orleans when Harry and Mariana dress as bullfighter and Spanish lady and Amy as a Dresden china shepherdess, with Gabriel as her attendant swain in knee breeches (184–85). The unreality of their world becomes clearer when Harry shows his daughters Gabriel's poem about the lost

Amy as a singing angel. To Maria's question about whether Amy sang, their father answers, "Now what has that to do with it? . . . It's a poem" (181). And Amy justifies her near-suicidal ride to the Mexican border with the view of herself as "the heroine of this novel" (189).

As the focus of the family romance, Amy embodies the family's view of "the romantic value of tragedy"; in their perception "she had been beautiful, much loved, unhappy, and she had died young" (173). More important, Amy's legend demonstrates the saga convention that earlier generations were more noble than later, declining generations. Young Amy is the best dancer at present parties but "the first Amy had been lighter, more smooth and delicate in her waltzing; young Amy could never equal her" (177). Cousin Isobel "rides almost as well as Amy" but "Amy had the pure Spanish style" (177). At the racetrack, Maria and Miranda are "pretty as pictures," Gabriel says, "but rolled into one they don't come up to Amy, do they?" (197). In effect, the Amy legend preserves the ideal of the belle out of which future matriarchs develop and beside which lesser men like Miranda's father Harry and Uncle Gabriel show the need for matriarchs.

In response to the legend, members of the third generation of grandchildren, like Maria and Miranda, must discover the discrepancy between legend and reality and, as in the case of Miranda, must become rebels against claims of the family. They find that the family has entered a tacit conspiracy to deny or suppress facts that fail to fit the legend, as well as to glamorize the parts that do. When "every older person" said "how lovely" Amy was, Maria and Miranda, lacking the elders' memory, see a photograph of faded charm and dated fashion (173). When their father asserts categorically, "There were never any fat women in the family, thank God," they remember Great-Aunt Keziah, too heavy to ride her husband's fine horses (174). After hearing legends of Gabriel as Amy's romantic beau, they recognize the fat, loud, shabby drunkard when they see him (197).

Beyond denials, Maria and Miranda discover the dark underside of the family legend. They hear their grandmother tell Cousin Isobel of Amy's wish, contrary to the matriarchal code, not to marry dull, sulking Gabriel or anyone (183, 188). They learn of Amy's hemorrhages after the hunting and dancing and see their replication in the bleeding nose, wild eyes, and trembling legs of Gabriel's mare Miss Lucy IV after her surprising win at the racetrack (191, 199) and draw their conclusions about Amy's probable suicide after seeing the letters from Amy's nurse (192–93). From bitter Cousin Eva Parrington, Miranda hears and partially believes the alternate version of the Amy legend, that Amy's quick decision at last to marry Gabriel came because she had to get married to avoid disgrace and that the courtship rituals of Amy and her peers were really desperate sex-ridden rivalries in which "they simply festered inside" (212–14, 216). Although Miranda thinks Eva's version is in its way "every bit as romantic" as the family's, she begins to recognize the force of Eva's characterization of the family as a "hideous institution" and "the root of all wrongs" (217).

Demonstrating the effect of the research into the past on the researcher, Miranda ponders how to escape that "hideous institution." Elopement, she finds, is not an escape (212–13). For her the family is as smothering as it was for the matriarch-bound father and uncles. "I hate loving and being loved," she realizes and knows she will run away from the version of family duty taught by the grandmother, from life as "a progress of continued and various acts of the will directed toward a definite end" marked by good and evil, that is, from a sacramental vision of family destiny much like Lytle's. Despite her resolve to live without false hopes or without being romantic about herself, her promises are made, according to the hovering and retrospective family voice, in "her hopefulness, her ignorance" (221).

What exactly "her ignorance" portends is never made explicit. If inferential readers can judge from glimpses of Miranda later, her destiny is to be personally independent and captive of her memory at the same time. She has the capability of becoming the subject of a Miranda legend to future generations of the Rheas as well as to readers of the Miranda saga. To Miranda herself twenty years after in "The Grave," she is the exile in Mexico recalled briefly to memory, by the matriarchy, of the pregnant rabbit and its mysterious link with the birth-death-rebirth cycle of maternal claims and, in the vision of her brother Paul holding the silver dove from the grandfather's grave, to memory of those claims of resurrection pondered by Sophia Jane and Nannie Gay.[13] To Miranda in "Pale Horse, Pale Rider," living as liberated woman in Denver at the close of the Great War, the family is one of her talismanic memories when she is near death from Spanish influenza. In dreams she is still linked to family memory:

13. Thomas F. Walsh, "Miranda's Ghost in 'Old Mortality,'" *College Literature*, VI (1979), 58, 60; George Cheatham, "Literary Criticism, Katherine Anne Porter's Consciousness, and the Silver Dove," *Studies in Short Fiction*, XXV (1988), 113.

No more sleep. Where are my boots and what horse shall I ride? Fiddler or Graylie or Miss Lucy with the long nose and wicked eye? How I have loved this house in the morning before we are all awake and tangled together like badly cast fishing lines. Too many people have been born here, and have wept too much here, and have laughed too much and have been too angry and outrageous with each other here. Too many have died in this bed already. There are far too many ancestral bones propped on the mantelpiece, there have been too many antimacassars in this house . . . and oh what accumulations of storied dust never allowed to settle in peace for one moment. (179–80)

Continuing the pattern of the matriarch whose husband deserted her by death, Miranda tells herself she does not want to love Adam because she knows she will lose him to death, as indeed she does. What is left to her as she recovers from influenza is to emerge as the enduring, self-sufficient, and duty-bound woman her grandmother was. Her duty, however, is to recover the story of the matriarchy and to perpetuate it in recorded and recreated memory. Her growth in stories of her encounters with the family legend has been preparation for her to act as the matured narrator presiding over the scattered saga of her family.[14]

In *Delta Wedding* in 1946 and *Losing Battles* in 1970, Eudora Welty shows how family sagas derive from family occasions such as weddings and reunions, those brief moments in the present with far reaches back in family time evoked by stories or memories of those in the present. A new development in managing family sagas, this device also shows the power of matriarchy in the memory and present of the Fairchild and Renfro-Beecham families but matriarchy by oligarchy rather than by a single dominant figure like Sophia Jane in Porter's Miranda stories. Here matriarchy is exercised by envelopment rather than drive, and men in the families are controlled by the women's loving expectations of them rather than by claims of "the womb that bore them, and the breast that suckled." As in Porter's stories, though, the matriarchs of the past in the Fairchild and Renfro-Beecham sagas come to power as grandmothers when they take over raising children after the children's mothers have died. Acting as links with the past, they domesticate history as a public event and make it subordinate to the dynamics of private family occasions. Through these

14. Nance, *Porter and the Art of Rejection*, 150; Kay Gibbon, "Planes of Language and Time: The Surfaces of the Miranda Stories," *Kenyon Review*, n.s., X (1988), 74–76.

ritual occasions the Fairchilds in *Delta Wedding* become not only a family but *the* family and central institution in southern life.[15]

As Eudora Welty has noted and numerous commentators have observed, she did not, however, write *Delta Wedding* as a reflection of the South or "the Southern problem." She chose 1923 as the time of present action in the saga to avoid the claims of public history. That year was, according to her calculation, a time when "all the men could be home and uninvolved" in wars, floods, or other urgent external events. Her aim, she said, was to "write a story that showed the solidity of this family and the life that went on on a small scale in the world of its own." To write her book about the Delta, Welty, as a woman of the city, had to become familiar with delta lore and ways of feeling. For that, she turned not to histories and almanacs but to family stories: "I had some friends who came from there and I used to hear their stories. . . . Some family tales and sayings are right in the book, though by now I can't remember which are true and which are made up." [16] In effect, by a kind of authorial adoption, she makes another family's past and lore her own.

As she envisioned, "the solidity of this family" in "a world of its own" becomes the ruling attribute of the Fairchilds. With no single hero or heroine, the Fairchild family collectively is protagonist of the saga. Insular, proud, and self-sufficient, for all their attractiveness they are defensive in protecting themselves from outside intrusions and are capable of denying unpleasant parts of the past, present, and probable future in order to maintain their legend of happiness and perfection. In their view the Delta is an enchanted land appropriate for their legend of happiness, a magic circle within which they need not be concerned about the outer worlds of Memphis or New Orleans.[17] They live the dream of Arcady, concerned but not troubled by possible challenges to their dreams, able to see the challenges as opportunities to validate their self-legend. Those challenges

15. Melvin E. Bradford, "Fairchild as Composite Protagonist in *Delta Wedding*," in *Eudora Welty: Critical Essays,* ed. Peggy Whitman Prenshaw (Jackson, 1979), 202.

16. Charles Bunting, "'The Interior World': An Interview with Eudora Welty," in *Conversations with Welty,* ed. Prenshaw, 49–50; Ruth M. Vande Kieft, *Eudora Welty* (New York, 1962), 108–109; Linda Kuehl, "The Art of Fiction XLVII: Eudora Welty," in *Conversations with Welty,* ed. Prenshaw, 89.

17. Noel Polk, "Water, Wanderers, and Weddings: Love in Eudora Welty," in *Eudora Welty: A Form of Thanks,* ed. Louis Dollarhide and Anne J. Abadie (Jackson, 1979), 100; Carol S. Manning, *With Ears Opening Like Morning Glories: Eudora Welty and the Love of Storytelling* (Westport, Conn., 1985), 73–74; Jennifer Lynn Randisi, *A Tissue of Lies: Welty and the Southern Romance* (New York, 1982), 30–32, 43.

function as demonic interludes in the apocalyptic vision of their blessed life: the Yazoo river of death, the Yellow Dog train, and the haunted Indian mound are all dark spirits lurking on the edge of the circle of beauty and happiness, threatening but finally impotent before the magic of the family's self-love.[18]

Within their circle the family members themselves repeat their incantation of perfection. The eldest Fairchild daughter, Shelley, for example, notes in her diary that "we are self-sufficient against people that come up knocking, [that] we are solid to the outside" and that "Papa takes us all together and loves us by the bunch." [19] Her mother Ellen similarly realizes that considering a family member individually rather than as part of the whole is a null concept, particularly to Aunt Shannon (62). Their cousin Laura comes to understand that the Fairchilds think of themselves only in the present, and when "people were at Shellmound it was as if they had never been anywhere else" (134). After the wedding Laura also hears Shelley reproach her parents about adding another baby member to the family: "Mama, we don't *need* any more. . . . We're perfect the way we are" (229). Outsiders such as Dabney's fiancé Troy and George's wife Robbie likewise note the closeness, to them overcloseness, of the family. At the plantation store Troy concedes to Robbie that it is more difficult for a woman than for a man to marry into the too-close circle of high-strung Fairchilds. Robbie, struggling for the individual love of George against the claims of his family, recognizes that her love contrasts unfavorably with the enveloping Fairchild love and that he is lost in the fairyland of Shellmound (148). To her, the Fairchilds love themselves in each other and, knowing George has their love, are unable to understand that he would need to beg for love from his wife (165, 162).

Robbie is nevertheless a potential matriarch in the Fairchild family and participates in the feminine perspective from which the action is observed and pondered. The key to recognizing the dynamic of Fairchild family life in the saga is to see that all the observers and chroniclers are women. From Laura's opening perceptions as she approaches the Delta and Shellmound from Jackson to her closing perceptions at the family picnic three days after the wedding, women and girls provide perspectives in

---

18. MacKethan, *Dream of Arcady*, 190-92; Jane L. Hinton, "The Role of the Family in *Delta Wedding, Losing Battles,* and *The Optimist's Daughter*," in *Critical Essays*, ed. Prenshaw, 121.

19. Eudora Welty, *Delta Wedding* (New York, 1946), 84.

the action. In between are alternated viewpoints of Ellen Fairchild, mother and most perceptive of the matriarchs, and of her daughters and surrogate daughters like Laura. The shifting perspectives among women of the family provide reflections on rituals of family life as they prepare themselves for an action that may mean loss or gain for their magic circle.[20]

The expansion of feminine viewpoints was the agency by which Welty developed *Delta Wedding* out of her unpublished story "Delta Cousins." In the story the narrative viewpoint is nine-year-old Laura Kimball's during her visit to her cousins, the Sheltons, at Innisola. Although numerous narrative details in the story were carried over into the novel, for example, Raymond Shelton as the paragon figure is changed to George and the old beeman made into Aunt Studney, the most significant change was "redistribution of the point of view" so that not only more women could perceive and ponder the action but dimensions of time could be added as well. Thus, as Ellen prepares to bake a cake for George from Aunt Mashula's recipe, the action becomes a secret ritual for the success of George and Robbie's marriage and the occasion for remembering how Denis was killed and George was wounded in the recent war (23–25). When Dabney and India visit Aunts Primrose and Jim Allen at Grove house, their visit becomes the occasion for Primrose to remember old family losses back to the time of the Civil War, when brother Battle and brother Gordon were killed and Lucian Miles and Duncan Laws failed to return (45). In the shifting power of family legend, however, such old disasters and losses have become only stories for retelling in the family's myth of current happiness, mourned ritually and comically in the rivalry between Aunts Shannon and Mac "over which one agonized the more or the more abandonedly, over the fighting brothers and husbands" (188–89).[21]

It soon becomes clear that both the family attribute and the viewpoints of the women narrator-historians are functions of the matriarchal vision of the family as conservatively protective of its members collectively. The women are watchguards over men who may break out of the magic circle, go off into the world, and in their fragility become lost to the family. Guardians of the family's social fabric and keepers of its mystical links with nature, they form an "ancient order of powerful moth-

20. Madelon Sprengnether, "*Delta Wedding* and the Kore Complex," *Southern Quarterly*, XXV (1987), 126; Louise Westling, *Sacred Groves and Ravaged Gardens: The Fiction of Eudora Welty, Carson McCullers, and Flannery O'Connor* (Athens, Ga., 1985), 70.

21. Michael Kreyling, *Eudora Welty's Achievement of Order* (Baton Rouge, 1980), 55–61; Manning, *With Ears Opening*, 123.

ers." [22] It is also clear, though, that the matriarchy is not monolithic. Among the women different versions of the matriarchal order exist, and among the matriarchs some are wholly absorbed into the family creed, some are still on probation, and some still on the threshold waiting to be admitted. Tempe, for example, sees Ellen as still too innocent in her treatment of Robbie Reid, thus not yet a real plantation woman (190).

Because they are not yet fully insiders of the matriarchy, Ellen, Laura, and Robbie see more clearly the workings of the sisterhood than do those fully initiated. Among the initiated, the system of belief is so much taken for granted and seen as a natural thing that they can advise only about particulars within the general framework. Lacking Robbie's insight that the Fairchild women have a "thousand little polite expectations in their very smiles of welcome" and exact adoration from their men (146), Tempe advises Dabney not to let her husband know she can cook (99). And as Ellen notes when Troy brings the Delectable Mountain quilt from his hill-born mother, the Fairchild women do not sew (113).

The most frequently observing and responding matriarch, partially from the outside, Ellen Fairchild sees that even though the men define the family character as reckless and pleasure-loving, underneath their surface bravado the "fineness in her men called to mind their unwieldiness," and she knows that "the fineness could so soon look delicate—nobody could get tireder, fall sicker and more quickly so, than her men" (23). For all their fineness, they are, she understands, peripheral to important things that happen in the family. On the day of Dabney's wedding, Battle enters to confer his "paternal blessing" and is ignored while Dabney, Tempe, and Ellen arrange her bridal bouquet (204). A comic moment, it is nevertheless indicative of men's place in this world. Ellen also sees that the Fairchild men are controlled by the women's heroizing of them. Like Denis before him, George has become the family's hero, "sometimes almost its sacrificial beast" (63). Recognizing the danger, she urges him, "don't let them forgive you, for anything, good or bad" (166).

Still a partial outsider, Laura can see that George is smothered by the family's love: "They all crowded him so, the cousins, rushed in on him so, they smiled at him too much, inviting too much, daring him not to be faultless" (76). But as potential child of the family and incipient matriarch,

22. Sprengnether, "*Delta Wedding* and the Kore Complex," 127; Westling, *Sacred Groves*, 77; Kreyling, *Welty's Achievement of Order*, 71; Peggy W. Prenshaw, "Woman's World, Man's Place," in *Form of Thanks*, ed. Dollarhide and Abadie, 48.

she also feels the power of women and grieves for herself as "a poor motherless girl" (103). She has a father waiting for her in Jackson, but in the Fairchild world, she realizes, it is the mothers that count.

Besides noting how Fairchild women control by exacting adoration and a thousand small sacrifices, Robbie Reid sees that they wear masks of pleading (147). She interprets the trestle incident, when George stays on the railroad track facing the oncoming Yellow Dog engine to rescue Denis' brain-damaged daughter Maureen, as an example of the demands Fairchild women make and sacrifices they require of their men (146). She also sees how the women hold power by possession of the land and houses: "The women it was who inherited the place—or their brothers, guiltily, handed it over. In the Delta the land belonged to the women— they only let the men have it, and sometimes they tried to take it back and give it to someone else" (145). Beneath the smiles is the power to command. "All the men," she thinks, "lived here on a kind of sufferance!" (145).

Full claimants to matriarchy by right of birth in the family, Dabney and Shelley ponder the order they are about to enter. Although she and Troy Flavin will live at Marmion, Dabney realizes that, in the matriarchal order, the place really belongs to Maureen, inherited from her mother Vergie Lee. But in the Fairchild world, where unpleasant things like women "not of sound mind" are denied reality, their possession of the house will be, according to Battle, "not legally, but really" (341). Pondering her sister's coming marriage to Troy, Shelley thinks, as she sees him stop the fight among Negro fieldhands over Pinchy, that Troy as man imitates other men but women are original, though their powers are hidden: "Men were no better than little children. . . . Women, she was glad to think, did know a *little* better—though everything they knew they would have to keep to themselves" (195–96).

Within the matriarchy, the elder members particularly act to preserve and interpret the tradition. Although Aunts Shannon and Mac are keepers of family memory in their mourning of the lost men of the family, they also have their place in family legend as women who raised their nieces and nephews when James was killed in the duel with old Ronald McBane and Laura Allen died soon after and who taught them the family code (67, 120). Maiden aunts Primrose and Jim Allen, like vestal virgins at the Grove, keep the inherited night lamp and memories of the uncles killed during the Civil War. Tempe Summers is the archmatriarch, power figure, manipulator, and announcer of the code. As Ellen recognizes, "marital bullying" is "the breath of life to Tempe" as she takes "pleasure in demanding one more little old thing from Pinck," her husband (125). As priestess of the family legend, Tempe conveys to Dabney that Denis, though dead, is not gone: "His spirit haunted just where she knew. Not at large, not in transit any more, as in life, but fixed—tied to a tree" (117). She similarly interprets the trestle episode as a tribute to Denis. "Naturally," she says, George "did it for Denis" (115). When confronted with the unsuitable spectacle of George marrying below his class, she announces the matriarchal principle that it is the woman who determines the power of the family: "When people marry beneath them, it's the woman that coarsens the man. The man doesn't really do much to the woman, I've observed" (205–206). As keeper of the family legend of perfection and completeness, she is outraged at George and Troy for planning changes in the Grove. To her, change is a challenge to the matriarchal order. "You just want to provoke your sisters," she charges (246).

Despite her probationary status in the eyes of the delta plantation women, Ellen best embodies the matriarchal spirit of the Fairchild house and lands, including their mysteries. She senses, if she does not fully comprehend, that the matriarchy is not as complete and perfect as the family legend supposes. She carries the keys to the household, but as she tells Shelley, some of them are mystery keys—"Some of them are to things I'll never be able to think of or never will see again" (182). After the wedding, she walks in the yard and garden, thinks of herself as restorer of order in nature, and equates tending the garden with tending children, appropriate since she is the only current childbearer at Shellmound (226). She also realizes that the mysteries extend to matters beyond her control. Somewhere she has lost her garnet brooch, and she senses a warning in her dream it is to be found under a giant cypress tree at the bayou (66). During her walk to Partheny's, beside the bayou she meets the strange girl, links the lost girl with her lost pin, senses danger for the girl who is heading out into "the world," and feels "like a mother to the world" (70). At such a time she becomes more than a mother to the Fairchilds and takes on mythological implications of a fertility figure to the land, a Demeter "who rules the natural fertile world, presiding over birth and death of the vegetable and animal species, oblivious to separate human psyches." [23] Protector and

23. Prenshaw, "Woman's World," in *Form of Thanks,* ed. Dollarhide and Abadie, 60; Westling, *Sacred Groves,* 83; Sprengnether, "*Delta Wedding* and the Kore Complex," 122.

presiding presence, she tries by sympathy and mystery to draw a circle of security around the fairyland of Shellmound.

Type scenes in the family's life echo this double image of the protective circle and the intrusion from outside. In the life of the Fairchilds, the circle is particularly associated with eating. Soon after her arrival at Shellmound, Laura observes the family in circle at the dining room table and thinks how characteristic is that gathering (11). The scene is repeated throughout actions of the wedding week as the family celebrates Battle's birthday with a barbecue, Primrose and Jim Allen serve a guinea fowl dinner for George at the Grove, and the family welcomes Troy and Dabney back from their wedding trip with a picnic at the riverside.[24] The contrasting type scene is the trestle incident, never witnessed in the present action but repeatedly described and interpreted. For all their common bond in their legend of unity, the Fairchilds find different meanings in the event. With their frequent retelling of the Yellow Dog episode, they have already begun making it part of the family lore; clearly, as a family story it will become part of family history for future generations. Ellen realizes that to the Fairchilds the trestle incident was only a diversion and romance to be savored, but to her their varying interpretations show the complexities beneath the surface of Fairchild life. The differences, she senses, are not so much among family members as within them (163), and their unity is more superficial than real.

Like other established families, the Fairchilds have their talismanic objects, embodiments of memories of the past, if not of the past itself.[25] In the ancestral portraits are not only images of Great-Grandmother Mary Shannon at the Grove and Great-Great-Uncle Battle at Shellmound but those images as rendered by the family. That is, they represent the ancestry as the family want them remembered. At the Grove are two portraits of Mary Shannon, one done by Great-Grandfather George Fairchild that shows the image of the wife "for whom he had cleared away and built the Grove." The other, painted by John James Audubon in Feliciana, "nobody liked" (41). The portrait of Battle at Shellmound, significantly, was "done from memory by his brother" and shows the man according to family legend with his horse and dogs (55). The painting of Great-Great-

24. Elizabeth Evans, *Eudora Welty* (New York, 1981), 101.

25. Manning, *With Ears Opening,* 63; Bradford, "Fairchild as Composite Protagonist," in *Critical Essays,* ed. Prenshaw, 203–204; Sprengnether, "*Delta Wedding* and the Kore Complex," 124–26.

Uncle Denis, though by a "real painter," agrees with family memory, show-ing him "changelessly sparkling and fair" and "marching on a foreign land" (55). Other portraits demonstrate the family tendency to submerge indi-viduality in common legend and "could not be told apart" (55).

For the two talismanic objects in the present generation, the keynote is their fragility and transience. Although both also are sensed as cryptic warnings, like the portraits of the ancestors and stories about George and Maureen on the railroad trestle, they have the potential of becoming fam-ily lore. For the wedding gift to Dabney, Aunts Primrose and Jim Allen choose the night lamp associated with Great-Great-Aunt Mashula's long, vain wait for Great-Great-Uncle George to return from the Civil War and with Mashula's ghost "crying up the bayou" (45). When Dabney casu-ally accepts and then accidentally breaks the lamp, without crying, in her run to Troy (53), Shelley later thinks of the accident as a mark of the fragility of the Fairchilds' life (193). The other talisman, Ellen's garnet brooch given her by Battle, has been lost. To Ellen it represents not only a gift from her husband but a mark of love and children, potentially lost. Near the bayou she asks the lost strange girl about it and later sends Shelley to the Sibylline Partheny to ask if she might have "seen it floating around somewhere" (128). Although to Laura Partheny seems oddly casual about looking for the pin, the occasion of her search becomes an excuse for Partheny to send George a patticake, the powers of which will regain lost love (131). After Roy finds the pin in the grass at Marmion, site of Aunt Studney's cryptic release of the bees as invocation of many children for Dabney and Troy at Marmion, Laura loses the pin again when Roy dunks her in the Yazoo (177–79). Loss of the pin is the cost of Laura's descent into the River of Death with its "dark water and fearful fishes" and of her reemergence from the deep place. Immediately upon her return from de-scent into the Yazoo, Laura learns that because of Lady Clare's chicken pox, she can be a full participant in the fertility rite of Dabney's wedding.

In the comic world of the Fairchilds, no displacement of inheritance takes place, though it is threatened. Like George Posey in *The Fathers,* Troy Flavin represents the intrusion of strange forces into the Fairchild fairyland. Literally an outsider by coming from the hill country rather than the Delta and by being an overseer rather than suitor from the plantation-owning class, Troy represents to matriarchal Aunt Tempe a potential threat to the Fairchilds (152). To her he is associated with other threats to Fairchild integrity, with George's marrying old Swanson's granddaughter Robbie

Reid and with Mary Denis Summers' marrying the Yankee Buchanan and having a child by him in Illinois (101–11). If her theory on the greater influence of women is correct, though, the present mésalliance of Dabney and Troy will affect fortunes of the Fairchilds less than the earlier mésalliances of Denis and Vergie Lee and George and Robbie.[26] However, comic resolutions are still in prospect. Although Troy will bring strange ideas about fixing up Marmion and about introducing new crops at the Grove, Dabney sees that Troy is potentially more like the Fairchilds than she is (33), that he venerates women in a way satisfactory even to Tempe (185), and that his induction into the Fairchild world begins with the wedding rite. Despite her alienation from the Fairchilds for their heroizing George away from her, Robbie, probably pregnant with George's child, prepares to enter the Fairchild matriarchy, even if they live in Memphis (243–44). Mary Denis shows her continued loyalty to Fairchild legend by naming her baby for George, as Ellen and Battle's new child will be named Denis (114, 241). Like baronial families, the Fairchilds keep, through naming, the interchangeability of family members. In true comic tradition, threats of displacement are temporarily nullified and the wedding week ends with a dance and feast at the riverside.

The subtitle of *Losing Battles* should be "or the Triumph of the Family Story," for the novel demonstrates the capacity of family stories to expand into a generations-long family saga. Ultimately, telling stories becomes the story of *Losing Battles*.[27] The stories demonstrate, however, not so much an attempt to recover the past as the Renfro-Vaughn-Beecham family's attempt to recreate the past to fit the needs of their present. In effect, Eudora Welty's contribution in *Losing Battles* to the southern family saga tradition is to let the stories speak for themselves rather than to filter them through the memory of a narrator-historian presiding over the action. By one estimate, 90 percent of the narrative in *Losing Battles* is dialogue.[28]

26. John Edward Hardy, "Marrying Down in Eudora Welty's Novels," in *Critical Essays*, ed. Prenshaw, 93–94.

27. J. A. Bryant, Jr., "The Recovery of the Confident Narrator: *Curtain of Green* to *Losing Battles*," in *Critical Essays*, ed. Prenshaw, 80-81; Manning, *With Ears Opening*, 41, 150; Douglas Messeroli, "A Battle with Both Sides Using the Same Tactics: The Language of Time in *Losing Battles*," 360, and Mary Anne Ferguson, "*Losing Battles* as a Comic Epic in Prose," 324, both in *Critical Essays*, ed. Prenshaw; Richard J.Gray, *Writing the South: Ideas of an American Region* (New York, 1980), 246; Hinton, "Role of the Family," in *Critical Essays*, ed. Prenshaw, 124.

28. Robert B. Heilman, "*Losing Battles* and Winning the War," in *Critical Essays*, ed. Prenshaw, 273.

Welty indicated that in her plan for *Losing Battles* the family's need to tell stories is a product of its historical place and time. Set in the 1930s, in the Depression-poor hill country of northern Mississippi, the story of the family is a demonstration how, when the outside world has failed it, the family has itself to depend on, she said: "I wanted a clear stage to bring on this family, to show them when they had no props to their lives, had only themselves, plus an indomitable will to live with losing battles. . . . I wanted to take away everything and show them naked and human beings. So that fixed the time and place." Public history is largely absent from the action of the novel, and so long as the family has its private history, that is all it needs. The few references to the outside world of public history are inferential and related to family events. Sam Dale Beecham died in the Great War, but that is important only as it places him in family memory. The uncles' sons have moved away to the cities, ostensibly because the land has failed through drought and erosion, but their leaving is more important to the clan because they left home to live with their wives' families.[29] Perhaps the clearest indication they are cut off from documented history is Judge Oscar Moody's recognition that all legal evidence of births, marriages, and ownerships was lost in the courthouse fire, and the clan's stories are not evidence as the outside world recognizes it (322). Whether in terms of public or private history, though, the clan recognizes that its life is a diminished thing and has been in decline since the Renfros ran the trading post for Indians and passing immigrants and lost it the year Beulah Vaughn and Ralph Renfro married (32).

The implicit recognition in the family is that the men have failed in their encounters with public history and the outside world. Some, like Sam Dale Beecham, died in the war. Some, like Nathan Beecham, went into exile and wandered. Most recently, Jack Renfro has spent time in the penitentiary at Parchman. To make up for the men's forfeiture, women in the family have been its preservers and survivors. The present occasion for the family reunion is a recognition of its matriarchal order as all gather to celebrate the archmatriarch's birthday. Granny Vaughn embodies the nurturing power of women in the family, having raised her seven grandchildren after their parents Euclid and Ellen Beecham died when their buggy fell from Banner Bridge into the Bywy River (179). Matriarchal pride in nurturing can be seen in Beulah's oblique comment on Gloria's being

29. Bunting, "The Interior World," in *Conversations with Welty,* ed. Prenshaw, 50; Eudora Welty, *Losing Battles* (New York, 1970), 64, 66, 194.

raised in an orphanage: "We didn't believe in letting nobody go orphans in our family" (220). Granny's granddaughters provide cohesion to the family while the men play their games of feuding with the Stovalls and trying to run Judge Moody's car off Banner Top.[30] The women's role is not to control the men by commands or blandishments but to make them into figures of family legend by heroizing them and making their exploits the matter of family stories. The men's role is to look after concerns beyond the hearth. "Granny," says Uncle Curtis, "licked us all into shape . . . with Grandpa towering nearby to pray over our failings" (219).

Besides their office as nurturers, the matriarchs act as priestesses and as confessors of the family's failings, keepers of the dark secrets that lie behind the legend of survival. Beulah knows of Sam Dale's injury in infancy that could have kept him from fathering a child by Rachel Sojourner (323), and in her Bible Granny Vaughn has the card from him to someone named Rachel referring mysteriously to "our-baby" (267). To the extent that Miss Julia Mortimer is a member of the family during her residence with the Vaughns, she also acts as confessor to Nathan when, according to Lexie Renfro, he tells of killing Dearman and letting a Negro be convicted of the murder (344). Beulah and Granny also hear Nathan's confession to Julia and keep it as one of the dread secrets until he finally confesses to the whole family. Julia hints in her letters to Judge Moody and Gloria that she knows the secret of Gloria's parentage and the dire consequences of her marrying Jack Renfro (330, 314). Even though their memories conflict, like good family stories they become part of the legend, juxtaposed for incorporation despite their discrepancies.

In presiding over the family, the matriarchs, especially Beulah, act to assign roles to members, even perhaps remaking the current hero Jack into a reincarnation of Sam Dale, the family hero and hope before his death.[31] To her, Jack has been the chosen one, the hero and favorite since birth. She tells Birdie that she brought him up on praise (63), and to doubting Cleo she reveals the matriarchal bias in her preference: "He's Renfro-size! . . . But he's all Beecham, every inch of him!" (30). That her preferential view is shared by most of the clan is evident when Granny waits for him to come home as "the joy of life," when Aunt Nanny Beecham says the

---

30. Louise Y. Gossett, "*Losing Battles:* Festival and Celebration," in *Critical Essays,* ed. Prenshaw, 350; Ferguson, "*Losing Battles* as Comic Epic," in *Critical Essays,* ed. Prenshaw, 322–23.

31. Randisi, *Tissue of Lies,* 95.

reunion starts when Jack arrives (15), and when he is greeted by general shouting, hugging, and kissing (71). His role in the family is to bring back hope, to "haul [them] out of [their] misery" (194), and to receive the family's forgiveness for leaving home to serve time at Parchman (185). Leaving home and the family, not showing contempt for lawful authority, was his "crime" in the eyes of matriarchs. To them, his unnecessary carrying of Curly Stovall's safe across the fields to retrieve Granny's gold ring is "placed" as a man's sort of thing to do. "But he's a man! Done it the man's way," notes Aunt Nanny (63). If women define roles, not all, however, agree with their heroizing. Ella Fay notes that the girls got whipped when Jack did not (63), and Vaughn provides the dissenting undertone when he tells Aunt Birdie Beecham he does not care if Jack fails to get home for the reunion (11). To Beulah, Vaughn is the less heroic son because he resists matriarchal order: "He'll never be Jack. . . . Says the wrong thing, does the wrong thing, doesn't do what I tell him. And perfectly satisfied to have you say so!" (12). Although in matriarchal eyes Jack may be "the sweetest and hardest working boy in Banner and Boone County and maybe in all Creation," to Vaughn the problem created by the family, with Jack's consent, is Jack's belief in his own heroism.[32]

To the gathered matriarchs at the reunion, the main issue is whether Gloria as the hero's wife will show herself worthy of induction into the matriarchy. In their eyes, the problem with Gloria is that as a child raised in an orphanage, without clear matrilineal descent and with the ideals of Julia Mortimer instead of those of the Renfros, Beechams, and Vaughns, she wants a conjugal rather than consanguine family life. To Gloria, clan life smothers. The dead as well as the living crowd in on them, she complains to Jack (171). When it appears she does have a known descent through Rachel Sojourner and Sam Dale Beecham, the matriarchs rush to induct her into the circle, and in ritual oddly primitive and savage they hold her down and cover her face with watermelon, "with its blood heat," while they call on her to say "Beecham" (269) and Granny watches. Even though Beulah tells her to "get up and join your family," Gloria continues to protest she is not a Beecham and to claim she married Jack "to save him" from "this mighty family" (320).

The circle of matriarchs around Gloria is a repetition of the type scene within the saga. The circle of kin telling family stories is the scene not only repeated each reunion but, according to family lore, repeated in past gen-

32. Prenshaw, "Woman's World," in *Form of Thanks,* ed. Dollarhide and Abadie, 50.

erations and to be repeated in those of the future. Noah Webster Beecham notes this conviction when, near the end of the celebration, he talks with this future matriarch: "Gloria, this has been a story on us that never will be allowed to be forgotten. . . . Long after you're an old lady without much further stretch to go, sitting back in the same rocking chair granny's got herself in now, you'll be hearing it told to Lady May and all her hovering brood" (354). For what Noah Webster implicitly recognizes is that the storytellers are creators, more than recounters, of family history. The past is already essentially known to the family, and the stories are examples of phatic communion, of talk more for the sake of reaffirming relationships than for conveying information. The stories remind the clan who they are by recounting their past.

During the day's talk, presided over by a descriptive voice linking the actors with the natural world surrounding them, different kinds of narrative voice emerge.[33] Cleo, Noah Webster's wife and newcomer to the family, serves as interlocutor to prompt stories family members have to tell. Although the stories may be new to her and the reader, they are known tales to the others, and frequently the story is started by one member and supplemented or completed by others. When Cleo wants to know why Jack was sent to prison, Nanny designates Percy to tell Jack's story, and his account is soon added to by others (22, 32–60). A second kind of narrative occurs after Jack arrives and various members tell him of events that occurred while he was gone and Jack recounts how he left Parchman a day early to arrive in time for the reunion. Despite their recitation of defeats, their tone is self-congratulatory. A third kind comes from neighbors who mockingly report how Jack unknowingly helped Judge Moody get his car out of the ditch. A fourth is the ritual recitation of family history "in the argumentative voice of one who habitually brings comfort to others" by Brother Bethune, accompanied by the family's sotto voce comparison of his performance with Grandpa Vaughn's. As Birdie notes, Brother Bethune "ain't measuring up" because "what he's reeling off is tailored to any reunion he's lucky enough to get invited to" (177–80). That his performance fails to measure up to the ritual occasion becomes clear when, after his talk, he forgets to forgive Jack. "He was on the track, but he swerved," notes Uncle Curtis (213). Other narratives are told in explanation of documents produced and told about rather than read at the reunion—documents such as Sam Dale Beecham's card kept by Granny

33. J. A. Bryant, "Confident Narrator," in *Critical Essays*, ed. Prenshaw, 77–78.

in the family Bible, Julia's letter to Judge Moody, Julia's will in the blue-back speller, Julia's letter to Gloria warning her not to marry Jack, and the photograph of Ralph and Beulah's wedding. Nathan's confession of killing Dearman, of letting a Negro hang for the murder, of cutting off his hand in penitence, and of wandering in exile adds another dimension to the narrative developed by dialogue and family story.

Out of stories told and retold, the continuity of the Renfros, Beechams, and Vaughns emerges as a living past. The underlying message of the stories is that the clan has a heroic past that belies its present poverty. Its ancestors were among the first in the country. As Brother Bethune recognizes, Captain Jacob Jordan, Granny's grandfather, built the house the family lives in now "the year the stars fell," kept his stage stop, married a Carolina woman, begot his son Jack Jordan, and "died brave" (180). Ralph Renfro tells the Moodys how his ancestors kept a stage stop near Banner Top, rang bells to guide Carolina immigrants through the wilderness, and remembered tales of the Bywy Indians, who drowned themselves to resist removal to the west (335). His story is also one of lost fortunes as he recalls how the Renfros lost the store that developed from the trading post. "Come down to me and I lost it," he confesses (32). Brother Bethune also recites how later generations spent their lives at Banner and how Billy Vaughn built the first house in town, lost it to fire, built his church, married Thurzah Elvira Jordan, now Granny Vaughn, moved into the Vaughn house, and helped raise seven grandchildren (184). In his recitation of family history, however, Brother Bethune omits the generation of Billy and Elvira's children, and in connection with their reluctance to cross the Banner Bridge, Ralph Renfro has to tell the Moodys of the puzzling episode of Ellen Vaughn and Euclid Beecham falling from the bridge to their deaths.

In the family's later reconstruction, the Euclid-Ellen story is another case of destiny and love at first sight. "Clapped his eyes *one time* on Ellen Vaughn stepping out of her father's church one pretty Sunday, and it was all over for Euclid Beecham," reports Beulah (215). In echo of repeated family stories, Ralph Renfro wishes he had a penny for every time he had heard that one. As Beulah notes in her correction of Ralph, though, he is on the verge of telling that story "from the other side." Euclid and Ellen's story is the mysterious one in the chronicle of generations. Why, after bringing seven children into the clan, they rushed headlong into death is the puzzle for later generations to ponder. In Beulah's view they died because Euclid did not know how to stop a runaway horse; in Ralph's "other side" view, "Maybe he'd done better if his wife hadn't been holding the reins." This echo of generations-long matriarchal-patriarchal tension comes down to the "deep question" about "what errand" they were both so "bent on when they hitched and cut loose from the house so early" that morning. As Uncle Curtis admits, "that part of the story's been lost to time," and completing his "other side" version, Ralph decides, "Something between man and wife is the only answer, and it's what no other soul would have no way of knowing" (218).

That story, though central to family memory and family honor, as the mystery of the lost wedding ring shows, joins other mysteries emerging from retold stories: What was the nature of Sam Dale's injury? What was the real relationship between Sam Dale and Rachel Sojourner? Whose daughter is Gloria Short? That such questions will linger in family memory becomes clear as Jack, Gloria, and Lady May visit the family cemetery at Banner at the time of Julia Mortimer's funeral. At Sam Dale's grave, Gloria observes that if he had not died young, "he'd be old, and expecting to be asked to tell everything he knew" (427). At Euclid's and Ellen's graves, Jack thinks of their early deaths and wonders, "Like somebody had whispered to 'em 'Quick!' and they were smart enough to take heed" (426).

The wedding ring recovered from Ellen's body and kept by Granny in her Bible becomes, along with Billy Vaughn's bois d'arc tree, one of the family's talismanic objects (219). A memorial of that old puzzle about what went on between dead patriarch and matriarch, the ring comes back into current issue when Ella Faye takes it with her to Gloria's school and loses it to Curly Stovall at the store formerly belonging to the Renfros in payment for credit given the family (24). Jack fights Curly for the ring as for family honor, carries home the safe in which the ring was placed, loses the ring along the way, and ends up going to prison. Although at the time of the trial Judge Moody convicts and sentences Jack for contempt of lawful authority, to the family the key issue is what the ring means to the family. "The ring itself," says Beulah, is "exactly what old Judge Moody lost sight of!" (63). That no other of the present generation except Ella Faye recognizes the sexual as well as the memorial associations of the ring becomes clear in Percy and Birdie's account of Curly's ring snatching. They seem oddly innocent in recalling how Ella Faye had grown "a little during the summer," became "as pretty as she [could] be," and kept the ring "tucked in where Granny tucks her snuff box" before flaunting it in front of Curly (22–24). That the fight over the ring two years before was about sisters as well as grandmothers becomes clearer when Jack fights Curly the day after the reunion for ogling Ella Faye and she shows the pocketknife given her by Curly and kept on a neck string and says she can be a bride, too (411–12). When they fight again, Curly whips Jack and cuts off his shirttail to signal his victory and entry into the family (413). Apparently, a pocketknife, if not a ring, will become a talisman for new generations of the family.

The bois d'arc tree in the yard not only dates from the time of the great-grandparents' youth but clusters about itself the aura of miracle and mystery. Originally one of Billy Vaughn's switches for urging his horse when he came courting Elvira, the switch developed from a shaft stuck in the ground and forgotten until it sprouted and grew (181). Now "a veteran of all the old blows, a survivor," it has become an emblem of the family with its wounds and scars and circles of growth, the family totem.[34] At the end of the presentation of gifts to Granny, the clan sings "Gathering Home," and the switch tree becomes part of the family's vision of themselves moving on the stream of time, "and it all was unmovable, or empowered to hold the scene still fixed or stake the reunion there" (223).

The Jordan-Vaughn-Renfro house itself originally and finally becomes the focus of the clan in place for generations. Unlike the quasi-aristocratic country houses of southern gentry in its modesty, it nevertheless tells of the joining of families over time with its new house joined to the original cabin by a wide center passage and galleries back and front (6). With a new roof bought by Ralph Renfro at the cost of Jack's truck, it tells of the sacrifices endured to maintain family pride. As Ralph understands, Jack noticed the new roof as a Renfro gift to the Vaughn place; as he translates it, the roof is substitute for "a word from your father" (94). Indeed, the house embodies what Welty came to understand about the sense of place as a moment in history:

> I think Southerners have such an intimate sense of place. We grew up in the fact that we live here with people about whom we know almost everything that can be known as a citizen of the same neighborhood or town. . . . We know what the place has made of these people, what they've made of the place through generations. We have a sense of continuity and that, I think, comes from place. It helps to

34. Kreyling, *Welty's Achievement of Order*, 152.

give meaning—another meaning to a human life that such life has been there all the time and will go on.[35]

Although Shirley Ann Grau's *The Keepers of the House,* published in 1964, appears on first reading to be a traditional form of the family saga with its chronicle of generations, it soon becomes clear that the work represents a new dimension in the method of narrating a family saga. All the saga is filtered through the consciousness of Abigail Howland Mason Tolliver, matriarch, but is not entirely narrated by her. Rather, as she says in one of the sections she does narrate, she depends on knowledge gained through family stories and family memory so that her intimate knowledge is vastly greater than what she knows by personal experience: "Everyone tells stories around here. Every place, every person has a ring of stories around them, like a halo almost. People have told me tales ever since I was a tiny girl squatting in the front dooryard, in mud-caked overalls, digging for doodlebugs. They have talked to me, and talked to me. Some I've forgotten, but most I remember. And so my memory goes back before my birth. . . . When I want to, I can see my grandfather William Howland as a young man." [36] What further she brings to narration of her family story is the chronicle of a patriarchal family seen from a matriarchal perspective.

Her narration then is a re-creation of those half-forgotten family stories from childhood, enhanced by specific encounters with storytellers and by her re-creation into story of things observed earlier but not understood until later, when the pressure of events causes her to recall them for insight and strength. For her the agency for remembering the past is her linkage with the Howland family place. As in the southern manner of identifying place with history, she has only vague and passing memories of places other than her home but a vivid sense of enlarged memory associated with the ancestral home. Of the ten years she lived with her mother and father in Virginia while he was a professor at Mary Baldwin College, she wonders "if it had happened at all," for she remembers "so little." Because of her yearly visits to the Howland place, though, on her return there with her mother when her British father left in 1939 to fight a war, "Within a single day [she] felt that [she] had always lived there." Everyone "as-

35. Jean Todd Freeman, "An Interview with Eudora Welty," in *Conversations with Welty,* ed. Prenshaw, 179–80.

36. Shirley Ann Grau, *The Keepers of the House* (New York, 1964), 1, 14.

sumed I would have an atavistic memory" of the place, she says. "And maybe I did" (139, 142).

Beyond that atavistic memory, however, Abigail also has opportunities and occasions for supplementing it with stories told in her adulthood based on sights and events of other times. After her grandfather William Howland dies, she visits Margaret Carmichael, the part-black woman he lived with for thirty years in the Howland house, and hears from Margaret what her life with William had been like and how it was for her to live away from her children, who were sent to the North (221). Although she does not tell how she got the "news" of Margaret's death four years to the day after William's death, apparently from one of the anonymous messengers sent periodically by Margaret (233), Abigail has enough details to reconstruct stories told by the New Church settlement people about how Margaret heard someone call and walked out into the night to her death in the New Church baptistry (234). Earlier, after her visit with Margaret in New Church, she drives back to Howland with a sense of William sitting beside her telling her how it was to live the best of his life with Margaret (222). Although at the time she wonders why he had never told her before, out of such encounters she can narrate the experiences of William and Margaret in an earlier generation as though she had been there with them. Out of her inherited and ghost-haunted memory, Abigail gives embedded accounts of informants' stories and integrates them into her own tale of the generations.

Such a method of narration and dependence on family stories is not only Abigail's but Shirley Ann Grau's as well. As she said on several occasions, Grau drew on family stories in general and in particular when she wrote *Keepers of the House*: "I grew up with the usual family stories of births and wars and killings, of Indians and feuds," and the novel "was taken from places and events I knew in my childhood." She also noted that Howland "was [her] grandfather's name," that "Will Howland . . . [was] based somewhat on [her] grandfather," and that she had been raised by a woman much like Margaret Carmichael in the novel. She saw her reliance on family stories as characteristically southern. Like Eudora Welty, she saw that, despite all their travel and experience in the nonsouthern world, southerners like storytelling better than do people of other regions: "Perhaps because the South was the last one into the modern world . . . we still tell stories. . . . Everybody told stories, the cook and the yardman and my grandfather. . . . I can remember going hunting with my grandfather and his missing any number of shots because he was storytelling at the time. He was just walking and talking." [37] Her regional and personal memories merge in *Keepers of the House,* in which Abigail arrives at the time when she as matriarch embodies the family, feeling, she says, "the pressure of generations behind me, pushing me along the recurring cycles of birth and death" (5).

More than in most matriarchal sagas, the Howland chronicle is tied closely to events in public history. As Abigail reviews the generations, historical events serve as markers for identifying ancestors. The beginning of family memory coincides with removal of the Howlands from east Tennessee to the Deep South. Memory begins not with the life in the mountains but with the first Will Howland, veteran of the Battle of New Orleans, who abandoned his return to the razorback ridges and instead settled in the "friendlier country, cut to the measure of a man, where hills could be walked over, and the land turned easily under his plow" (11). To the extent that Margaret and her children become part of the dark, unacknowledged side of the family, their heritage, too, comes from the same historical time. She is a descendant, on her mother's side, of the Freejacks, slaves freed by Andrew Jackson for services at the Battle of New Orleans and named for their emancipator. The period between the War of 1812 and the Civil War is marked for the Howlands with each generation producing a Will Howland and with the generations together realizing the promise of their ancestor's choice of ground by prospering through farming, trading at Mobile, and acquiring slaves, but not growing rich or becoming cotton snobs. Not until after the Civil War, during which one Will Howland burned to death in fighting at the Wilderness north of Richmond and Cousin Ezra was shot at Tim's Crossing (248), does the family gain financial power it will enjoy in the next century, and that development, true to the realities of history, comes not by agriculture but by commerce. Abigail's great-great-grandfather William H. Howland marries Aimée Legendre of New Orleans, who brings with her the Civil War profits of her cotton-trading father (15). Those war profits of the old matriarch introduce new dimensions into family history and effect a displace-

---

37. "Shirley Ann Grau," in *World Authors, 1950-1970,* ed. John Wakeman (New York, 1975), 570; Shirley Ann Grau, "The Essence of Writing," in *The Writer's Handbook, 1977,* ed. A. S. Burack (Boston, 1977), 17; Carlton Cremeens, "An Exclusive Tape-Recorded Interview with Shirley Ann Grau," in *Writer's Yearbook* (New York, 1966), 22; Nancy Campbell, "Miss Grau Eyes Her Novel," New Orleans *Times-Picayune,* June 27, 1965, Sec. 3, p. 15; John Canfield, "A Conversation with Shirley Ann Grau," *Southern Quarterly,* XXV (1987), 48.

ment in the inheritance as Aimée buys land that will make the fortune of the family in the twentieth century by timbering rather than farming (13, 154). She also introduces French Catholicism into the family, which, with the scandal of war profits, divides sentiment in later generations (164).

Besides the Howland whose death in Cuba links the family with the Spanish-American War (170), the two world wars and the intervening Depression similarly serve as markers for later generations in family memory. In keeping with world events, Will Howland, Abigail's grandfather, almost dies of Spanish influenza near the end of the first war (25). During the Depression the family helps drifter children abandoned by their families (158). Her father, Gregory Edward Mason, British-born professor at her mother's college in Virginia, returns to England in 1939 talking of an Armageddon with the Nazis, and she never sees him again (142). If later generations could not forget Legendre's war profits, Will Howland remembers the first generation and wonders what they would say about a daughter of the family marrying a descendant of the British they fought at New Orleans (42). True also to history, Abigail notes changes resulting from World War II, when the outside world intrudes in planes flying overhead on training missions, agricultural workers desert the fields for better-paying jobs in shipyards on the coast, and Will Howland stops raising cotton and raises cattle and cuts timber for more war profits (166). Finally, the Korean War becomes part of Abigail's family memory when her first lover Tom Stanley dies in Korea and her husband John Tolliver serves grudgingly at a desk job in Washington, D.C. (187, 203).

If Grau was particular about history for the Howland family, she was even more particular about being unspecific about their geography. Her Wade County and Madison City are as apocryphal as Faulkner's Yoknapatawpha and Jefferson. Knowing that "Southerners are touchy and love to litigate," she scrambled her geography: "It's no one place. It's a bit of everything. For that same reason, I went very carefully through the Atlas and checked the names of every county and town in the Southern states against my counties and towns." Although the general impression is that the Howlands' state is Alabama, she suggests Louisiana geography in her swamp scenes and mention of the Red River. She implies Mississippi in references to North Trace, to the Battle of Tim's Crossing, and to northern tier counties, like the Tolliver Nation, with histories of slave-breeding. Alabama points of reference include Mobile, Birmingham, and the Black Warrior River as nearby sites. In scrambling references, she also broadens implications of her locale to match southern experience.[38]

The reason for close correlation of family history and public history becomes clear as public history of the South impinges on Abigail's generation. The novel keys its present action on the segregation-civil rights controversies rocking the nation in the early 1960s. In effect, current news as well as family history becomes the matter of the saga. In contrast with Welty's practice of placing the family outside the currents of history, Grau shows how the family is shaped by and responds to history. Asked twenty-five years later why she wrote about the black-white conflict, she noted it was "*the* issue" of the decade. It also afforded a combination of family and public history: "So those two just happen to come together. . . . The thing just presented itself, I think, stimulated by the issue of the day. A lot of family stories fitted themselves together and I was able to move them that way." She recognized how the two could profitably interact in the novel: "[*Keepers of the House*] turns on race discrimination, basically, and that is the law of the area. It's not something the characters plan. It's a problem that the characters must deal with. It's a problem from outside impinging on them. . . . It isn't nature any more. . . . It's customs, laws, rules, but man-made this time." [39]

For Grau, history reflected in the saga is a time of moral complexity. "I've always been fascinated by, to quote [Bertrand] Russell, 'the harm that good men do'—an action from the best of motives proving to be the worst thing possible." Moral perplexity lends itself, she thought, to the easy hypocrisy of simple answers to hard questions, of the "cheap ego trip" of "the thrill of being the good guys against the bad guys." That fiction can deal with human predicaments more accurately than can polemics was clear to her in responses to her novel. "After that book, I can't tell you how many people called me up and said (anonymous calls), 'How can I change my birth certificate?' In a little town in Plaquemines Parish there are pages of the birth register missing. You could just rip it out and there goes that." The mob of whites who attack the Howland house show again the conflict between the local code on race and the law, though the law has changed from the time of Stribling's saga.[40] As John Tolliver tells Abigail, his association with the White Citizens Council and other

38. Cremeens, "Exclusive Interview," 22; William T. Going, "Alabama Geography in Shirley Ann Grau's *The Keepers of the House*," *Alabama Review*, XX (1967), 64, 67–68; Paul Schleuter, *Shirley Ann Grau* (Boston, 1981), 53.

39. Canfield, "Conversation with Grau," 43–44, 41.

40. *Ibid.*, 44; Schleuter, *Shirley Ann Grau*, 59.

segregationist organizations is just playing the political game by the other code, and he does not propose to be a white knight fighting injustice (253).

In the manner of other saga writers, Grau also makes the Howland house the measure of change in family history. In the house built by her great-great-grandfather (5), Abigail remembers how it has been identified with the family as the Howland house despite Aimée Legendre's attempts to have the place called "Shirley" (154). A sprawling structure with twenty-two bedrooms at the time of Abigail's mother's wedding (57), shaped according to the needs of succeeding generations, the house is remodeled to its original shape by Abigail's husband John as he takes off "most of the wings and sheds that had grown on it like mushrooms and barnacles over the generations" (225). Like the commercial new rich restoring other country houses, he acts from political rather than familial motives: "It looks better for me to live in an old house. . . . Substantial, like a wool suit in summertime" (208). When the scandal breaks about Will Howland's marriage to Margaret and threatens his political ambitions, though, John Tolliver retreats to the Tolliver Nation in the north of the state. Abigail refuses to leave not only because she knows the townspeople would burn the Howland place but because it is the locus of family memory.[41] By the time she has repelled the raiders, Abigail can tell the ghost of her grandfather she has kept the house for future generations (289).

Not only the house itself but special parts of the house accrue talismanic significance for Howlands and in the process show the special attribute handed down through the generations. The charred handrail on the hall staircase is the object that best epitomizes the family past and family attribute. The handrail was charred in the old days by bandits who killed the sister of Will's great-great-grandfather. The ancestor and his sons then, Abigail recalls Will telling her, "drove the robbers into the canebrake in the dark and killed them there, one by one as they wallowed hip deep in the swamp," and, as she remembers later, "dragged the bandits out of the swamp, and hanged them, living and dead, from the tallest trees" while "Mrs. Howland stood under those white oaks, looking up, and laughing" (133, 279). When the house was remodeled, the charred handrail was kept "to remember by," for "generation after generation." After Abigail disperses the raiders, she chooses, like a true Howland, not to repair anything. "Howlands keep such things to remember by" (296).

41. Anthony Buloski, "The Burden of Home: Shirley Ann Grau's Fiction," *Critique*, XXVIII (1987), 193.

The talismanic handrail is also an index to the family attributes of living independently of the town and of taking vengeance. As narrator Abigail recalls stories told by her grandfather, it emerges clearly that Howlands have from the earliest times lived by their own code, have taken revenge on violators of their code, and have remembered acts of vengeance for future reference. Whether these episodes recount vengeance taken on the bandits who killed the Howland girl and charred the handrail or vengeance taken on Indians who killed and scalped the first Will Howland and were themselves brought back to hang from the white oak in front of the house, Abigail recalls in them the earlier matriarch's response to the family code, of Mrs. Howland laughing at the bandits hanging from trees. Abigail invokes that old code as she and Oliver, the only hand who does not desert at the prospect of trouble, burn the raiders' cars and hear them explode: "One for one. Like it was before. You kill my child in the kitchen and I murder you in the swamp" (285). As she fires at raiders in the yard, she again invokes family memory for present need: "I didn't hunt them down in the swamp but I'm going to kill them just the same" (288).

If readers have deplored Abigail's insensitivity to the plight of Margaret's children and her "insensitivity in the face of racial and regional antagonisms," they fail to recognize that in terms of the saga she is a product of her family and inheritor of the family attribute.[42] A resourceful defender of her half-black uncle and aunts in the manner of their ancestors during their childhood and school days, she becomes their enemy when they violate the family code and join those against whom she defended them. For her, the issue is family loyalty, not race. She knows, if others do not, that the type scene repeated through generations is vengeance wreaked.

That she and the earlier Howlands must have revenge, though, is an indication of family resolve to live by its own code rather than the community's. Will Howland shows the tendency to outrage community pieties when he doubts publicly that his great-uncle was happy to be burned to death at the Wilderness for the Cause (29). And he shows himself indifferent to local sentiment about his "reading the Yankee press" when he subscribes to the New York *Tribune* for Abigail's mother and indifferent to local expectations that, as an eligible man of property, he will find a wife

42. William J. Stuckey, *The Pulitzer Prize Novels* (Norman, 1981), 211; Louise Y. Gossett, *Violence in Recent Southern Fiction* (Durham, 1965), 192–93; Schleuter, *Shirley Ann Grau*, 56, 65.

among the local women after his Atlanta-born first wife dies (28). He outrages local sensibilities again when he decides to bury his tubercular daughter in Santa Fe rather than bring her back to Wade County, where "all the
Howlands had been buried" (170–71). Indeed, Will's decision to follow
the example of his Creole grandmother Aimée in exploring the edge of
the known world (71) is what takes him into Honey Island Swamp to find
the Armstrongs' hidden still and on to New Church to meet Margaret
Carmichael, the action that sets up the climactic confrontation between
the Howlands and Madison City. In taking Margaret first as his housekeeper and soon as his mistress, Will stays within the allowable code of the
community, but when he marries her and makes his children by her legitimate, he violates the community's code. It is the consequences of that
"old crime" that Abigail has to live with.

Thus, the influence of the matriarchy in family history becomes the
dominant issue for Abigail's generation. Over the span of generations,
three matriarchs before Abigail stand out: the Howland mother laughing
at the hanged bodies of her daughter's killers; Aimée Legendre, whose
memory split the family over her Catholicism and her father's war profits;
and Margaret, who became an unacknowledged part of Howland family
life for thirty years and was more like a mother and grandmother to Abigail than was her own blood mother (78, 143). Against the examples of
family matriarchs, Abigail senses the role of nameless southern matriarchs
on the porch:

> It was a sure thing they prided themselves on, this ability to tell Ne-
> gro blood. And to detect pregnancies before a formal announcement,
> and to guess the exact length of gestation. Blood and birth—these
> were their two concerns. . . . I've spent my time sitting on porches on
> a sunny dusty afternoon, listening to the ladies talk, learning to see
> what they saw. . . . They taught me my Bible lessons the exact same
> way, and to this day I am very good at spotting signs of Negro blood
> and reciting the endless lists of genealogies in the Bible. It's a
> southern talent, you might say. (143)

Although in family history, Will remembers, it was the men in the family, not the women, who kept alive the memory of old killings and vengeance
(133), in Abigail's time the matriarchs must affirm the old attribute because the men have defaulted. She recalls how her mother refused to see
Gregory Mason after World War II and burned his unopened letters (142,

150), and she knows in her own experience how John Tolliver abandoned her and her family to save his own political ambitions. Even though she has a sense of being regarded as a horror by John after the scandal breaks about William and Margaret's marriage, in her view the horror was in her choosing the wrong man (257). As she faces the night raiders with only Oliver's help, she feels abandoned by men when she needs them and, in effect, though still a matriarch, assumes the patriarchal role (275). In retrospect she can see that this displacement of roles and inheritance has been in the making for generations. In place of a Will Howland in each generation, now there are Abigails—her mother, herself, and her daughter—as keepers of the house.

Through stories told her by William and Margaret, Abigail can also see in retrospect the connection between the matriarchal presence and the family attribute of living on the edge of the known world. In Margaret the matriarchy is associated through local stories about Alberta and Stanley Albert Thompson with the legendary, which Grau had explored in "The Black Prince." [43] After his trip into the primal swamp, William Howland sees Margaret Carmichael at the baptistry stream near New Church community and, wondering "for a minute if she were really there at all," remembers the stories of "Alberta, the great tall black woman who lived up in the hills with her man Stanley Albert Thompson" and occasionally came south to the swamps during the cold of blackberry winter (75). As he approaches Margaret he still keeps the tales of Alberta in mind (76), and when he first sees her in his kitchen at Howland house, he again confuses her with Alberta (128). Notably by this time and thereafter, Alberta exists in family legend. In effect, Will Howland replaces Stanley Albert Thompson in the family's reconstitution of the legend. The implications of Alberta-Margaret and Stanley-Will as outsiders to the conventional life of the community are ominous. For in Margaret's mind at least, fate is at work. As she recalls to Abigail, she was not surprised by Will's appearance because she remembers telling him, "I knowed you was coming. . . . I know it ahead of time" (118). The reason she knows is that she, too, has made her journey into the swamp, has glimpsed her di-

---

43. As she told Canfield, Grau moved from "trying to create a kind of legendary, mythological time, a non-real approach, a storytelling in the legendary sense of storytelling" in "The Black Prince" to a more realistic presentation in *The Keepers of the House* but wanted to go beyond limits of realism as well. "Perhaps myth-making is the way to go," she speculated. Canfield, "Conversation with Grau," 45.

vided heritage of black and white, has had her vision of generations that have wept and will weep, and has chosen her white destiny (85, 105).

Through her years with Will Howland, Margaret and her shadow identity as Alberta become part of the matriarchal family lore. Abigail's mother tells her "the old Negro stories about Alberta" as she overlooks Will's relationship with Margaret in her lady-of-the-manor way of explaining to Abigail how Margaret's children "had just come to her, without a father . . . just come sneaking into her body when she was asleep in the soon [*sic*] of a foggy morning" (144). After Will's death and her visit with Margaret at New Church, Abigail has a better sense of Margaret's importance to her grandfather. Accompanied by his ghost on her return from New Church, Abigail recognizes that Margaret reminded him of "the free-moving Alberta of the old tales" (223). In her way Margaret completes the cycle of identifying with Alberta when she returns to New Church after Will's death and dies at the baptistry where he first saw her as Alberta.

In any case, for Abigail, Margaret has become part of the matriarchal family, signaled by Abigail's naming her last daughter Margaret as if for a member of the family and as she named another daughter to perpetuate the line of Abigails. Abigail's Margaret serves as Margaret Carmichael's reincarnation, for during her pregnancy Abigail is haunted by the dead woman: "Margaret lurked around the corners of the dark spots of all my dreams. She even called to me out of the color-streaked ether-filled cold when the child was born" (235).

If, for Abigail, Margaret is part of the matriarchal heritage of the family—a heritage against whose consequences she must defend the House of Howland—Margaret is also separate from the patriarchal heritage of vengeance needed to defend the House. While she is firing at the raiders, Abigail realizes that Margaret is not among those ancestral ghosts watching her (290). As John saw when Abigail named their last daughter, Margaret's ghost had been exorcised from the family.

More than most family sagas, *Keepers of the House* affords moments of vision for the characters as they contemplate their role in family history. That all moments of vision come through Abigail's narrating consciousness suggests they may be functions of her mind rather than of others'. Because she is collector and repository of family memory, the visions of William and Margaret, as well as her own, nevertheless become part of that sustained memory. William's vision, as Abigail recalls it, is the sameness of generations when children come to tell their parents they are ready to marry someone of whom the parents hardly approve (199). His vision occurs within the context of his warning to Abigail that love is not by itself enough for dynastic purposes (180–81). Margaret's secret life, as Abigail comes to understand, is filled with visions both before and after she meets Will Howland. During her girlhood, at the time of her great-grandmother's death, she sees a vision of the old woman calling her into the house to "be with my blood" (98), and again at the time of her great-grandmother's burial she sees the old woman's ghost muttering, "Flesh and blood" (103). As Margaret listens to the blues singing during the wake, she envisions "the generations of weeping that had been done, the generations of weeping that were to come," and feels herself enlarged until "she could feel the earth move under her feet, breathing slowly as it passed from season to season" (105). When she prepares to leave New Church and goes to say goodbye to her grandfather Abner Carmichael, she again realizes that "it takes two generations to kill off a man," that "first him, and then his memory" go (109). If Abigail reconstructs Will's visions as those of individuals struggling against dynastic destiny, she sees Margaret's as struggles of conflicting claims of blood within the generations, ominous for Margaret and even more for her children.

Abigail's own visions are not only of ancestral ghosts watching as she reenacts the family past but also of the consequences of that reenactment. The sources of her visions are, besides family stories, her imaginative empathy with matriarchs in the long line of family retribution. Abigail obviously cannot know from direct testimony Margaret's state of mind when she heard the call outside her house at New Church, put down her handwork, and went outside into the night and to her death, apparently by suicide in the baptistry. But Abigail has a vision of what it means: "This was the order re-establishing itself. This was the way I'd known all along it would be, without realizing it. It wasn't something you cried over. You didn't even grieve in the ordinary sense of the term. You just curled up where you were, curled up in pain and fear, and you stayed shriveled and shivering" (235).

She also remembers the earlier matriarch who watched the hanging bodies of her daughter's killers and laughed. As Abigail tells her own daughter, the matriarch's laugh had not been glee at vengeance taken but empathy at suffering experienced: "And she'd been seeing her daughter's death agonies repeated over and over in the agonies of her murderers"

(279). When Abigail has exacted her own vengeance on the town by closing down the hotel, slaughterhouse, and ice cream plant and on Margaret's son Robert by calling him in Seattle, telling him she has found him, and threatening to expose his bloodline to his white wife, she reenacts her visions about Margaret and the old matriarch. Like the old matriarch, she laughs and cries, and like her imagined response to Margaret's death, she huddles in a fetal position and shivers (309). Her response is not so much contemplation of a bleak naturalistic world as it is her dynastic vision of generations that have wept and will weep and her participation in their agonies.

At the time of Margaret's death, Abigail envisioned order restored by that death. Her vision of the old matriarch laughing she thought of as "the old tragedy, its violence and its pain, all of it" (279). In her final fetal hysteria Abigail reenacts the tragic dynastic vision of order restored at the cost of violence and pain. Her image of death and birth combined is fulfillment of her opening vision of "the pressure of generations behind [her], pushing [her] along the recurring cycles of birth and death." Ah, Abigail; ah, family.

5

REACHING FOR AFRICA
THE BLACK FAMILY SAGA IN THE SOUTH

In his essay "The South as Field for Fiction," written after the close of Reconstruction, Albion W. Tourgée pondered the phenomenon of black freedmen as a new source of literary interest: "Undoubtedly the richest mine of romantic material that has opened to the English-speaking novelist since the Wizard of the North discovered the common life of Scotland," he thought. The problem was that the black freedman lacked a distinctive individual past. "The white man traces his ancestry back for generations, knows whence they came, where they lived, and guesses what they did. To the American Negro the past is only darkness replete with unimaginable horrors. Ancestors he has none. Until a quarter of a century ago he had no record of his kindred." [1] Since the middle of the twentieth century, writers of black family sagas have worked to prove Tourgée wrong.

Yet even before midcentury, some black families kept alive traditions that told of ancestors held in family memory, if not made subjects of sagas. In his now-classic study *The Negro Family in the United States*, first published in 1939, E. Franklin Frazier recorded previously unpublished stories by informants about their ancestors, as well as accounts of memoirs, autobiographies, and biographies of prominent black Americans, many of them southern. Some reached as far back as their African originals, including, for example, the story of an ancestor's being lured to capture by curiosity about a red flag. Since such a story was also common among published accounts, though, Frazier concluded that family traditions were dying out: "Except in rare instances the few memories and traditions of African

---

1. L. Moody Simms, Jr., "Albion W. Tourgée on the Fictional Use of the Post–Civil War South," *Southern Studies*, XVII (1978), 405–406.

forebears that once stirred the imagination of the older generations have failed to take root in the minds of the present generation of Negro youth. Here and there one finds among the family traditions of college students a story of an African ancestor portrayed in more or less distinct outlines." He concluded more generally that attempts to "resurrect the forgotten memories of their ancestors" from an alien culture were exercises in race pride growing out of the Harlem Renaissance.[2]

Traditions from the period of slavery were more numerous but still largely isolated. Usually they were remembered to explain how ancestors met or how the initiator of the line of descent was conceived or born. Traditions from emancipation and Reconstruction told of families rejoined after separation during slavery or families separated because of Klan activity, of emerging dominant matriarchs who made their men beg for doles, of the family's work and sacrifices to clear the mortgage on the farm still held by the family. As Frazier noted and Nathan Glazer emphasized in his foreword to the reissue of Frazier's book, stability of the black family was severely tested by the three great crises of slavery, of emancipation and Reconstruction, and of removal to northern cities during the great migration, each stripping the family of its former supporting structures.[3]

The context for development of the black family saga was the progression in black writing following sociological, economic, and political trends affecting blacks. The period from 1900 to 1920 was marked by apologetic and propagandist writings reflecting attitudes of blacks toward themselves; in the period 1920 to the late 1930s, the Harlem Renaissance celebrated black primitivism; the late 1930s to the early 1960s protested the pain of living in a racist society; and after the late 1960s it was marked by the beauty of "living black." During these times of change, black writers tended to record typical rather than individual lives reflecting the unique and individual behavior of particular persons. The black search for family roots emerged as the fulfillment of the "largely generalized" search for origins during the Harlem Renaissance.[4] In their search for roots, black family sagas have emphasized correlations between family history and documented public history.

2. E. Franklin Frazier, *The Negro Family in the United States* (Rev. and abr. ed; Chicago, 1966), 13, 15–16.

3. *Ibid.*, 53–54, 57–58, 78, 120–23, 132, 154, viii.

4. J. Lee Greene, "The Pain and the Beauty: The South, the Black Writer and the Convention of the Picaresque, " in *The American South,* ed. Rubin, 286–88; Elizabeth Schultz, "African and African-American Roots in Contemporary Afro-American Literature: The Difficult Search for Family Origins," *Studies in American Fiction,* VIII (1980), 129.

When she came to write *Jubilee* in 1966, Margaret Walker depended largely on generalized history to tell the story of the first generation of her family. Although she assures the reader in her dedication that the novel is the story of her maternal great-grandmother Margaret Duggans Ware Brown, told by her maternal grandmother, the family story is located within typical historical situations and contains little that is distinctive to the family. Even though in the acknowledgment she points to the particularizing evidence of a hundred-year-old "true photograph of my great-grand-mother, who is the Vyry of this story," and to records in the Terrell County Courthouse, Dawson, Georgia, of the real estate transactions of her maternal great-grandfather Randall Ware, so named in the novel, the actions of family characters in the novel are similar to those described in slave narratives and in histories of public events.[5] As a family saga, *Jubilee* is a fictionalization of history from the late 1820s to 1870. History dominates the novel and excludes or obscures many of the other conventions of the novelistic saga.

That history does so is consistent with Walker's purpose in writing *Jubilee*. "I wanted to tell the story that my grandmother had told me, and to set the record straight where Black people are concerned in terms of the Civil War, of slavery, segregation and Reconstruction. I believe that the role of the novelist can be, and largely is for me, the role of a historian. More people will read fiction than will [read] history, and history is slanted just as fiction may seem to be. People will learn about a time and place through a historical novel." But it was history with personal meanings for her. Born the same year, 1915, that her great-grandmother (the Vyry of the novel) died, Walker early sensed a sympathy with the matriarch and began planning her story when she was nineteen but took thirty-two years to bring it to maturity. Over those thirty-two years she learned by experience to deal with "the childbirth problems" and other cares of a mature woman that she had to know from the inside to write about her fictionalized great-grandmother. From both writing and "living through it," she concluded, "I was meant to write *Jubilee*."[6]

If a gap in family continuity loomed between the end of *Jubilee* in 1870 and her assertion in 1966 that the novel was part of a continued family

5. Margaret Walker, *Jubilee* (Boston, 1966), Dedication, Acknowledgment.
6. Charles T. Rowell, "Poetry, History, and Humanism: An Interview with Margaret Walker," *Black World*, XXV (1975), 10; Phyllis R. Klotman, "Oh Freedom: Women and History in Margaret Walker's *Jubilee*," *Black American Literature Forum*, XI (1977), 139, 142–43; Claudia Tate, ed., *Black Women Writers at Work* (New York, 1983), 191–92.

tradition, Walker expected to close the gap in a sequel. For the next part of the saga, she planned to write about Vyry's daughter Minna, Minna's children, and Vyry's death after the family removed to Mississippi. Again, the family would appear within the context of larger history and black institutional life: "The sequel is . . . the story of the black church and the black school. It's about benevolent societies, about jazz and blues. It's about Alabama, Mississippi and Florida." [7]

Because she chose the role of social historian in her novel, Walker had to adopt the point of view of the omniscient narrator to provide the historical context of the family. Although the focus is on Vyry, the narrative consciousness commonly shifts to other persons as well and gives history from their points of view. The viewpoint is still within the family, though, when Sully tells Vyry how Shady Oaks plantation in the southwest corner of Georgia came into family hands because the present owner's grandfather fought in Virginia during the Revolutionary War, received the land in Georgia for his war service, and passed it on to his heirs (43).

The family's link with public history, then, comes through two kinds of historical information: what is known to the white gentry during the three decades before the Civil War and the early years of Reconstruction and what is known of historical movements from the slave and freedman perspective. The first kind includes the talk of political guests at Shady Oaks about the Missouri Compromise and resolutions on states' rights by Robert Toombs and Alexander Stephens (79), the countywide concern in 1851 over possible slave insurrections (81), John Dutton's participation in the Confederate Convention of February, 1861 (180), jubilation among the gentry over Robert E. Lee's decision to support the South (201), and Salina Dutton's decision to invest in Confederate bonds (257). Conceivably, slaves on the plantation know of such events by overhearing talk, but the historical accounting is given from the author's point of view. Other kinds of historical developments beyond the plantation filter through the slave and freedman families because they may affect life in the black quarter. News on stricter application of the Black Code translates to no instruction in reading and writing for slaves, and news of the organization of abolitionist societies means somebody in the outside world is encouraging slaves to escape (49). Rumors of slave insurrections in Virginia and South Carolina mean closer watches by overseers and patrollers (79); news of General William Tecumseh Sherman's capture of Atlanta and his march through

7. Claudia Tate, ed., *Black Women Writers,* 200.

the countryside to Savannah offers a nearer hope for deliverance and protection (263–67). After the war, rumors of white resistance to tax-supported
education for freedmen and poor whites mean diminished chances of es-
caping the new bondage of tenant farming, as does the more general recognition that the South is being reclaimed by Redemptionists (420–22, 473).

Among the kinds of knowledge and of action that slaves and freedmen think of as local to themselves but that are in fact typical of slave narratives from across the South are Brother Zeke's roles as preacher and tutor on the plantation and as secret agent for slave escapes (56), Randall
Ware's link with the Underground Railroad (91, 96), John Dutton's ad-
vertisement in newspapers of a reward for the return of runaway Lucy,
identified by the R branded on her forehead (127–28), slaves' tension when
the slave trader visits the plantation and when they are being stripped and
auctioned in the barn (156, 162), and Vyry's lack of feeling at the death of
her white father and her recognition that his promise to free her in his
will was not kept (196, 200). Occasionally, though, historical reconstruc-
tions, and perhaps family memory, become anachronistic. When Vyry and
Innis Brown see the Klan burn a cross on the hill beside their burning house
in 1870 (377), they see a practice that did not begin until the Klan's revival
in the twentieth century. Early Klan intimidators did, however, leave warning signs such as gallows and miniature coffins at the gates of their victims.[8]
The saga incident shows how family stories impose later images on early
events.

History and typical action are further domesticated in this saga by the
use of black folklore. Each chapter has its epigraph to serve as a comment on the action of the chapter, and most are excerpts from black songs
and sayings. In the opening chapter, for example, the death of Vyry's mother
in exhausted childbirth is foreshadowed by "Swing Low, Sweet Chariot,"
and the chapter ends with singers in the quarters chanting, "Death come
knocking at my door." In Chapter 8 Randall Ware's beginning courtship
of Vyry is signaled by the ditty "Gwine to Have That Yeller Gal." In chapters concerned with the white Dutton family, however, epigraphs echo the
white world. Chapter 23, detailing the Duttons' early enthusiasm for the

8. The Klan got the idea of cross burning from Thomas Dixon's novel *The Clansman*
(1905), and Dixon got it from an old practice in the Scottish highlands for calling clans together. Inspired by *The Birth of a Nation*, the film version of the novel, William J. Sim-
mons of Atlanta revived the old Scottish practice by burning a cross during Thanksgiving
weekend of 1915 on Stone Mountain outside Atlanta. Allen W. Trelease, *White Terror: The
Ku Klux Klan Conspiracy and Southern Reconstruction* (New York, 1971), 55–56, 421–22.

Civil War, carries the tag "Hurrah for the Bonnie Blue Flag," and Chapter 25, the account of Johnny Dutton's fatal wounding at Chickamauga, sets the tone with lines from the sentimental ballad "Just Before the Battle, Mother." As the war turns against the South, epigraphs for the white family become gloomier and those for the blacks more jubilant, though they become increasingly ironic when Chapter 36, marked by "Hurrah, Hurrah, We Bring the Jubilee," tells not only of the Union army's arrival but also of its plunder of the plantation for black and white alike. In such cases, historical event serves as background for folk experience, and folklore assumes greater validity than does public history. Walker herself noted that she wrote *Jubilee* as "a folk novel based on folk material" to increase its realism.[9]

Because the story of Vyry is told by a matriarch to a matriarch, it is not surprising that *Jubilee* is the story of the rise of matriarchal power in the first generation. It is also consistent with trends in public history and in history of the black family that authority of black men during slavery was commonly supplanted by authority of the master, or plantation matriarch in the case of house servants, and that during Reconstruction women and children often had to survive in the absence of family men who were away to work on railroads and in lumber camps. In the black world, Sally initiates Vyry into the matriarchal code at the time of her first menstruation, instructing her that women are strong and men are weak and "nothing but trouble" and that such knowledge is part of their African heritage: "My Maw say that us colored folks knows what we know now fore us come here from Affriky and that wisdom be your business with your womanhood" (54). That wisdom becomes evident to Vyry through the institution of the black granny as midwife when Caline and May Liza act as grannies for Vyry when her first child is born. That wisdom finally becomes the basis for Vyry's family's protection in Butler County, Alabama, when she agrees to act as granny to white women (149, 434). This turn of events, more than most, has the ring of actual family history, though the attendance of black grannies at births in white families is one of the givens of southern family history. Like other matriarchs in the transition between slavery and Reconstruction, she also faces the task of choosing between husbands, not they choosing her, when she has to decide between Randall Ware, the husband separated from her by slave codes, and Innis Brown, her husband of freedom.

9. Klotman, "Oh Freedom," 144; Margaret Walker, *How I Wrote Jubilee,* quoted *ibid.,* 139.

That her dilemma is not unusual is indicated by Frazier in his account of the disruption attending emancipation.[10] Just as many other black matriarchs did, Vyry chooses the husband of freedom because he is the father of her youngest children (465, 471). That is to say, she follows the code taught her in her youth.

The saga convention of moments of vision occurs thus within contexts of history and matriarchy and, interestingly, comes through the fathers of Vyry's children. When his son is born in slavery, Randall Ware has the conventional vision from slave narratives that his son will one day be free (150). Innis' vision comes when he sees how Vyry embodies all the strength and decency, the power of spirit and forgiveness, despite her scarred back, of the family matriarch: "She was only a living sign and mark of all the best that any human being could hope to become. . . . Peasant and slave, unlettered and untutored, she was nevertheless the best true example of the motherhood of her race" (485–86). If the insight is Innis', the language and the moment are Walker's as she sums up the generation of her great-grandmother. Although the novel is rounded out for Vyry of the first generation, the saga is just beginning for her descendants. In effect, the saga loops back to the dedication and acknowledgment to tell what eventually happens in subsequent generations.

Any consideration of Alex Haley's *Roots,* published in 1976, as a family saga has to reckon with its vast popularity and its existence as an icon of black self-awareness since the mid-1970s. However, that popularity came about more from its dramatization as an eight-part series on ABC-TV, shown from January 23 to 31, 1977, than from its existence as a literary family saga. If television data can be believed, 85 million to 135 million watched the dramatization of *Roots.* The popularity of the television series had the effect of prompting sales, and presumably reading, of *Roots* as a book, so that the initial printing of 200,000 hardback copies was soon sold out, and the hardback edition together with the Dell paperback edition sold well over 1,000,000 copies within the first year of publication.[11]

As a literary family saga, *Roots* is significant because it introduces the

10. Frazier, *Negro Family,* 33–49, 102–13, 80.

11. In Haley's view the paperback sales were too popular. He sued Doubleday for premature paperback publication of *Roots* on the grounds that paperback sales by Dell, a subsidiary of Doubleday, deprived him of higher royalties from hardback sales. M. Reuter, "Why Alex Haley Is Suing Doubleday: An Outline of the Complaint," *Publisher's Weekly,* April 14, 1977, p. 25; M. Reuter, "Doubleday Answers Haley: Denies All Charges," *Publisher's Weekly,* September 6, 1977, pp. 34–35.

new dimension of "faction" into the genre. Haley described his new concept in this way: "All the incidents are true, the details are as accurate as very heavy research can make them, the names and dates are real, but obviously when it comes to dialogue, and people's emotions and thoughts, I had to make things up. It's heightened history, or fiction based on real people's lives." What that meant, he said near the end of *Roots,* was that specifics about his family had to be filled out with deductions based on general knowledge: "Since I wasn't yet around when most of the story occurred, by far most of the dialogue and most of the incidents are of necessity a novelized amalgam of what I *know* took place together with what my researching led me to plausibly *feel* took place." As he wrote later of his research, "my idea was to siphon into each notebook, representing each successive year, whatever the boy Kunta *plausibly* could have experienced through any one or any combination of the human senses." [12] In making his new form of saga, Haley ran into the paradox that the further he went back to the sources of his particular family, the more he had to depend on general knowledge of the social and historical context of the family; the closer he came to the present generation, the less history he invoked.

That Haley depended perhaps too heavily on history and historical reconstruction can be seen in the suits brought against him charging plagiarism. Harold Courlander, folklorist and novelist, charged that Haley had drawn significantly on certain thoughts, scenes, dialogue, concepts, and imagery from Courlander's novel *The African,* published in 1967, the story of a young man captured in Dahomey and sold as a slave in Georgia in 1802. The suit was settled amicably out of court before the case reached the summation stage, with Haley acknowledging debt to Courlander's book, though his publisher refused to sign the agreement on grounds that Haley's use of Courlander's material was not substantial enough to be subject to copyright law. The other suit, dealing with Haley's depiction of slave conditions on the Waller and Lea plantations, was brought by Margaret Walker, charging that *Roots* "was largely copied" from *Jubilee.* Although the charge did not stipulate particular copyings, she offered both books in evidence. The suit was dismissed with the judge's ruling that the similarities were insignificant. [13] Despite his twelve years of researching *Roots,* Haley claimed he had not read *Jubilee.*

12. J. F. Baker, "*PW* Interviews: Alex Haley," *Publisher's Weekly,* September 6, 1976, pp. 9, 12; Alex Haley, *Roots* (New York, 1976), 584; Alex Haley, "Foreword," in *From Freedom to Freedom: African Roots in American Soil,* ed. Mildred Bain and Ervin Lewis (New York, 1977), xv.

13. M. Reuter, "Two Writers Question the Originality of 'Roots,'" *Publisher's Weekly,*

The important point for saga writing is that in a family chronicle of seven generations, despite the contributions of family stories, the convention of keeping parallels with public history plays a large part. Haley stresses that point in the closing pages of *Roots* as he tells of his travels and researches to track down clues about the family's African ancestor. He stresses it even more when he recounts in his "Foreword" to *From Freedom to Freedom* how he spent two years of research to establish the family lineage through seven generations, two years researching eighteenth- and nineteenth-century African culture, and additional time in London reading accounts of African travelers and assembled enough materials for four or five books on African culture. In *Roots* and on other occasions, he also reported his psychological research of spending nights in the hold of a ship making the transatlantic run from Africa to the United States in order to get the feel of Kunta Kinte's passage in the slave ship, later identified as *Lord Ligonier*. That historical research played a large part in Haley's thinking about *Roots* can be seen in his plan, announced soon after publication of the saga, to recount "My Search for 'Roots,'" described as a "strictly nonfictional account of the details of his long odyssey, a huge expansion of the material only sketched in the closing pages of 'Roots.'" Long postponed and no doubt impeded by suits and charges of plagiarism, "My Search for 'Roots'" nevertheless was intended to authenticate the reading of personal and public history implicit in Haley's faction. Although he cites family stories in *Roots* as the stimulus for his initial search, he apparently did not rely on them for authentication of his story. As he said near the time *Roots* was published, he began his search in hope of finding specific facts about "the African" in his ancestry, but if that search was unsuccessful, he was "prepared to make the book a black American family saga," that is, a typical story.[14]

Why Haley was prepared to write a black American family saga can be partly seen in his previous association with Malcolm X and his ghost writing *The Autobiography of Malcolm X*. In Chapter 118 of *Roots,* just before he begins his account of the long search for Kunta Kinte and his descendants, Haley mentions spending two years interviewing Malcolm X

May 2, 1977, p. 20; M. Reuter, "Haley Settles Plagiarism Suit, Concedes Passages," *Publisher's Weekly,* December 25, 1978, p. 22; Herb Boyd, "Plagiarism and the *Roots* Suit," *First World,* II (1979), 31, 33; Reuter, "Two Writers Question," 20.

14. Haley, "Foreword," xiv–xv; "A Symposium on *Roots*," *Black Scholar,* VIII (1977), 40; Baker, "*PW* Interviews," 12, 8.

and writing the account of his life. Although in *Roots* he establishes no other than a chronological link between the two projects, Haley describes in his "Epilogue" to the *Autobiography of Malcolm X* the process not only of his research-interviewing to write the autobiography but also of his growing involvement in Malcolm X's search for his own and other blacks' place in American life and of the black leader's change from radical Black Muslim separatist to seeker for American black and African connections. Malcolm X wanted, Haley remembered, "to make the Africans feel their *kinship* with us Afro-Americans" (Haley's emphasis) and to make them realize "we all came from the same foreparents."[15] Haley remembered that when he and Malcolm X first signed their contract to work on the autobiography, Malcolm X told him he wanted a writer, not an interpreter. Haley admitted at the end of his "Epilogue," though, how much the black leader influenced him: "I tried to be a dispassionate chronicler. But he was the most electric personality I have ever met, and I still can't quite conceive him dead. It still feels to me as if he has just gone into some next chapter, to be written by his historians."[16] Shortly after writing that, Haley began his twelve-year search for *Roots*.

In writing his family saga as faction, Haley necessarily stresses some conventions of the genre and obscures or minimizes others to fit the demands of his new form. Among those emphasized, continuity of the family through seven generations is reminiscent of the African griot's biblical style of narration, as he notes in *Roots*: "Something like: '—and so-and-so took as wife so-and-so, and begat . . . and begat . . . and begat.' . . . He would next name each begat's eventual spouse, or spouses, and their averagely numerous offspring, and so on" (718). *Roots* is curiously disproportioned, though. More than half the book, 83 of 120 chapters, is concerned with "the African" Kunta Kinte, who then drops from the narrative except as a memory. Kizzy of the second generation enters the narrative in Chapter 69 and overlaps the chapters with her father and son George until she is separated from the younger generations in Chapter 104, but she has only three from her perspective in the family succession, Chapters 84 through 86. Chicken George, third-generation member, dominates Chapters 87 to 103 with his gamecock fighting and his adjusting to the world of slavery in a way his grandfather was never able to do, until he disappears

15. Alex Haley, "Epilogue," in *The Autobiography of Malcolm X* (New York, 1973), 419.
16. Haley, "Epilogue," 456. See also David A. Gerber, "Haley's *Roots* and Our Own: An Inquiry into the Nature of a Popular Phenomenon," *Journal of Ethnic Studies,* V (1977), 87–88, 101.

from family importance during his absence in England for almost five years. The closer the family gets to freedom, the less is told about each generation. George's son Tom assumes headship of the family in Chapter 103, guides the family through removal from Caswell County to Alamance County in North Carolina and through emancipation and the family's removal to Henning in west Tennessee in Chapter 113 and to the marriage of his daughter Cynthia in Chapter 116. In barely a chapter and a half the next generations are begotten, married, and moved into the first third of the twentieth century, and history is reduced to genealogy.[17]

A consequence of the disproportion in presenting generations is that Haley suggests the pattern of decline in significance of the generations. Paradoxically, as the generations gain freedom and status in the world, they lose distinction in the narrative. As they come closer to success, with an artistically resourceful blacksmith, a prosperous lumber company operator, a college professor, a government official, and a famous author in the succession, they become less memorable than the mutilated slave and the picaresque gamekeeper. No one says that author Haley or blacksmith Tom is a lesser descendant of "the African," but it is the noble and humiliated first generation whose memory is celebrated.

The disproportion also shifts emphasis to the convention of historical context in the family chronicle, with the attendant problems of the nature of time and chronology in family memory. During Kunta Kinte's early life in Juffure, time is non-calendrical. Life in Juffure is measured by the cycle of seasons, of droughts, harvests, and feasts, and, in the case of Kunta Kinte, by his progress through stages of his manhood training. As Haley found in his research, the perspective is that of an anthropologist's notation of rituals, not a historian's linear chronicle. The effect of the descriptions of Kunta Kinte's progress to manhood is to make his early life the common experience of his village.[18] Once he is captured, though, he falls into time and becomes subject to the iron will of history. The historical context serves to measure the family's progress, at least during the first three generations, through American history. The remarkable knowledge of public events brought to the awareness of slaves on remote rural plantations occasionally tends to inject a false note in their family chronicle. Haley accounts for that knowledge through conversations overheard

17. Gerber, "Haley's *Roots*," 90.
18. Merrill Maguire Skaggs, "*Roots*: A New Black Myth," *Southern Quarterly*, XVII (1978), 45.

by house servants and through news brought by Kunta Kinte after his travels as coachman with Dr. Waller. Haley also invokes the elaborate underground communications network practiced by slaves and hidden from masters.

Even though the bones of Haley's historical research show through at times, most of the history the slaves discuss has at least tangential bearing on their hopes for freedom and their despairs about new restrictions. Their talk about the Thomas Jefferson-Aaron Burr conflict for the presidency, for example, leads to further talk about the Jefferson-Sally Hemmings scandal and Jefferson's plans for emancipating slaves and returning them to Africa. In any case, talk about public history, ranging from heavy British taxes before the Revolution to news of the surrender at Appomattox Court House, shows the steady induction of Kunta Kinte's family into black American ways of thinking and feeling and away from the African-centered memories of Kunta Kinte.

When he invoked historical context, Haley also opened himself to the discipline of history and the corrections of historians less concerned than he with family tradition. He has been cited for such inaccuracies as having Kunta Kinte captured by white men in the bush when records show that white slavers, too obvious and too clumsy in the bush, depended on the stealth of slatees, African hirelings of the whites, to kidnap slaves or depended on other blacks to capture and trade chattel after tribal wars; for having the Wallers grow the wrong kinds of crops in Virginia; and for depicting Mandinka village life as more idyllic than records show. His depiction of Juffure as a tranquil, isolated, and tradition-bound village has been especially challenged by historians of British colonies in West Africa. According to their records, Juffure was for two centuries a major transshipment point for goods and slaves from the interior and existed as a white trading post surrounded by white colonists. Also problematic was the reliability of the griot on whom Haley depended. As Mark Ottaway, British journalist, wrote in his attack "Tangled Roots" in the London *Sunday Times*, on April 10, 1977, the griot Kebba Kanga Fofana in Juffure, knowing what Haley wanted, apparently mixed fact and invention in his recitation. He was also not the official griot but a substitute for the real one, who was playing in the band to greet Haley. Still, Fofana was able to recite the complete Kinte family genealogy and to put Kunta Kinte in the correct context. Another problem was the discrepancy in accounts of Kunta Kinte given by Fofana in 1966 and afterward. In one telling, Kunta Kinte was held at James Island for seven years before being shipped to America. For dramatic purposes, Haley chose to ignore that possibility and had him put immediately on a slave ship to emphasize the contrast between his freshly remembered life in Juffure and the horror of life in the hold of a slaver.[19] In that instance Haley chose art over history to make his family legend.

Whether or not Fofana was a reliable narrator, Haley uses the griot as the model narrator in his family saga. Although in the concluding chapters of *Roots* he presents himself as the narrator-historian tracing back the family past, throughout the saga he presents griot figures as the sources from whom family lore is drawn. In his acknowledgment he recognizes that "the memories and the mouths of ancient elders [were] the only way that early histories of mankind got passed along . . . for all of us today to know who we are." During Kunta Kinte's manhood training, the griot, who is himself an example of continuity as only sons of griots may become griots, teaches Kunta's Kafo group about their tribal history and the great African empires (116–17). In Virginia, Kunta listens to Fiddler report his news and thinks of him as a griot figure (219). Later Haley himself hears his grandmother Cynthia and the older women talk on the porch during summer evenings and learns from them as Kunta Kinte had learned from the patriarchal griots. Part of their talk is apocryphal and part is mysterious. In the family apocrypha Kunta Kinte's mutilated foot is explained by his having had to make the choice between castration and loss of his foot. And though they do not know their significance, the grandmothers pass on the mysterious African words in Kunta Kinte's legacy (568). After the family stories came the linguistic and historical research. In effect, Haley presents himself as the successor to the griots, his recitation written, if not oral, historical, if not traditional.[20]

Within the narrative, each generation has its griots. In depicting the way each new child is told the story of their African ancestor, Haley makes the type scene in family history also the mark of their special attribute. For what distinguishes the family from others is that, despite the twists and turns of history, they know they have a direct link with their ancestral past. Although they may not know the significance of the African names, they have them in their tradition, and they know of a particular person as their ancestor. Unlike other slaves on the Lea and Murray farms, who have

19. *Ibid.*, 43; Gerber, "Haley's *Roots*," 98–99, 96–98.
20. Helen Chavis Othow, "*Roots* and the Heroic Search for Identity," *CLA Journal*, XXVI (1983), 314.

ancestral instincts but not ancestral memories, the family has its past concentrated in a story that can be remembered and told and remembered. Noticeably, though, the tradition changes as Kunta Kinte becomes an ancestral memory. In the old way, Omoro takes young Kunta out under the night sky and presents him to the stars and moon as Kunta does Kizzy when she is born (3, 290). After Kunta drops from the narrative as an active presence, however, presentation of the newborn to the moon and stars ceases, and instead Kizzy tells her new baby George the story of Kunta Kinte (377), and George tells each of his children the story but does not preserve the ritual (431, 437, 438, 444). When the younger Lea slaves are sold into Alamance County and Kizzy is left behind in Caswell County with the older slaves, she calls on the family to keep the story alive in later generations (495). George tells Vergil's son Uriah about the family lineage, and when he leaves North Carolina in order to stay free, George tells his son Tom to keep the story going. So the story continues as each generation tells the next. It is no wonder later that Will Palmer, successful lumberman, feels excluded as an in-law when he contemplates the family cult of memory he has married into, that because of "Cynthia's devotion to her ancestral memory," he is "considered as having married into Cynthia's family rather than the other way around" (561). As in other family stories, this family has its silent agenda of taking into the group those who agree with the family's image of itself.

Will Palmer's predicament suggests further the generations-long conflict of patriarchal and matriarchal influences in the life of Kunta Kinte's descendants. Unlike Walker's account of matriarchal endurance, *Roots* is a celebration of patriarchal authority in this black family. In *Roots* Haley's purpose was to revise the black male image from that of men who had defaulted in family influence to that of black male hero who dominates family memory and sets family values. Although the line of descent runs almost as often through daughters as through sons, the women as much as the men are careful to preserve the heritage of the patriarch. Kunta's heritage includes the corrective attributes that American slaves presumably lacked, "a nurturing father, a cultural tradition, a proud family heritage, an honored social rank, a complex idea of social structure, a thorough education, and an exceptional personal pride." [21]

However, the legendary black patriarch comes at a cost to the verities of black family history and suggests that if the heritage is true, it is

21. Skaggs, "New Black Myth," 44–47.

hardly typical. Haley's family image is more a goal than an actuality, and in this chronicle of generations the women are more passive and self-effacing than other records show. The shift reflects a perpetuated vision of Africa where Moslem patriarchy holds authority. In celebrating the heroic winners, Haley shows strong women like Tom's wife Irene acting resourcefully for a moment, then lapsing into submissive forgetability.[22]

Among other family saga conventions in this work of faction, the convention of moments of vision comes more from the imaginative than from the historical side of the saga. As he was able to identify himself with his ancestors, Haley could, with his perspective of the seven generations, imagine moments when ancestors paused in their labors to see the past and the future running in a design of destiny. During the vigil time of his manhood training, Kunta Kinte sees himself, his family, his village, and his tribe all living together with the past and the future, "the dead with the living and those yet to be born," all living "with Allah" (89). After emancipation and the family's removal to Tennessee, at the picnic celebrating the opening of New Hope Church, Matilda remembers Kizzy and wishes she could see how far the family has come, and George assures her, "She lookin', baby. She *sho* is!" (555). As he begins his search, Haley is assured by Cousin Georgia Anderson that the ancestors are up there watching him (571). In his own right as both family member and narrator-historian, Haley realizes the agony as well as triumph when he returns to Juffure and envisions the collective millions of ancestors enslaved like his ancestor, marched in coffles, beaten, stripped, branded, and shipped in packed holds. "My mind reeled with it all" (580). But on his flight home he senses the pattern of fate at work in leading him to write his account of Kunta Kinte and descendants and to make it "a symbolic saga of all African-descent people."

Ernest J. Gaines's *The Autobiography of Miss Jane Pittman,* published in 1971, is a family saga in the form of a fictional autobiography. So convincing was it as an "autobiography" that many readers thought the novel an edited transcription of a real person's memoir, and the editor at *Newsweek* was shocked to learn, when he asked Gaines for a picture of Jane Pittman, that she was a fictional person.[23] The further paradox is that it is a family saga without a family in the sense of blood kin and generations of descendants. Instead, because of her 110-year span of life, Jane Pittman func-

22. Gerber, "Haley's *Roots,*" 94; Skaggs, "New Black Myth," 50.
23. Ernest J. Gaines, "Miss Jane and I," *Callaloo,* I (1978), 23.

tions both as ancestor and chronicler of the generations of her men, for Ned Douglass, Joe Pittman, Tee Bob Samson, and Jimmy Aaron make her chronicle a story of men told by the brooding childless matriarch. Her story is the saga of three black men and a dissident white man struggling to realize their full manhood against the confining force of Louisiana history. Their struggles define the reach for freedom she began at age 10.

The Autobiography of Miss Jane Pittman developed as a consequence of Gaines's earlier story "Just Like a Tree," first published in *Sewanee Review* and collected in *Bloodline* in 1968. The story of an old black woman, Aunt Fe, who has to leave her home in rural Louisiana during the civil rights demonstrations and move to the North because of bombings near her house, "Just Like a Tree" is an inferential summary of her life and influence, told from the points of view of those who come to tell her goodbye. As he worked with the multiple points of view, Gaines realized, "You don't know her life—where she comes from, her children, her husband—her life in general, before that day." Recognizing that to develop the long background of his heroine he would have to make her 100 or more years old, he began the story of Jane Pittman, again from the multiple points of view of her neighbors telling her story on the day of her burial. Finding that method of narration too diffuse and digressive, however, he settled on the single autobiographical voice and let Jane tell her own story.[24]

The story has autobiographical dimensions for Gaines as well. As several commentators have surmised and Gaines has acknowledged, Jane Pittman was inspired by, if not modeled on, his Aunt Augustine, the crippled matriarch in Louisiana who raised him until the age of 14 after his mother left to join her second husband in California. In his early drafts on Jane Pittman he saw her as "a lady who had never walked in her life." He also saw himself in Jimmy Aaron and remembered he knew at least two years before he started writing the novel the direction it would take. "Maybe I had known it all my life, because it seems that I started writing it many, many years before when I used to sit on the porch or the steps and write letters for the old people." The undercurrent of resentment against restrictions in the saga was Gaines's, too. He recalled how in New Roads, Louisiana, his "little Bayonne," he could not eat or drink or go to the bathroom in certain places and had to ride in the back of the bus. Like Haley

---

24. Gaines, "Miss Jane and I," 34, 36–37; Marcia Gaudet and Carl Wooten, "An Interview with Ernest J. Gaines," *New Orleans Review,* XIV (1987), 69; Marcia Gaudet and Carl Wooten, eds., *Porch Talk with Ernest Gaines: Conversations on the Writer's Craft* (Baton Rouge, 1990), 106.

in *Roots,* Gaines recognized that his saga was the product of family stories and porch talk presided over by his Aunt Augustine: "I did not know then that twenty or twenty-five years later I would try to put some of their talk [in *Autobiography of Miss Jane*]." [25]

For Miss Jane to tell her story of a century, Gaines also had to solve the problem of putting into form the scattered recollections of a centenarian who does not recall everything in chronological order. His solution came in the device of the history teacher, the technical narrator-historian, who records her stories and those of people in the quarter and edits them into a saga. The introduction presenting the history teacher, he said, was the first thing he wrote: "I could not see how a person who is a-hundred-and-ten years old could actually tell her story. . . . I've seen this kind of story-telling many times before. One person may be the main narrator but there were these other people around to help her along if she could not remember or if she got tired of talking." In effect, Gaines implies use of the African and African-American oral tradition of storytelling within his European-American written tradition. In the written tradition the teller, the story, and the audience are separate from each other. The oral tradition involves participation and responses by the hearers as the tale is told. With the teller and the tale inseparable, "the teller can be held accountable for knowledge about the ordering of events he relates, and the audience functions to insist upon that knowledge and ordering." [26]

This style of teller-response narration, however, results in shifts of focus in Jane's story. The chronicle begins as Jane's personal narrative, told as a kind of family story, but shortly before halfway through, as the scope of history expands, she ceases to be the principal actor and tells a larger story that she is present to observe and that is the story of her generations. Beyond her own story, Jane's is a folk account of the history of her time and place. As the historian-narrator of the introduction notes, her story is not in his official books of history. What is wrong with those books is that "Miss Jane is not in them." [27]

25. Gaines, "Miss Jane and I," 24; Jeanie Blake, "Interview with Ernest Gaines," *Xavier Review,* III (1983), 1; Gaines, "Miss Jane and I," 35–36, 25, 24–25.

26. Trudier Harris, " 'I Wish I Was a Poet': The Character of the Artist in Alice Childress's *Like One of the Family,*" *Black American Literature Forum,* XIV (1980), 24; John O'Brien, ed., *Interviews with Black Writers* (New York, 1973), 92–93.

27. Jerry H. Bryant, "Ernest J. Gaines: Change, Growth, and History," *Southern Review,* n.s. X (1974), 863; Greene, "The Pain and the Beauty," in *The American South,* ed. Rubin, 268–78; Ernest J. Gaines, *The Autobiography of Miss Jane Pittman* (New York, 1971), vi.

Although Gaines denies that Jane's story is "a capsule history of black people of the rural South during the last hundred years" and insists that "Miss Jane is Miss Jane," the context of his denial suggests she is typical and recognizable: "You have seen Miss Jane, too. She is that old lady who lives up the block . . . and thinks about the dead. . . . If you go to the history books, you will find that most of them would not agree with what she had told you. . . . Truth to me is what people like Miss Jane remember." Hers is rather an alternate version of the past that reflects the double consciousness of black Americans described by W. E. B. DuBois. In *The Souls of Black Folk*, written in 1903, DuBois saw the American Negro as "a sort of seventh son born with a veil, and gifted with a second sight, in this American world—a world which yields him no true self-consciousness but only lets him see himself through the revelation of the outer world." As a result, "one ever feels the twoness—an American, a Negro, two souls, two thoughts, two unreconciled strivings; two warring ideals in one dark body, whose dogged strength alone keeps it from being torn asunder." [28]

Gaines modifies DuBois' general view, however, by his insistence on the importance of place as a dimension of the past. He emphasizes the power of "this Louisiana thing that drives me" as the stimulus to his imagination. To him, even the examples of DuBois, Frederick Douglass and Booker T. Washington were too special to tell "the true story of blacks in this country . . . the story of the average black who has lived to that age [of Jane Pittman]." In his view even the narrator-historian of the introduction was naïve in believing that the great black leaders told the story of people like Jane Pittman. [29]

Like Margaret Walker and Alex Haley, Gaines resorted to the convention of public history to tell the saga of Jane Pittman's generations, but it was history from a special perspective, seen from the underside. Like Haley, he did his historical research, but it was research into the past as rural blacks of Louisiana, from 1860 to 1965, would know it. He got suggestions from black historians such as Alvin Aubert at Southern University on the ten or twelve significant things known to blacks in Louisiana since the mid-

28. Gaudet and Wooten, "Interview with Gaines," 37; W. E. B. DuBois, *The Souls of Black Folk* (1903; rpr. New York, 1969), 3; Jack Hicks, *In the Singer's Temple* (Chapel Hill, 1981), 83–84.

29. Charles T. Rowell, "'This Louisiana Thing That Drives Me': An Interview with Ernest Gaines," *Callaloo*, I (1978), 40; Gaines, "Miss Jane and I," 28; O'Brien, ed., *Interviews with Black Writers*, 93.

nineteenth century: the Civil War, Reconstruction, the floods of 1912 and 1927, the construction of spillways to control floods, Huey Long, the civil rights movement, and athletes like Jack Johnson, Joe Louis, and Jackie Robinson. He asked other people, such as drinkers in bars, and listened to their opinions of Huey Long, read books and newspapers of the times, and, like Ernest Hemingway, learned how the weather was when events took place. Having learned his past, Gaines then had to convert it into the language and perspective of his "illiterate black woman a hundred years old talking about these things." He had to have her say what he wanted her to say but to say it in her own way.[30] How one should look at such history Mary Hodges indicates in the book's introduction: "[You] take what she say [sic] and be satisfied. . . . You don't tie up all the loose ends all the time" (vii).

In the stages of the saga, shown in the four parts of *Autobiography of Miss Jane*, Jane shows the particular double consciousness of the Louisiana black version of history.[31] For whites, "The War Years" means defeat of the Confederacy, disillusionment of southern soldiers willing now to let Yankees have the blacks despite their own, however wobbly, scriptural justifications for slavery, and the plantation mistress' lament for "the sweet precious blood of the South"; from the northern soldiers' view, they mean freeing Ticey from whippings and giving her the nonslave name of Jane Brown (6–8). For Jane, the war years mean her freedom to head north but also to be killed, the massacre by patrollers, the Freedom Bureau house run according to a northern white ethic, the old man's Faulkneresque calculations on how long it will take Jane and Ned to reach Ohio, and finally her recognition that the South, not Ohio, is her home as she xes her labor contract with Bone. For whites, "Reconstruction" runs from 1867 to 1877. In Jane's version, it lasts until early in the twentieth century and is a time of losses and reduced expectations: of schools offered and closed down, of Ned's flight to Kansas and intimidations by the night riders, of Joe Pittman's break with tenant farming, of Ned's call for black unity, of dreams of the devil horse that will kill Joe Pittman, and of invoking the Chariot of Hell to haunt Albert Cluveau for killing Ned. Despite the losses, though, Reconstruction means that people like Joe Pittman and Ned Douglass are made into real men, not former slaves.

30. Gaines, "Miss Jane and I," 35–36; Rowell, "This Louisiana Thing," 47; Gaudet and Wooten, "Interview with Gaines," 238–39.

31. Bryant, "Change, Growth, and History," 860–61; Hicks, *In the Singer's Temple*, 84.

The sense of double consciousness continues in the saga's last two sections. For whites, the years of "The Plantation" section mean the transitional period when the South opens to new economic forces such as industrialization and the chamber-of-commerce mentality while still holding to the dream of plantation gentility. To Jane and her co-informants, it is a period of repression and despair as segregation, building since the 1880s, settles in. It is a time so bad for Jane that she turns to other-worldly hopes and finds religion or talks to trees and has a kind of double secret life of the spirit. For whites in the South, the time of "The Quarter," from 1940 to 1962, is a period of war and a time when the cycle of rural poverty finally breaks as young people leave the farm for the cities and government jobs and work in manufacturing plants and mills. For blacks, it is a time of growing unity and blacks' progress in the outer world, when the army is integrated, when Joe Louis and Jackie Robinson become everybody's heroes, when black schoolchildren in Little Rock and Montgomery show their courage, and when people of the quarter learn they are not immune from demonstrations in the cities. It is a time when they learn that Jimmy Aaron, as The One long looked for, will lead from the streets rather than from the pulpit.

As Jane's dreams and talks with trees suggest, a further dimension of her alternate version of history is her reliance on black folklore. Although premonitory dreams may not be the stuff of official history, they are part of Jane's saga through the years. Drawing on the residual African element in her heritage, she has a kind of extrasensory knowledge common to folklore rather than to history.[32] Her knowledge becomes folk history when she dreams and thus knows of the coming fatal horse for Joe Pittman, foresees in her dreams Ned lynched by the Cajuns, by a wind of intuition knows that Ned has been killed even before the news comes, and senses death in the air the morning Jimmy Aaron is shot. As the fictive editor realizes, none of these hidden events will be in the history books.

For all their losses, though, Jane and her generations of men show a pattern and design in the past and demonstrate the saga convention of the special family attribute. Apparently, Gaines recognized this design when he noted that in the early stages of writing his book he kept going further into the past trying to find "some kind of meaning to our present lives." The pattern he found in Jane's "family" history is a running conflict through the generations between the forces to hold and preserve and the

32. Hicks, *In the Singer's Temple*, 84.

forces of change. Although she is slow to realize it, Jane is a force for change when in her encounters she reasserts, "We ain't going back." During the course of her long life, Jane changes from a vision of individual freedom to one of freedom through the unity of her people, gained through the loss of her four men. The apparent failures of Ned Douglass, Joe Pittman, Tee Bob Samson, and Jimmy Aaron become foundations on which others can build. "Someone else must pick up from there and go on," Gaines realized.[33]

The type scenes in *Autobiography of Miss Jane* thus dramatically measure progress in the family attribute of "going on." Central to that progress are scenes showing changes in relationships between white plantation owners and black workers—scenes that occur five times. First, at the time of emancipation the plantation master assembles the slaves to tell them they are free to go or stay and offers them work on shares (10–11). The second occurs when Bone calls together his workers and tells them the plantation has been lost to the "Secesh" and the Yankee army is leaving (69). At the third, soon after, Colonel Dye assembles all hands to announce the new order: no more black soldiers or politicians, no school, wages the same but drawable only through the plantation store (70). The fourth comes when Robert Samson calls together all hands and again tells them the rules: rent-free living on the place but banishment if they or their families are involved in demonstrations (218). The climactic fifth comes when Samson meets the plantation people at the bus stop, tells them Jimmy Aaron has been shot, and tells them to "go back home" (243–44). This time, as Jane passes him and they look at each other "a long time," there is no going back and the black-white relationships of a century are broken.[34]

For all her 110-year perspective, Jane's account is curiously lacking in moments of vision, of glimpses of a governing design within which individual struggles find their meaning. Certainly she implies design in her refusals to go back, but Jane's one true moment of vision is shared with Jules Reynard after Tee Bob Samson stabs himself to death in the Samson library and Sheriff Sam Guidry holds his impromptu hearing. As Jules takes her home in his car, he and Jane conduct their own inquest on what happened

---

33. Gaines, "Miss Jane and I," 34; William L. Andrews, "'We Ain't Going Back There': The Idea of Progress in *The Autobiography of Miss Jane Pittman*," *Black American Literature Forum*, XI (1971), 146–49; Bryant, "Change, Growth, and History," 853, 859; O'Brien, ed., *Interviews with Black Writers*, 84.

34. John Callahan, "Image Making: Tradition and the Two Versions of *The Autobiography of Miss Jane Pittman*," *Chicago Review*, XXIX (1977), 53–54, 61.

and why. After speculating on Tee Bob's state of mind when he knocked down Mary Agnes LeFabre and imagining that he saw her for a moment as her submissive grandmother and himself as her Creole master and lover, they ponder the generations-long complicity between races. In light of Jimmy Caya's recitation of "the rules we been living by ever since we been here"—rules he describes as "what my daddy told me . . . [and] what my daddy's daddy told him" about the right of white men to take black women at their pleasure—Jules sees the design in Tee Bob's suicide: he had to kill himself "for our sins" (196). To Jane's lament for "Poor Tee Bob," Jules answers, "Poor us." To Jules's view that their vision is "gospel truth" because it is shared by black and white, Jane remains silent before the claims of history, and Jules, for all his decency, invokes history to justify his inability to cancel the claims of the past on the present.[35]

As the scene with Jules ends without explicit comment or interpretation, so does the final scene when Jane walks past Robert Samson and on into history. The end, however, is in the beginning, and the saga loops back to the introduction with emphasis on telling the story. Jane returns to the quarter, tells her story, and dies. At her funeral the fictive editor faces the problem other narrator-historians of sagas have. Although most other tellers generally agree with Jane's version, others refuse to say anything after hearing his tape, and some say not everything is correct. In saying that "Miss Jane's story is all their stories, and their stories are Miss Jane's," the narrator-historian recognizes that this folk saga, though reduced finally to written form, exists for use and interpretation as later tellers need it.

Toni Morrison's *Song of Solomon*, published in 1977, introduced a new development in the black family saga by appealing to legend beyond history rather than to history itself. The process of discovery in this saga involves searching out meanings hidden in legend and folklore beneath or behind history. The meanings are largely those hidden in names that linger into the present but whose significance is not clear until Milkman Dead goes on a near-mythic quest into his family past. Although his quest involves an inquiry into the southern roots of his Detroit family, it reflects at the same time the historical and sociological phenomenon Frazier saw as the third crisis in black family history, black families' leaving the rural South for new lives and new structures in cities of the North. To the extent that Milkman's search goes beyond the sober facts of history to the

---

35. Jack Hicks, "To Make These Bones Live: History and Community in Ernest Gaines' Fiction," *Black American Literature Forum*, XI (1977), 19.

wonder, finally, of African legend, the narrative also introduces elements of magical realism into the tradition of the family saga.[36]

The convention of the consanguine-extended family assumes a more prominent role in Morrison's saga than in Haley's or Walker's in the sense that Milkman Dead, child of the latest generation, discovers he has such a family and a past that extends beyond the persons of his father, mother, and sisters. One of the chief themes of his venture is the discovery of earlier generations, of previously unknown kinships, which proceeds through his discovery of names and meanings of names in the family. By the end of his search in Virginia, Milkman reads road signs "with interest now, wondering what lay beneath the names," for "under the recorded names were other names . . . names that had meaning." [37]

That names are clues to the family past, and to the mystery of the family past, comes home to Milkman when he learns that the family name Dead came from his illiterate ancestor's registration as a freedman by a drunken registrar in Alabama after the Civil War. When asked where he was born, the freedman said, "Macon." When asked what his father's name was, he reported, "He's dead," and he entered recorded history as "Dead, Macon." Like other former slaves and freedmen, he discovered the puzzling necessity of having two names, one a family name, but rather than take the name of a former master, he kept the name Dead because "it was new and would wipe out the past" (53–54). What his "real name" was is left to Milkman's generation, concerned with recovering a past all but wiped out.

As Milkman continues his search, he becomes aware that family legend more than family history explains names and relationships. Although Milkman's grandfather had named his own daughter Pilate during a fit of melancholy over the death of his wife as she bore Pilate and he wanted to consign the slip of paper with her name to "the Devil's flames" rather than to the family Bible, Pilate at age twelve accepts the name and keeps it in the brass box hung from her earlobe, giving it a mysterious significance in her life. She is condemned to a life of wandering and exile because she was born without a navel, a mysterious mark of her separation from the ordinary human community. Her life of wandering, however, suggests that Hagar is her type name, and it is significant that her granddaughter is so

36. Sanford Pinsker, "Magic Realism, Historical Truth, and the Quest for a Liberating Identity: Reflections on Alex Haley's *Roots* and Toni Morrison's *Song of Solomon*," *Studies in Black American Literature I: Black American Prose Theory*, ed. Joe Weixlmann (Greenwood, Fla., 1984), 191–93.

37. Toni Morrison, *Song of Solomon* (New York, 1977), 333.

named and that Milkman should wonder what Hagar's true name is. His mother Ruth Foster Dead likewise has her secret fantasized identity as the miller's daughter in the tale of Rumpelstiltskin who could save her child only by learning the name of the little man who spun gold from straw for her (13). His father Macon Dead, too, has his legendary identity as the ogre father beyond his ordinary identity as local businessman and property owner. Seen early as the malevolent father who stunts his family (10), Macon assumes the role of malign father of the hero of a quest, the father who tries to kill the future hero at his birth.[38] Although he warns Milkman about the snakelike charms of Pilate, Macon also recognizes that Pilate and he are the true inheritors of their African ancestors and look little like their light-skinned mother with the also-cryptic name Sing (54).

Believing at first that he is searching for gold buried by his grandfather, Milkman soon hunts for ancestral bones in Pennsylvania and learns that his true quest is for ancestral names in legendary Shalimar, Virginia. There he hears children chant that "Jay the only son of Solomon" can "whirl about and touch the sun" and realizes that the song Pilate sang, "O Sugarman don't leave me here," is a cryptic version of the children's song "Solomon don't leave me here" (303). That recognition is rounded to completion when he can sing to dying Pilate the certification of her kinship to the first Solomon: "Sugargirl don't leave me here" (340).

His discovery of Solomon's name thus enables Milkman to understand the role of removal in establishing family identity and the special attribute that has endured in the family through the removals. From Africa to the South to Pennsylvania and finally to Detroit, the family has shifted its outward identity and changed its name but kept its inner secret attribute of believing it can fly away from oppressors and limitations. Milkman retraces those removals as he rides from Detroit to Pittsburgh to Danville to Shalimar and at the place of origins wonders "why black people ever left the South" (263). If Shalimar is not Africa, it is Milkman's vision of Africa as he looks at the strange people "with wide sleepy eyes that tilted up at the corners, high cheek bones, full lips blacker than their skin, berrystained, and long necks" and feels natural and at home (266). Like legendary Africa, "Shalimar was not on the Texaco map he had, and the AAA office couldn't give a nonmember a charted course — just the map and some general information" (263).

38. Pinsker, "Magic Realism," 193; Charles De Arman, "Milkman as the Archetypal Hero: 'Thursday's Child Has Far to Go,'" *Obsidian*, VI (1980), 57–58; A. Leslie Harris, "Myth as Structure in Toni Morrison's *Song of Solomon*," *MELUS*, VII (1980), 70–71.

The family attribute has been all but displaced in Detroit by Macon Dead's new zeal for material possessions and his denial of the past.[39] A hard-headed businessman and collector of rents, he thinks the keys to rental houses are keys to success (23), drives his family in his Packard on Sundays to show his success (31), has money but fails to enjoy it (32), tells Milkman that having money is the "only freedom there is" (163), and urges Milkman as his inheritor to learn to own things: "And let the things you own own other things. Then you'll own yourself and other people too" (55). Macon Dead's behavior is representative of that Frazier noted about the black bourgeoise after their move to the North. Their emphasis on conspicuous consumption, their attempt to establish status through wealth in the black community, their mixing genteel traditions with the folk tradition all led to a confusion of values, sometimes creating "a world of make believe." [40] To Milkman, Macon's faith in money is a displacement of the inheritance. As he discovers, Pilate, though shunned and marginalized, is custodian of the original family attribute. In contrast with Macon's grim household, hers is a house of life and singing, and she claims to be one of the last Deads alive (29, 38). She knows the inheritance of the flying ancestor.

The family lore on their flying ancestor is not unique to them, however; it comes from black folklore in the South. B. A. Botkin records several stories of flying Africans from John Bennett's *Doctor to the Dead: Grotesque Legends and Folk Tales of Old Charleston,* published in 1946. Africans could once fly like birds, so the legend goes, but lost their wings because of sins. A few in the Sea Islands and low country, though, were overlooked and kept their power of flight. When a cruel master overworked and beat his people, a woman with a newborn baby spoke to an old man near her in a mysterious language and was told, "Not yet." Beaten again, she asked, "Is it time yet, daddy?" The old man said the time had come, gave her his blessing of peace, and stretched his arms to her. She leaped into the air and went away like a bird. Others, also beaten, spoke to the old man in an unknown tongue in words forgotten, laughed, leaped into the air and flew away. When the master ran to beat him, the old man laughed and said something to the other Africans. They all recalled the power once theirs, leaped into the air and flew away as the men clapped their hands, the

---

39. Susan Blake, "Folklore and Community in *Song of Solomon,*" *MELUS,* VII (1980), 81–82.

40. Frazier, *Negro Family,* 82.

women sang, and the children laughed and sucked their mothers' breasts. Morrison reported that in her own family stories part of the given lore was that in the old days black people could fly, a trait she found as well in slave narratives: "They always talk about it. They all either know somebody who flew, or they saw somebody who flew, or they knew somebody who said they saw somebody who flew. . . . Somebody whirls around, whirls around, then he gets up and flies away." [41] In *Song of Solomon* she adapts that lore as a family attribute of the Solomon family—an attribute not to be assumed but to be nurtured and rewon in each generation.

How Milkman learns of that family attribute and of the names in which it is hidden involves him in the saga role of narrator-historian. During the course of his search he hears the often-conflicting versions of the family past, both historical and legendary, and has to evaluate them all until he has a new legend of his own. By the time he reaches the Reverend Cooper in Danville, Milkman feels a growing sense of reality in the old stories "that he'd heard many times before but only half listened to" (233). By the end of his quest, Milkman has become the tale teller as he tells his father about their flying ancestor. Like saga narrators before him, Milkman must construct his new legend from the pieces told by others but fashioned for his own needs as a child of the present.

To construct his legend Milkman has to work his way through public history to the myth behind history. The beginning of his quest is shaped by such events in contemporary history as the news of Emmett Till's murder by whites in Mississippi (80–81), information about the insane murderer Winnie Ruth Judd (99), talk of Jews hunting down fugitive Nazis (161), and reports that four black girls were killed in Montgomery (174). Guitar speaks for blacks caught in recent history as he denigrates Albert Schweitzer and Eleanor Roosevelt as whites potentially as guilty as the klansmen who shot Emmett Till (157–58). Guitar's participation in the Seven Days brotherhood dedicated to random killing of whites to avenge deaths of blacks and finally his targeting Milkman as a victim are based on material values of history. For Guitar, Milkman's quest was to find ancestral gold, not ancestral bones and legends. Without material comforts but concerned instead with human relationships, Pilate represents for Milkman escape from individual material history to the legend of the greater family, and his knowledge is measured by his turn from Macon's values to Pilate's as he

41. Botkin, *Treasury of Southern Folklore*, 480–82; Schultz, "African and African-American Roots," 145, 148.

moves south and passes from a historical family past to a mythical past where Africans can fly.[42] Notably, however, that African past points not to a particular tribe or village like Haley's Mandinka village of Juffure in The Gambia but to a kind of transcendent pan-African legend, truer in idea than in fact.

Even though he learns the secret of family names during his quest into the legendary past, Milkman realizes in Shalimar that he does not understand the values of his past. Like the Genesis writers puzzling over motivations of the ancestors, Milkman sees that knowing what is not the same as knowing why, and in his puzzlement demonstrates the saga convention of wondering at the values of his ancestors. After his first session with Grace Long and Susan Byrd, he ponders why his father denies interest in the Virginia background and why Pilate is so absorbed in it:

> The questions about his family still knocked around in his head like billiard balls. If his grandfather, this Jake, was born in the same place his wife was, in Shalimar, why did he tell the Yankee he was born in Macon, thereby providing him with the raw material for the misnaming? And if he and his wife were born in the same place, why did Pilate and his father and Circe all say they "met" on the wagon? And why did the ghost tell Pilate to sing? . . . Here he was walking around in the middle of the twentieth century trying to explain what a ghost had done. (297–98)

His perplexity comes out of his more general puzzlement about "why black people ever left the South" (263) and why rural blacks hate him as a city black. To them, he has "the heart of the white men," who do not know blacks' language of names, who see blacks as "anonymous, faceless laborers" (269). Only later does he fully come to see that their values are embedded in a primal language he scarcely understands. During the hunt for the bobcat with men from Shalimar, he realizes his ignorance of the calls and signals by which hunters talk to each other: "It was all language. . . . No, it was not language; it was what there was before language. Before things were written down. Language in the time when men and animals did talk to one another . . . when men ran *with* wolves, not from or after them" (281). Milkman has to pass through the initiatory rite of the hunt before he can gain the Shalimar hunters' acceptance and begin to learn their

---

42. Susan Blake, "Folklore and Community," 77–78; Chiara Spallino, "*Song of Solomon: An Adventure in Structure*," *Callaloo*, VIII (1985), 512–13.

silent language. Then he is ready to understand the children's chant about Solomon's flight.

His earlier puzzlement also extends to the perplex of patriarchal-matriarchal conflict in the family. In the world of Macon Dead he has seen how moneyed men treat their women as conspicuous examples of their success. His sister Corinthians tells how their father has made dolls of the daughters, and his sister Lena swears there will be no more male superiority and laments how she missed college in order to protect Ruth from Macon (197, 217). That the patriarchal-matriarchal conflict goes further back in family lore is clear when Circe tells Milkman that his grandmother Sing's trial was that she loved her husband "too hard" and was nervously protective of him (245). What Circe does not say is why Sing was so watchful of Jake. Not until he hears how Solomon flew away from Ryna and tried to take Jake with him can he glimpse the cost to matriarchs of the heritage of flying Africans. For the line of desolated matriarchs runs through the family story as a counterpoint to the men's freedom in flight. Sing apparently knows of the matriarchs' abandonment by their flying men and fears it. Milkman reenacts that family practice in his affair with Hagar as he deserts her. After hearing Ryna's story, Milkman realizes that her predicament has been repeated through the generations.[43]

Type scenes in the saga similarly show the clash of values at work in Milkman's family through the generations. Singing and flying are associated with the heritage Pilate tries to preserve; urinating is the mark of values Macon has embraced. From his first meeting with Pilate to his last song for her, Milkman recognizes that not only has the dream of flying been the family attribute but singing about it has been the family scene.[44] That it has been corrupted in the present generation is evident when insurance agent Robert Smith, now one of the Seven Days trapped in history, tries to fly from Mercy Hospital while Pilate sings "Sugarman done fly away" (338, 5). That corruption is more definitely marked in Macon's world by the act of urination. When Macon goes to Porter's tenement to collect his rent, Porter holds off the crowd with his shotgun, "pee[s] over the heads of the women" gathered on the street (26), and links his predicament with that of "Mr. Smith." During one of the family's proud Sunday drives to the beach in the Packard, Milkman as a small boy wets on Lena while she picks violets (35). Later, when he tells Macon about Corinthians'

43. Spallino, "*Song of Solomon*," 518.
44. Schultz, "African and African-American Roots," 142; Spallino, "*Song of Solomon*," 522.

meetings with Henry Porter, Lena accuses him of peeing on the family again, saying, "You've been doing it to us all your life," and then points out the dying maple in the yard, the one that Milkman wet on at the beach and that was brought back as a twig with the violets she picked (214–16). As he leaves behind Macon's version of history for Pilate's legendary past, however, Milkman also exchanges one kind of type scene for another.

If Macon's rental house keys have talismanic significance to him as markers of success, Pilate's green bag becomes the family talisman from earlier generations. Unknown to Milkman until he meets Pilate, her heavy green bag is "Pilate's inheritance," according to Hagar. Whether it contains gold or bones, the green bag accrues ancestral significance for Milkman during his search for a family past. After he learns of the strange lives of his grandfather and great-grandfather, he can understand why Pilate keeps the bones of the man who almost flew away but remained to marry, beget children, and die defending his bit of "Lincoln's Heaven." Back in Detroit, he can assure Pilate that the bones she has are indeed her father's and that her father wants her to bury them at Solomon's Leap (337). As Milkman and Pilate carry out the rites of familial reverence and bury the bones, though, they still embody the contradictions of their heritage. To Guitar they are reburying not bones but gold needed for his violent version of history, and he shoots Pilate. To Pilate the burial is completion of a cycle of family history as she buries her name-bearing earrings and Sing's snuff box with the bones and calls on Milkman to sing the ancestral chant as she dies. While he sings, he has his moment of vision, derived from the family talisman, and realizes that singing is like flying (340). With this recognition, Milkman sings for the first time in his life and joins the long line of family singers reaching back to his great-grandmother and including Pilate and the chanting children of Shalimar.[45]

Morrison's novel thus makes important new advances in the black family saga in the South. Although earlier writers of black family sagas appealed to history for authentication of their family claims, in *Song of Solomon* Morrison denies the claims of history and takes the family story into the dimensions of legend as a necessary way of understanding the past and of coming to terms with it. In her saga the reader is forced to accept a different reality—the reality of flying Africans and of people born without navels. In that legend beyond history, family names take on magic quali-

---

45. Schultz, "African and African-American Roots," 142.

ties and undergo metamorphoses so that exploring the past and its meanings becomes an exploration of mysteries. For Toni Morrison, the South in the family past, seen from the perspective of black removal to northern cities, becomes the threshold of Africa, as legendary as Africa.

6

THIRD GENERATION
SAGAS AFTER THE RENASCENCE

By the late 1970s and the 1980s southern families had gotten far enough from the Civil War that it was no longer the great watershed in family memory. Writing within the context of studying changing social types, John Shelton Reed observed, "It could be that we are seeing an example of what has been called the 'third generation' phenomenon, in which ethnic revival is found among the third-generation Americans, children of parents who were at some pains to disown *their* parents' embarrassing 'foreign ways.'"[1]

Numerous writers and observers in the South have agreed that some deep sea change has taken place. Among writers of the older generation, Katherine Anne Porter saw that later novelists "don't have the tragic feeling about the South that we had," and Eudora Welty rejected the Civil War as a reference point, as did Flannery O'Connor and Walker Percy, saying that their generation "had no more interest in the Civil War than the Boer War." Shirley Ann Grau also thought more recent southern writers "value only the immediate past." Frederick Hoffman perceived an intellectual and moral shift "from the Southern past to the contemporary universal," Louis D. Rubin, Jr., believed new southern writers had moved from interest in the community to "little private things," and Lewis Lawson feared that younger writers, too conscious of "the image of the South postulated by the generation of the Renascence," would use up "the capital which was deposited in the bank by Mr. Faulkner and others" and write parodies of the earlier generation. Fred Hobson similarly recognized that in a Sun-Belt

---

1. John Shelton Reed, *Southern Folk, Plain and Fancy: Native White Social Types* (Athens, Ga., 1987), 73.

South "not noticeably haunted by God, and not likely to take sin and guilt or redemption so seriously," power and public relations replace moral compassion as the matter of concern for polemical writers. From a sociological viewpoint, Reed noted that the media rather than poets and novelists tend to set the values for southern types.[2]

As a third-generation writer of family sagas, Reynolds Price has embodied and expressed most of those revisionist views stated more generally by other writers and critics. Seeing himself as a novelist, not a southern novelist, he nevertheless found his stories of people struggling with their destinies located in southern settings. "Insofar as the South is a unique world, my work reflects that uniqueness, but my work is not, never has been *about* the South." He preferred, he said, to think of *The Surface of Earth,* written in 1975, as an American novel more than one specifically southern. He saw the "enormous force, even tyranny, of family organization in absolutely every aspect of Southern life until down perhaps into the 1950s and 1960s" and judged "the enormously complex symbiosis of the races" in that novel as "powerfully Southern" but not unique to southern life. Such southern institutions as the family and the influence of the country, he observed, persist despite their changes and weaknesses in recent decades. Writers of his generation, he thought, will thus still encounter "claustrophobic families" and children drowned in the rhetoric of those families.[3]

As the child of a later generation, Price acknowledged reference points different from those of early saga writers. "The Depression was my generation's Civil War, the force which shaped and confirmed my earliest fears,

2. Givner, ed., *Porter Conversations,* 49, 57; Albert J. Devlin and Peggy W. Prenshaw, "A Conversation with Eudora Welty," in *Welty: A Life in Literature,* ed. Albert J. Devlin (Jackson, 1987), 19–20; William F. Buckley, Jr., "'The Southern Imagination': An Interview with Eudora Welty and Walker Percy," in *Conversations with Welty,* ed. Prenshaw, 105–107; Canfield, "Conversation with Grau," 48; Hoffman, *The Art of Southern Fiction,* 10; Louis D. Rubin, Jr., "The Boll Weevil, the Iron Horse, and the End of the Line: Thoughts on the South," in *The American South,* ed. Rubin, 365–68, and in Givner, *Porter Conversations,* 50–51; Lewis Lawson, "Twentieth-Century Southern Literature," in *Southern Literary Study,* ed. Rubin and Holman, 151–52; Fred Hobson, *Tell About the South: The Southern Rage to Explain* (Baton Rouge, 1983), 358; Reed, *Southern Folk,* 72–73.

3. Wallace Kaufman, " 'Notice I'm Still Smiling': Reynolds Price," in *Kite-Flying and Other Irrational Acts,* ed. John Carr (Baton Rouge, 1972), 77; Reynolds Price and William Ray, *Conversations: Reynolds Price and William Ray* (Memphis, 1976), 61, 77; Reynolds Price, "Dodo, Phoenix, or Tough Old Cock?," in *Things Themselves: Essays and Scenes* (New York, 1972), 170–71.

demanded the building of my earliest defenses against the anonymous forces of ruin, humiliation before one's kin, in one's love." Although he thought the Civil War still as little understood as the Mariana Trench, he believed the writers of his generation had equally unknown traumas to explore—not only the Great Depression but the "manless years" of World War II, the black rights struggle, and the agonies of Vietnam. Showing the anxiety of influence, he recognized the "special and enormous case" of Faulkner but admired him "with a cold, distant admiration for a genius whom I know to be grand but who has proved irrelevant to my own obsessions, my own ambitions." Rather, he turned to writers such as Eudora Welty, who wrote about ordinary people like those he knew.[4]

When he came to write his family saga *Surface of Earth,* and its continuation and sequel *Source of Light* in 1981, Price turned from the crush of southern history to search out the meanings of a southern family within the context of mythic, especially biblical, insights. More than most family sagas, *Surface of Earth* and *Source of Light* exist for their moments of vision, afforded by an intricate narrative of four generations struggling through circumstances to find a design beneath the surfaces of action. With paradigms of the potential sacrifice of Isaac by Abraham, the actual sacrifice by Jephthah of his daughter as told in the book of Judges, and the myth of Tristan, Iseult, and King Mark, the saga assumes a level of reality, beyond quotidian events, where dreams, visions, and memory projected into the future are part of the narrative action. As in the Old Testament, visions come not only through dreams but as well through the pronouncements of angelic messengers. As it progresses, the saga narrative changes, shifting more and more toward a visionary reality.

As he indicated in his accounts of the composition of *Surface of Earth,* Price did not at first realize that he would write a family saga. He began planning the story as early as March, 1961. The initial situation was that of the interdependence of an alcoholic father and his young son, initially named Phil, both of whom travel through eastern North Carolina during summers of World War II as part of the father's job. The boy's mother is dead, the father feels guilt over the mother's death but has an affair with another woman, and the boy knows of his father's mistress and turns for love to the aunt who looks after him when he is not with his father.[5] The

4. Kaufman, "Notice I'm Still Smiling," 88–89; Price, "Dodo," in *Things Themselves,* 174; Kaufman, "Notice I'm Still Smiling," 75–76.

5. Reynolds Price, "Given Time: Beginning *The Surface of Earth,*" *Antaeus,* XXI (1976), 57–64.

father's guilt comes from the promise he made to God, during his wife's difficult labor when the boy was born, to stop drinking if the child is saved. The boy survived but the mother died, and the father realized he had forgotten to ask for her life, too, so the boy grows into recognition that he is both his father's pledge to God and the one responsible for killing the woman his father loved.

As he worked with widening implications of the story, Price became aware of his own analogous involvement in the lives of his parents and his own sense as a child of having assumed "the burden of an immensely heavy human relation." He, too, had a "very difficult birth" and his mother, a "nearly fatal labor," with the result that the story of his birth "resonated through [his] own childhood." Thus was he initiated into family stories of mothers dying in childbirth and husbands surviving with the guilt of those deaths. In *A Palpable God* Price remembers how his alcoholic father made a vow to quit drinking if his wife and child lived. By the time Price was five he had learned to see himself as "a pledge, a hostage with more than normal duties and perils." [6]

By mid-1963, after time spent away from the South during his residence at Oxford University, Price began to think of his story as a "family novel" and determined to "examine intensely, unflinchingly, and forgivingly the interlocked members of a family." He began to see his real story as a cycle of courtship, marriage, marriage troubles, difficult childbirth, husband's vow, and wife's death and pondered whether to bring the story full circle with the son's courtship and marriage. Realizing the novel had to be about fathers as well as sons, he decided to write a chronological scenario of the generations in order to see how to break it up into intense scenes. By July, 1963, he thought of the son imagining his father and mother beginning him and seeing "the whole network of love and hate that lay around his father that night"—a network of others waking and sleeping in North Carolina that night. [7]

When he returned to the story in 1968, he began to discern its visionary implications. At that point, he remembered in *A Palpable God*, he thought of the story as "a kind of realistic allegory of [his] own peculiar relation to [his] father" and wrote his "meditations on the narrative implications of Rembrandt's four pictures" of the sacrifice of Isaac, "a conscious calisthenic for the novel." By 1971 he could see that the story de-

---

6. Price, "Given Time," 59–60; Reynolds Price, *A Palpable God* (New York, 1978), 13.

7. Price, "Given Time," 62–63.

manded a "return to its source" and "a forty-year trek through a crowd of lives in numerous places." By then, vision was becoming paramount, with tracks of the fathers and sons leading to "*the goal set for them by their clamorous past and the hope of rest, God's fiercest prod.*" By then, he had also come to realize that his "story may be finally nearer to the story of Jephthah (in all its details, not simply the sacrifice of his child) than to Abraham." By August, 1974, he envisioned his novel as "a kind of summary book of a larger part of what [he knew] as a person who has lived his life and watched many others for four decades." [8] Like those biblical narratives he translated in *A Palpable God,* his was a story of God working in history.

Having seen how the initial story situation required returning to its source, Price expanded the father-son unit until it led to the generations of Mayfields, Goodwins, and the black line running from Elvira to Rover to Grainger on the father's side and the Kendals and Watsons on the mother's; the Hutchinses of Goshen, Virginia, for Rob Mayfield's marriage; and the Drewry line in Richmond for Forrest Mayfield's long life with Polly. Price found a recurring motif in the disruption of family closeness through generations as children establish themselves in their own lives and households. [9] By the time he was finishing *Surface of Earth,* Price considered the father-son relationship of Rob Mayfield and his son Hutchins as "the latest visible stop in a very long chain of causes and effects and accidents in a family over a period of nearly a hundred years." By the time of his own manhood in *Source of Light,* Hutch feels that family past as a web and a burden. Before leaving for his years at Oxford, he tells his lover Anne Gatlin that, with "all the layers of Mayfields and Kendals and Hutchins piled on me," he feels not cursed but crowded: "My people abandoned so much on my doorstep—or had it snatched from them and set down here. There's no one but me left to use it all, consume it, convert it, redeem back all my people pawned away—their generous starved hearts." [10]

The black strand in the Mayfield family line, embodied primarily in Grainger in the foreground of the narrative, serves repeatedly to enforce the theme of family as fate. At times acting like a messenger angel, Grainger is that part of the family known but not acknowledged. Coming from the black branch that removed to Maine after emancipation, he does not

8. Price, *A Palpable God,* 12–13; Price, "Given Time," 58; Price and Ray, *Conversations,* 19, 53.

9. Constance Rooke, *Reynolds Price* (Boston, 1983), 113.

10. Price and Ray, *Conversations,* 48; Reynolds Price, *The Source of Light* (New York, 1981), 38.

know at first of his family connections. Old Veenie realizes that such knowledge is sorrow and makes Forrest promise not to tell Grainger of his link with the family through old Robinson Mayfield and Elvira. But Forrest's is one of the unkept promises in the family, and he later admits to Rob his error in telling Grainger who Grainger is and raising the black man's hopes beyond Forrest's power to help him.[11] The unkept promise becomes part of the family heritage. As Forrest told Rob, Rob tells Hutch that Grainger feels deserted by Rob as Grainger will later feel deserted by Hutch (514). If Grainger is fated never to gain full acknowledgment, he nevertheless participates in the family's key occasions, such as Rob and Rachel's wedding supper (249), and in the exchanges of promises offered and withheld that are embodied in Robinson and Anna Goodwin Mayfield's gold wedding ring.

Among the families involved in the saga, the Mayfield men, from generation to generation, demonstrate the special attribute that causes the complications in the family. They are the seekers and sometimes the bringers of vision that penetrates the surface of earth, the stratum of circumstance that limits them. For these men, sex is the opportunity and occasion for that vision. Because of their restless seeking, they are also wanderers, and their history is one of loving and leaving the women of their lives. In no one of their generations is there a permanently established conjugal family unit. Rather, the Mayfields' women are left as waiting survivors in consanguine families. The patriarchal-matriarchal conflict through the generations thus derives from the family attribute. The further complication is that the men's sexual demands result repeatedly in their women facing the peril of childbirth in pre-antibiotic years, and the family history is marked by a series of women dying or nearly dying in childbirth and a series of men carrying the guilt of their wives' suffering. The saga opens on that note, with Bedford Kendal telling his children how their maternal grandfather Thad Watson shot himself at his daughter's cribside after her mother died bearing her and how the Kendal family took the Watsons' daughter Charlotte, later his wife, to raise after the deaths of her parents. Among Bedford's hearers is his daughter Eva, who elopes with Forrest Mayfield and enters the legacy of old Robinson Mayfield.

As Robinson tells Forrest, his gift has been to bring life to women

---

11. Louis W. Chicatelli, "Family as Fate in Reynolds Price's *The Surface of Earth* and *The Source of Light*," *Mid-Hudson Language Studies*, V (1982), 134; Reynolds Price, *The Surface of Earth* (New York, 1975), 254.

through sex. Forrest's mother Anna Goodwin was "dying on the vine" until he changed that: "But I brought her new life. That was my line—
don't you see?—back then. It was what I could do" (109). But his motto,
he says, is "*Don't never stand still,*" and his daughter Hatt Shorter reminds
Robinson's grandson and namesake Rob that Mayfield men always leave
(154). His father Forrest similarly tells Rob that Mayfield men run while
their women stay and smother what is left (222). Rob continues the Mayfield legacy when he impregnates Rachel and she dies bearing Hutch.
Approaching Fontaine later, Rob wonders at the moral consequences of
promises broken and ponders the legacy of old Robinson Mayfield as he
thinks of his own "gift for pleasure, a true seed within him from Robinson
his grandfather" (341). By the time of *Source of Light* Hutch tells Rob that
the ability "to make women think they've been rushed to Heaven before
their time" is "a danger that runs in your family, you've noticed—the Mayfield side" (6–7). Later, waiting to die of cancer, Rob reviews the way sex
has been his means for breaking through the surface of earth, through "the
lovely sad crust of this present world into glimpses of permanence," always "in the company of women" (68). Still puzzling his legacy in England, Hutch senses the problem: "It's the soul that's in danger. . . . The
Mayfield Soul. Or is it a Kendal or Hutchins Soul?" Although he may be
outwardly proud, he insists, "Inside I'm doubting—a Mayfield as I said"
(148).[12]

The continuity of Robinson Mayfield's legacy, however, has its answering legacy in the endurance of the Mayfield men's women. For them,
patient waiting upon the surface of earth provides moments of insight,
though their hold on circumstances can be smothering. Even when they
have been married, legally or de facto, these women tend to lead lives of
single survivors. Robinson's wife Anna is left to raise their son and
daughter while he wanders. When he later takes Polly Drewry as his live-
in mate and nurse, she accepts a life of waiting and being passed on from
Robinson to Forrest to Rob to Hutch, quasi-wife to the first two, consoler
to the others. As she tells Hutch in *Source of Light,* she did not call her feeling for Robinson love but waited for it to "name itself in time." By the
time of Rob's funeral, she realizes the name of her life is waiting—waiting
for Robinson to die and waiting forty years for Forrest to make up his mind

12. William Claxton, "With This Ring I Thee Wed: The Mayfield Men," in *Reynolds
Price, From "A Long and Happy Life" to "Good Hearts," with a Bibliography,* ed. Sue Laslie
Kimball and Lynn Veach Sadler (Fayetteville, N.C., 1988), 33–34, 37–40; Rooke, *Reynolds
Price,* 117.

about her (247–48). Forrest's wife Eva demonstrates the hold of her own family when she takes their son Rob to visit her father, sister, and brother for Christmas and never returns to Forrest. Living the rest of her life as daughter and sister rather than as wife and mother was, Price saw, "a perfectly authentic choice" in southern families before World War II. Rob has not only his biological mother Eva, who is more like an aunt than a mother, but his Aunt Rena, more like a mother than Eva, and, after Rachel dies in childbirth, Min Tharrington in a circumstance much like Polly's. As the line of family women extends, Hutch has not only Eva, Rena, Polly, and Min but also Rachel's friend Alice Matthews as his surrogate mothers. What Rena, Alice, and the other women have learned is that the dream of ecstatic union fails, but waiting provides opportunities to love, to work, to find openings in the surface of earth that give glimpses of eternity.[13]

Because of the male legacy of sexual potency and the women's legacy of waiting, the recurring type scene in family history becomes that of women dying or nearly dying in childbirth and men suffering the guilt resulting from those crises. The other main type scene depicts the patriarchal legacy as father lies on son in a kind of conferral of sexual potency from generation to generation.[14] Forrest remembers waking in the night before Robinson leaves, with his father lying on him, their eyes four inches apart, but what the look in his father's eyes was he never knew (24). Since Forrest was separated from Rob during the boy's youth, that generation missed the ritual act. Later, however, Rob, untutored by example, still covers Hutch when the boy is four or five years old (347), and Hutch covers Rob during their stay at Virginia Beach (401–403), ritually giving him up and into Min's arms.

Like type scenes, family talismanic objects hold promises and memories of the clan together through generations. A major motif running through the narrative is the passing along of the gold wedding band first given by Robinson to Anna Goodwin Mayfield. Although Price recognized that "chords of repetition and recurrence and cycle were beginning to sound" by the time he completed Book One of *Surface of Earth*, not until he was nearly finished with the novel did he realize that "the actual end of the novel was going to complete the history of a physical object,

13. Constance Rooke, "On Women and His Own Work: An Interview with Reynolds Price," *Southern Review*, n.s., XIV (1978), 713; Bess Spangler, "'A Dry Rag to Suck': Old Maids in *The Surface of Earth*," in *Reynolds Price*, ed. Kimball and Sadler, 93–96.

14. Rooke, *Reynolds Price*, 141; Claxton, "With This Ring," in *Reynolds Price*, ed. Kimball and Sadler, 40–43.

a gold ring," that "one of the things the novel has been about was the history of a ring." [15] When they are first separated, Forrest sends Eva his mother's ring to wear or to keep for Rob, but the package is refused and returned by Bedford Kendal (90, 96). Forrest later offers Anna's ring to Polly, but she refuses it, too, having heard its history from Robinson (118). After Forrest gives the ring to Grainger as a Christmas present, he sees Grainger wearing it at Rob's wedding supper (122, 250). Polly later explains how much she resented seeing the ring on Grainger's finger because it represented Forrest's greater obligation to Grainger than to her (410). By the end of *Surface of Earth*, Grainger has passed the ring along to Hutch (491). In *Source of Light*, before he leaves for Oxford, Hutch refuses to let Anne Gatlin wear the ring in New York so they can stay at the hotel as husband and wife. When he later offers it to her, she, too, refuses because it means not commitment but keeping her on a string (33, 40–41). In Rome at Christmas he gives her the ring but not the accompanying words of commitment (125, 173). After her abortion, Anne takes the ring to Polly Drewry and asks Polly to keep it since she is the only one who has known all the men involved in handling it (315–17). When Polly accepts the ring, though, she does so in the spirit of promises unkept and commitments withheld. She will keep it under the bed for Hutch but not wear it herself (318).

Two other family talismans of continuity are the carved priapic dolls made by old Robinson and the gold coin he gives his black children. The priapic dolls, Polly tells Hutch in *Surface of Earth*, are old Robinson's joke icons of "Mam and Pap," and she gives them to Hutch as continuants of the priapic heritage of the Mayfields. In *Source of Light*, Hutch takes one priapic doll to Oxford, keeps it with souvenirs of his trip to Cornwall, and studies it as part of the legacy he must carry into the future (312–13). The five-dollar gold coin dated 1839 was sent by Robinson to Rover in Maine when Grainger was born and is his cryptic good luck wish for his black descendants (456). Grainger, however, gives the coin to Hutch as his way of saying they share the same heritage (511).

Although the sections of *Surface of Earth* are explicitly dated and letters in both *Surface of Earth* and *Source of Light* mark their points in time, the family events in the saga depend little on public history for their significance. In this respect Price shows how far he has come from those sagas keyed to the Civil War and how close to putting actions within the context

15. Claxton, "With This Ring," in *Reynolds Price*, ed. Kimball and Sadler, 31; Price and Ray, *Conversations*, 59.

of the mythic universal. The family actions of *Surface of Earth* are depicted against the backdrop of two world wars, which provide perspective for measuring "the exaggerated suffering" of family members.[16] At the close of *Surface of Earth,* while Rob remembers how his life has been shaped by the "single and barren," by people "like old Bible figures, tall forms in dark figures on whom the sky leans," Hutch dreams of "children, real children a little smaller than he, seated far apart in a bare Normandy field, consumed by real flames—no man in sight or hearing, no woman," and sees in that vision "real agony" (590–91). By the time of Hutch's sojourn in England in *Source of Light,* Alice Matthews writes to tell him of watching a parade of blacks in Richmond on July 4, 1955, and of wondering why they keep silent about "Virginia's jackass display of 'massive resistance' to school integration" (120-21). For the most part, however, the family has its own agonies to deal with.

When Price decided to write *Surface of Earth* from third-person point of view in order to provide perspectives of several family members rather than from the viewpoint of the boy who was to become Hutch, he apparently gave away possibilities of providing a focused narrator-historian for his saga. The dramatized scenes and summarized continuities, the letters carefully dated, the family stories told by one member to another, and the pictures of family members on significant occasions all wait for an ultimate collator. In *Source of Light,* however, Hutch becomes aware of his potential role as family historian when Rob asks him to try to find the "diagram" in the generations. "Eva, Grainger, me, and maybe some of the dead," Rob says, "would be grateful if anyone looked back on us (not down) and saw that we'd made anything like a diagram in these fifty years, anything more than harum-scarum tracks in the dirt as a handful of scared souls scuttled for cover" (56). He can ask Hutch, Rob says, for this reason: "Somehow you're the one named Kendal-Hutchins-Mayfield that escaped having whatever worm gnawed us. . . . The thing, passed on to you through me and Rachel, may have been exhausted or somehow fed. Or all of us have learned a kind of peace in you, learned it for you" (56). To aid Hutch's search for the diagram, Rob spends his last days composing letters to Hutch telling of his best moments and leaves three shoe boxes of documents for Hutch "with prayers for mercy, not judgment" (118, 214).

Hutch himself recognizes his potential for the role of narrator-historian when he tells Polly he realizes his talent to watch things and peo-

16. Rooke, *Reynolds Price,* 127.

ple and copy their motions (317). His recording of the family, though, is complicated by his seeing the family's struggles in terms of literary analogy, particularly in terms of the Tristan-Iseult-King Mark myth with its hints of incestuous love. During his trip to Cornwall with Lew Davis, at Tintagel they see the marker near Fowey with the inscription "Here lies Drustan son of Cunomorus." Hutch equates Drustan with Tristan and Cunomorus with King Mark and wonders: "In all the stories Tristan was Mark's nephew. Did the inscription signify 'son of his loins' or 'adopted son'? Had the poets made a hard tale softer?—incest, real or legal, smoothed to household adultery?" (90). Excluding himself from the storm of family passions both in history and myth, Hutch sees his role as that of watcher, like "Gorvenal, Tristan's empty-handed handy man, unworn as a baby after all his long witness," and feels Gorvenal's sense of abandonment, "left suddenly with nothing to show but memory" (110). In effect, he learns to substitute art for love in showing the family design.[17]

In making the role of narrator-historian one of artist-observer, though, Hutch displaces himself from the family legacy, and in choosing an unpaired life he portends decline of the family line.[18] With his bisexuality he becomes, like Rosa Coldfield, "all polymath love's androgynous advocate." Although he may find design in the family's struggles on the surface of earth, in searching for the source of light he ceases to be part of that struggle. The displacement is foreshadowed by Rob's speculation that the life force in the family has been exhausted in Hutch; the displacement comes true when Anne Gatlin aborts the child she and Hutch conceived in Rome. Anne may dream that Rob thanks her for bringing "life again to the clean dead house" (276), but awake she accepts Min Tharrington's view, gained after long association with Mayfield men, that the child is hers, not Hutch's, to abort (269). After his sense of revulsion at discovery of the abortion, however, Hutch turns again to Rob's last letter as a "map toward what he still meant to have, the life Rob missed; a chart-by-omission" (312). When Hutch writes Polly that his talent is to watch, record, and find the still center of peace, he recognizes, as he told his Oxford tutor Mr. Fleishman, that his life, since his birth and his mother's death, is "a solitary journey with skirmishes of company" (292). That recognition provides the answer to the puzzle he had earlier sensed with Anne: "Is he *designated* by whatever hand of God, Fate, The Past" to share "a well-paired life" or "to

17. *Ibid.*, 137.

18. *Ibid.*, 141; Claxton, "With This Ring," in *Reynolds Price,* ed. Kimball and Sadler, 40–43.

stand on the edge alone and stare inwardly"? (39). His recognition about himself extrapolates the insight he gained from the Tristan-Iseult myth, that ecstatic love leads to art and death rather than to the mundanities of "the well-paired life." Like Denis de Rougemont in his study of the Tristan myth, he sees that "passion and marriage are essentially irreconcilable." [19]

The moments of vision in *Surface of Earth* and *Source of Light,* which constitute the dominant convention in the saga and to which the other conventions lead, derive from Price's recognition that a sense of the supernatural is a key part of human consciousness. "I do strongly suspect, even avow the existence or presence of forms of reality quite beyond those forms we encounter in our daily routines," he told William Kaufman. "And whether or not those forms do manifest themselves—ever, in observable, sensually perceptive ways—certainly there can be no question that the dead linger, most powerfully, in our lives; the meaningful dead, those people who by the time most men have reached the age of twenty-one stand as one's ancestors on the black side of death in relation to our present continuing lives." Going further, he saw that "the supernatural in the form of ghosts is still a possible, occasionally a necessary, component of a serious novelist's vision." [20]

In *Surface of Earth* and *Source of Light* those supernatural moments commonly take one of three forms: visions, dreams, or poems, the last by Hutch in *Source of Light.* The visions are generally related to dynastic possibilities. In *Surface of Earth,* when Rob and Grainger are driving to Fontaine from Goshen in response to the night call that Bedford Kendal has had a stroke, Rob remembers that Bedford had promised the old Kendal place to him years before and has his brief vision of the Kendal place as the source of his future children (293). By the time Hutch has grown to consciousness of his place in the family struggle, he has his vision of ten lives warped by his grandparents' elopement (445), and Rob has his vision at Goshen that, though he had been "aimed" by Eva and Forrest, his life has been saved not by the paired of the family but by the single and barren, by Rena, Sylvie, Grainger, Polly, Della, and Kinnerly, and he blesses them (488). At the end of his life in *Source of Light,* Rob has his climactic vision of his own birth and finds peace: "Feasible center, discovered in time, revised now and right" (210).

---

19. Denis de Rougemont, *Love in the Western World,* tr. Montgomery Belgion (New York, 1940), 262.
20. Kaufman, "Notice I'm Still Smiling," 83.

Like the visions, the dreams are portentous, but they tell of loss. During their summer of wandering in 1944, Rob tells Hutch of the dream he had while he and Rachel were on their wedding trip. During their stop at the railroad hotel in Lynchburg, he dreams that an angel ("He was dressed like a real man . . . but I knew what he was") comes to their room and delivers his message with his eyes: "It was Judgment; he had been sent to tell us that message direct." His worst mistake, Rob says, was ignoring that dream (483). Hutch's recurrent dream is of finding his lost mother. He dreams of seeing her as a girl of his own age, found standing on a creek bank in the woods, who, though told to "Wait here," disappears when he brings Grainger to see her (346). In *Source of Light* Hutch's dream turns to his child instead of his mother. While staying at the Kendal farmhouse during Rob's last days, Hutch dreams of seeing a child entering the house and reaching for him. He realizes it is his child in Anne and moves toward it but wakes before the dream is completed (254). The dreams of loss are messages that his destiny is to stare inwardly and be alone.

Hutch's poem sent to Anne repeats, but attempts to revise, the secret dream of finding Rachel on the green bank. Instead of "the girl who bled to death in bearing him," he finds Anne "prepared to stay . . . obeying half a dream" (125–26). Although he tries to write a poem about the Tristan-Iseult-King Mark myth seen from the butler Gorvenal's viewpoint, he never finishes it. Instead, while snowed in at the New York airport during his return to Oxford after Rob's death, he writes his poem to Rob—a poem in which he recognizes Rob's charge to "find the figure made by our family's path"—and invokes the image of resurrection by remembering his mock-death by drowning at Warm Springs and his return to life (259–61).

That view of resurrection derives from Price's own view that life is a divine comedy. The real human story, he says in *A Palpable God,* is "credible news that our lives proceed in order toward a pattern which, if tragic here and now, is ultimately pleasing in the mind of a god who sees a totality and *at last* enacts His will," for "*History is the will of a just god who knows us*" (Price's emphases). He similarly observed to Constance Rooke that *Surface of Earth* is a comic action as in a divine comedy, reaching for "order, serenity, the dissolution of the self in some larger intention." That intention is apparently signaled in the epigraphs of both novels. The epigraph of *Surface of Earth,* taken from Augustine's *Confessions,* envisions a God at rest beyond the struggles and teachings of angels or men, and that of *Source of Light,* taken from Emanuel Swedenborg's *Heaven and Its Wonders and Hell,* invokes an angelic language so perfect it has "nothing in common with human languages." *Surface of Earth* can be seen as a running debate between Augustine's claims of divine and serene rest and a human family's struggles with the claims of a fallen world.[21] But if, as Price told Rooke, his stories are "an elaborate dialogue with the whole notion of free will and freedom, free will and compulsion," they are also, he said, about the limits of human freedom. In his saga Price is primarily concerned in *Surface of Earth* with showing limitations imposed by the mistaken choices and compulsions of the generations. In *Source of Light* those determinants provide the basis for Hutch's rising, tentatively at least, to transcendent insight.[22] The cost for the Mayfield-Kendal-Hutchins family, however, is transformation of the family from flesh and blood generations into art and legend.

Like Reynolds Price, Lee Smith has felt the anxiety of influence as a third-generation writer of family sagas and, like Price, has turned to the mid-South as the locus of unexploited materials. Even though she wrote one novel set in Alabama, *Fancy Strut,* she has recognized the problems inherent in writing about that area: "It's very difficult to do the deep South any more unless you stand it on its ear like Barry Hannah does. If you're from the deep South and that's what you know, it's very hard to write and not be trite." In contrast, "it's not quite as hard if you're from the mid-South, from the mountains, and it does seem to me that there's an awful lot of good writing that's coming out of that region now [in 1983]."[23] Unlike Price, though, she turned to folk culture in *Oral History* and popular culture in *Oral History* and *Family Linen* as the matrix of her sagas.

In *Oral History,* written in 1983, Smith uses the folkloric past of a family legend of witches rather than the Civil War as the reference point of family memory. Her saga explores the influence of the witch-haunted past as the governing family attribute and through multiple narrators shows the ambiguity involved in the mysterious witch legend. As her exploration shows, witchhood means love as a destructive force working through the generations.

21. Price, *A Palpable God,* 14; Rooke, "On Women and His Own Work," 707; Michael Kreyling, "Motion and Rest in the Novels of Reynolds Price," *Southern Review,* n.s., XVI (1980), 853, 868; Rooke, *Reynolds Price,* 112.

22. Rooke, "On Women and His Own Work," 708; Chicatelli, "Family as Fate," 131, 135.

23. Edwin T. Arnold, "An Interview with Lee Smith," *Appalachian Journal,* XI (1984), 251.

The saga grew out of her short story "Oral History," first published in *Carolina Quarterly* in 1981. The short story about a college girl going to her mountain kin to tape-record their quaint stories, leaving the tape running at the family cabin, and having a family member go back to get the tape was, she realized, a story with a hole in it waiting to be filled. "I kept wondering what would have been on the tape," she remembered. "So then I decided to write the novel filling in what would be on the tape." In effect, the short story became the frame story for the novel. Knowing how the novel would begin and end, she had to do "all this research, all this reading" in mountain lore, which she recounts in the "Author's Note" prefacing the narrative. The saga is "*all* the new *stuff* in the middle." [24]

Using the short story as a frame for the saga action, though, required changes and adaptations to fill the new middle. Like Faulkner adapting his stories to fit the McCaslin saga in *Go Down, Moses,* Smith changed names of characters and locales, added and deleted narrative details, and in the closing part of the frame added characters not anticipated in the original. Pappy in the original becomes Little Luther Wade, Fern becomes Jennifer, Hassell becomes Almarine, Darryl becomes Billy, Uncle John becomes Lewis Ray, and Margaret Fay becomes Pearl, but Ora Mae remains stolid, mysterious, and forbidding in both story and saga. Local names change as Clinch Valley becomes Tug Valley and the unnamed prosperous mill town where Fern lives becomes Jennifer's Abingdon. Among the dropped details is the notation that Fern stayed with the Cantrells while her father was away in the army and that he got her back six years before the present action. Among the details dropped from the original but left implied in the core story narration by Sally are Hassell's comments to Fern about Darryl: "I think he died of love myself. Eat up with it." Almarine tells Jennifer, though, "It was your own mother had to do with it [Billy's death], and that high school boy." Smith also added to the closing frame that Debra will have a hysterectomy, that Richard Burlage will publish his memoirs at Louisiana State University Press, and that Almarine will make a killing in AmWay, retire young, invest in a ski run on the mountain, and build the theme park Ghostland to exploit the haunted cabin legend. [25]

That the novel became a saga of generations was the outgrowth of Smith's recognition that she was ready to write about whole lives. When

24. Arnold, "Interview with Smith," 246, 249, 252.

25. Lee Smith, "Oral History," *Carolina Quarterly,* XXXIII (1981), 75–84; Lee Smith, *Oral History* (New York, 1983), 13–24, 281–86.

she was a younger writer, she said, short stories with youthful perspectives of a moment were right for her. As a mature writer she saw the value of depicting whole lives in a continuity of generations.[26] In *Oral History* when Jennifer comes to Hoot Owl Holler to tape-record the haunting sounds of the old family cabin on Hoot Owl Mountain, her purposes are not only to complete the project for her oral history course and please Dr. Bernie Ripman but, she thinks self-consciously, to gain "new knowledge of my heritage and a new appreciation of those colorful, interesting folk," of "my *roots*" (19). Less conscious are her casually stated wishes to know "a little more precise information," she tells her grandmother, about her blood mother Pearl, concerning whom her father in Abingdon has always said, "The subject is closed." Less conscious still is her wonder about the coincidence in time between her mother's death from pneumonia and her cousin Billy's being murdered by a mentally ill teenager. More puzzling is why Billy sat in the rocking chair at the cabin as if waiting to be killed (21–22). It takes whole lives to answer such questions, and if Jennifer never understands the answers, the reader, privy to stories she never hears, comes closer to, though never completely reaches, understanding.

Although continuity in the generations is signaled by recurrence of the name Almarine in the family, the genealogy is a tangle of marriages and quasi-marriages by several members in each generation, with children by different wives and husbands. The genealogy begins in mystery with the removal of old Charles Vance Cantrell and his wife Nell to the mountains of western Virginia, from Ireland, reports tradition, if not evidence. On the distaff side is the mystery of Pricey Jane's origins. She comes to the mountains with a family not her own and vague memories of a place called Matewan and of a gypsylike mother who wore gold earrings (28–29, 63–64). Among the whole lives recounted is that of the first Almarine, who also shows the genealogical tangles as he lives with Red Emmy the witch, marries and has children by Pricey Jane, and after her death lives and has children by Vashti Cantrell, who says she was his dead brother's wife. The mysteries and tangles of the genealogy also demonstrate the effect of the lingering attribute of the family, told in the epigraphic "Fair and Tender Ladies," that "love, it was such a killin' crime."

What sets the Cantrell family apart and gives it identity is its sense of being haunted by the lingering curse of the witch Red Emmy. Whether or

---

26. Arnold, "Interview with Smith," 252.

not the cause is real, the sense of being haunted is real in the family and for its neighbors. Since no impartial narrator or authorial voice can verify Red Emmy's witchhood, the family attribute becomes a function of narrative point of view. The "fact" of Emmy's witchhood reflects preconceptions of the narrators and observers and determines what they see and hear.[27] Like tellers of family stories, they shape the past to fit their present needs. Jennifer comes to Hoot Owl Holler knowing she will record quaint mountain ghost sounds because she has been conditioned to expect so by her folklore professor Ripman, and Granny Younger finds evidence of Emmy's witchhood because such evidence authenticates her own self-conception as a seer of things to come.

The indeterminacy at the heart of the narrative becomes part of the design as Smith purposely left the question of Emmy's witchhood unsolved. At her editor's suggestion that "it would be better to leave a central mystery at the core of the novel, which is whether Emmy was a witch or not and whatever happened to her," Smith left out a section on Red Emmy's background. What that section originally included, she said, was a stream-of-consciousness presentation through Red Emmy, indicating that her witchlike behavior was the result of her being sexually molested by a preacher when she was an orphan child. She accepted her editor's idea "to *never* explain" and instead to evoke "mythic elements, making the book mysterious and mystical in a way it would not be if everything in it had been explained away."[28]

As a result of her and her editor's decision, the lingering effect of Red Emmy's curse becomes the burden of the narrators' interpretations, and the novel sets up contradictions among narrators and between narrations and genealogical charts. Granny Younger says that the first Almarine Cantrell returned from his mysterious absence to begin life again at Hoot Owl Holler in August, 1902 (31). In the genealogy, written in cursive as if in a family Bible, Almarine and Pricey Jane's first child Eli is given the birth year of 1899 (95). Yet Sally says in her narrative that at the time of Pearl's graduation the family had no Bible (256).

Whether or not Aldous Rife is correct when he tells Justine Poole that the Cantrell mysteries are results of tales rather than facts (183), the tales flourish and are told to unnamed hearers. In several tales the narration is

27. Suzanne W. Jones, "City Folks in Hoot Owl Holler: Narrative Strategy in Lee Smith's *Oral History*," *Southern Literary Journal*, XX (1987), 102–103.

28. Arnold, "Interview with Smith," 254; Dorothy Combs Hill, "An Interview with Lee Smith," *Southern Quarterly*, XXVIII (1990), 15.

directed to an unnamed "you," by Granny Younger (27, 37, 49), by Ora Mae (208), and by Sally (233); and the tales are spread through time so that no one auditor, except the reader, could hear or read them all. Although several have the quality of family stories told during long evenings by the fireside, some, like Richard Burlage's memoir or Aldous Rife's postcoital talk with Justine Poole, are stories no Cantrell family member would have opportunity to know.

If no central focus of narration or reception exists in the saga, nevertheless, the legend of Red Emmy's witchhood continues as the central feature of the Cantrell family. Granny Younger explains Almarine's morose life by his encounter with Red Emmy and sets forth the legend of Emmy's curse on the family. Almarine senses the lingering curse when he finds Eli dead and Pricey Jane dying (74). Justine Poole repeats the Tug Valley view that Hoot Owl Holler is witch-haunted and that the Cantrells have a curse on them (126, 182). Richard Burlage remembers Rose Hibbetts saying Dory is cursed (160), and Ludie Davenport supplies supporting evidence, like hearing Almarine's ghost dog, that a curse is on the Holler and the Cantrell girls (176). Even Sally, who rebels against the family's sense of being haunted, recognizes both that her mother Dory lived in a waiting dream and on borrowed time before she was killed on the train track on which Richard rode away and that Pearl had the family curse of never being satisfied and of wanting to live several lives (239, 242, 245). Whether or not Almarine the younger believes in the family curse, he is willing to exploit the idea by constructing his theme park on it. When he returns from the mountain cabin with Jennifer's tape recorder and tells her he saw the chair rocking, heard wild laughter, and felt a cold chill (280), his whooping is ambiguous, as much enthusiasm for a profit-making idea as shock that Ora Mae's and Luther's claim the cabin is haunted might be true.

Smith's ambiguity of narration reflects her view that families are mysterious to themselves. She realized that families tell different stories about the same event and wrote *Oral History* to explore "how you can never know the truth, if it exists at all" because "you never know what really happened"; all you know is "what people thought about it." The mystery of the family is also the mystery of the past: "It is always the teller's tale, and you never *finally* know exactly the way it was." The mystery of the past is something "you never quite get at," and the paradox of trying to record the past is that the past loses its vitality as it is recorded.[29]

29. Hill, "Interview," 13; Arnold, "Interview with Smith," 244, 246.

In *Oral History* Smith uses a mix of narrative styles to reach for that ungraspable past. Third-person narratives focusing on one person's awareness include Pricey Jane's puzzle about her own dreamlike past as she enters Black Rock unaware she is about to begin a new life that will become part of Almarine's past (69), Almarine's sullen rage when he finds Pricey Jane dying and Eli dead and takes Dory to Granny Younger (74–81), the funeral two years later for Pricey Jane, Eli, Granny Younger, and Nan, seen from the viewpoints of Louella Hibbetts and Almarine (91, 93), and Justine Poole's and Aldous Rife's musings about the effect Richard Burlage has had on the Cantrells and the community (178–85). First-person narratives are shaped by Granny Younger's belief she has portentous second sight about Emmy's evil influence (27–68), by Rose Hibbetts' jealousy about Almarine's turn from her to Vashti and her willingness to lie that she has rejected Almarine's marriage proposal, by Little Luther Wade's secrecy in planning to shoot Richard Burlage and accept Dory despite family gossip (169–73), by Ludie Davenport's insistence she knows a witch when she finds one near (173–78), by Jink Cantrell's sense of loss as he changes from sensitive boy to hog-scraping and hard-drinking man (186–207), by Ora Mae's defensive plea that she sacrificed her chance to escape the hollow because the Cantrells needed her (207–16), and by Sally's bemused repetition of the story she told her husband Roy to explain how she escaped the family curse (233–78). Richard Burlage's memoirs of late 1923 and early 1924 and the later memoir of his 1933 visit to the area show the third style of narration, first-person written. Jennifer's written "Impressions" while she is visiting Hoot Owl Holler are also first-person but concern herself more than the kin she wants to record. Such documentary narration, Smith says, is another form of showing how the tale is shaped by the teller and how the truth of the past is vitiated in the recording.[30]

If *Oral History* proposes no final version of the Cantrell family past, it suggests at least a hierarchy of reliability in narrations, with written ranking lower than oral. The oral narrations presume a listening audience, though the "you" hearer is not identified. The written narrations, memoirs and "Impressions," are done primarily for the self or for a projected audience, for example, Dr. Ripman or the readers of Burlage's account of his mountain sojourn, and lack the immediacy of an exchange between teller and hearer. More important, they lack the effect of a message received.[31] The crucial

---

30. Hill, "Interview," 13.

31. Ann Goodwin Jones, "The World of Lee Smith," *Southern Quarterly*, XXII (1983), 135; Suzanne Jones, "City Folks," 104–106.

example of such a written message unreceived is Burlage's note to Dory asking her to leave Hoot Owl Holler with him. Stopped by Ora Mae, the undelivered written message changes the course of several lives and leaves Dory to live in a waiting dream, according to Sally.

A third family mystery concerns the gold earrings passed on through the generations as talismanic objects. Pricey Jane brings them into family history from her half-dreamed mother singing a song in words she could not understand (69). One might suspect that they, too, hint of the curse of love as a "killin' crime," for those who wear them live in a waiting dream of dissatisfied love. The two-year-old Dory wears them at Pricey Jane's funeral (94), and later, when she walks with Richard Burlage, they lead to kisses and hopes that cannot be realized (132). After Dory dies on the railroad tracks, Little Luther gives them to Maggie, who escapes their curse by passing them on to Pearl to wear to the Key Club awards banquet (250, 256). After Pearl dies of "complications," Sally sees Ora Mae, "that old, old ugly woman!," hold them briefly to her ears, "let out the awfulest low sad wail [Sally] ever heard," and throw them into the gorge below the family burial ground (277).

The Cantrell family's type scene is the taking of lived-out family members to the burial ground on the windy crest of Hoot Owl Mountain, an open space that is good for visions. As Almarine leads the group to the burial ground for Granny Younger, Pricey Jane, and Eli's funeral service by Brother Lucius Basnight, the occasion becomes one for visions about community and Cantrell fortunes. Louella Hibbetts has her vision of them all growing older and joining Cantrells at the summit (90), the Davenports speculate about the destiny of Red Emmy (91), Ora Mae recognizes she is trapped in the mountains (90), Almarine thinks how a man needs sons (93), and Ora Mae tells the Wade girls she lives in a haunted house (94). The scene is implicitly reenacted in the family's gathering for Dory's funeral amid sardonic laughter, as Sheriff Hubble keeps away the curious public, that it is the first time the law has been welcome at Hoot Owl Holler (250). At Pearl's burial—"the saddest burial [she] ever went to, and the smallest," in Sally's view—it is not only the time for Ora Mae to throw the gold earrings into the gorge but also the time to measure dispersal and vulgarization of the family. Maggie and Lewis Ray are too far away to come, Billy will not leave his rocking chair, and the minister, a friend of Almarine's from Junior Toastmasters, would rather talk about pick-up trucks than destinies (276).

Like the type scenes, references to public history and to folklore measure the Cantrells' progress through generations until finally the two merge in contemporary popular culture. During their early generations the Cantrells live remote from outside history, and only incidental mentions of events such as World War I mark progress through time until, as Richard Burlage notes during his return in 1933, the outside world intrudes and Tug Valley becomes a drab coal-mining company town of slag heaps, rusting machinery, and worn-out people. In the meantime the Cantrells and their kind have lived in a folk culture of birth rituals, hog killings, and religious ecstasies at the Free Will Followers Church on Grassy Creek. The mountain folk have learned to combine new history with old superstitions, as Rose Hibbetts shows when she says she had a phone call from Emmy in hell saying Dory is the one she claims (199). By the time of the narrative present, folk culture has given way to popular culture. Now folk music has become Grand Ole Opry on television, and Almarine and Debra's children, instead of hearing family stories at Ora Mae's knee, have "Magnum, P.I." and "Charlie's Angels" as the furniture of their minds. Almarine demonstrates the ultimate conversion as he sells AmWay instead of moonshine and exploits the family legend of haunted memory in his Ghostland theme park.

As the world of the Cantrells changes, it shows family decline. Richard Burlage and Jennifer Bingham may be exploiters from the outside, uncaring about what effect they have on the mountain family, but the Cantrells have the ghosts of self-destruction in themselves as well. For all their primitive strength, used to survive through generations of poverty and haunted dreams, they want to escape the mountains as much as they are held by them.[32] Dory would leave them all to go away with Richard Burlage, Ora Mae knows the dream of escape to Charleston with Parrot Blankenship, Sally runs away to Florida before she returns to find contentment with Roy, and Pearl, according to Sally, is cursed with wanting to live other lives in the outside world before she returns wounded and ready to die in the mountains. That decline is the intended pattern in the saga is indicated in Smith's observation that "everything gets weaker" in the generations. After the lumber and coal companies come in and the floods take out, the land is "not as strange and strong and beautiful" as it was. So, too, the people falter, and Pearl's "attempt at a grand passion" is "trivial compared, say, to Almarine's grand passion." Even Sally, who is apparently meant to be "a positive image of a woman as the speaker at the end," lacks the narrative

---

32. Suzanne Jones, "City Folks," 104, 110–11.

force of earlier tellers because she is hurried and compromised by the modern world and, lacking their isolation, is less "mythological" than earlier narrators.[33]

Although both Ora Mae and young Almarine can assert the privacy and integrity of the family in warning Jennifer not to come back again with her tape recorder, Almarine's solution to the family legend is not to suppress but to exploit it. In effect, he becomes a man more of the modern world than of the folk in setting up his theme park. To the extent that the family is identified with the cabin on Hoot Owl Mountain, Almarine reenacts, Poesque but modern, the Fall of the House of Cantrell.

In *Family Linen,* published in 1985, by contrast, Lee Smith shows the Hess family of modern southerners fully caught by and immersed in popular culture. The saga convention of linking family to public history now becomes primarily a linkage of family with pastless contemporaneous reference. This late twentieth-century version of a supposedly ordinary southern family, no longer keyed to the Civil War and old catastrophes and guilts, draws its values from the popular present rather than from tradition. The Depression is as far back as family memory can reach, change comes by fashion and economic developments rather than by political or social upheaval, and blacks are part of society but not of the family past or present. There seems to be no basis for a saga of the generations, no sense of a consanguine clan with coherence as a social and economic unit, but only a scattered conjugal family until the members begin to suspect that they are not so ordinary, that their ignored past holds a mystery, a special attribute, and they are forced to contemplate the past and make their peace with it. Then the saga conventions begin to exert their force.

Speaking in September, 1983, and already planning, perhaps working on, *Family Linen,* Smith predicted, "I'm going to write another novel . . . but it's going to be contemporary and about a family and the focus is going to be on versions of family love rather than an attempt to deal with the land and the setting and the lore." [34] She found the vehicle for her exploration of versions of family love in what she called the "Outhouse Murder," a sensational news story that ran in North Carolina papers in December, 1979.

With such headlines as "Horror of Murder Began 35 Years Ago" and

33. Arnold, "Interview with Smith," 246–47.
34. *Ibid.,* 251.

"After 35 Years, Raeford Murder Story Unravels," the Associated Press story told how a reading teacher at Valencia Community College in Florida, Annie Blue Perry, in 1978 was haunted by half-remembered images of her mother and father quarreling during Easter weekend of 1944, of her mother dismembering the naked body of her father, and of later seeing her father's face in the muck of the outhouse privy. Perry was then ten years old. After she had gone to the Federal Bureau of Investigation (FBI) with her story, she called her mother, Winnie Cameron of Timberland community in Hoke County, North Carolina, near Fort Bragg and near the small town of Raeford, shortly before Christmas, 1978, to ask about her father's disappearance. Winnie Cameron refused to answer the question. The FBI monitored the call. On law officers' suggestion, Perry went to a hypnotist to see if under hypnosis she could recover any other suppressed details. On the basis of such additional information and at the suggestion of law enforcement officers, she called her mother again on December 1, 1979, asked her if her father's body was still "in the toilet," and was told by Miss Winnie, "I will tell you after Christmas." On Wednesday, December 12, Annie Blue Perry and her sister June Ivey helped local law officers, directed by Hoke County sheriff David Barrington, locate the site of the old outhouse. Barrington was a long-time friend of Winnie Cameron, who in 1954 had divorced her husband Edward Leon Cameron, age thirty-four when he disappeared, on grounds of separation for more than two years. Winnie Cameron, sixty-nine, over the years had gained a reputation as a hard-working, church-going, single mother who had successfully raised her three children, two daughters and a son, and had become active in Red Cross volunteer work and civic affairs. She was known among neighbors as "the most Christian lady you could hope to come across" and was not known to have had any special men friends since her husband's disappearance. Her family enjoyed somewhat better than average wealth for the area because the Camerons had sold eight thousand acres to the federal government in the late 1920s for part of Fort Bragg.

While law officers dug and began to find bones in the early afternoon, Winnie Cameron watched, then disappeared about 8 A.M. the next morning. She was not located until late Friday. In the meantime, law officers found more bones, the associate chief state medical examiner determined that the body had been dismembered prior to burial, and her son Edward Cameron, Jr., had been summoned from New York. The son borrowed a plane to search the area and discovered his mother's body and her nearby car in a wooded area not far away. Winnie Cameron had shot herself once in the chest with a .32-caliber pistol and had left a confession in an envelope addressed to Sheriff Barrington. He confirmed that the contents contained a confession but refused to supply details to the press. The Fayetteville *Observer* reported that another person had helped bury Edward Cameron's body but that person had died before the case had been reopened.

Details recovered during hypnosis included the daughter's discovery on Easter morning, April 9, 1944, of her mother in the kitchen with the sink full of pots and pans of bloody water, her sight later that day of her father's nude body on the floor in an unused room with gauze wrapped around his hips and groin area, and her sight later that night of a large cardboard box on the back porch. She saw the face in the privy a week later. No information was given about the cause of the quarrel between Edward and Winnie Cameron.[35]

Smith read the story at the time it was breaking and shortly thereafter, discussing the matter with Reynolds Price, thought it would make a "great novel." The story had enough unanswered questions to invite interpretation. In 1985, after publication of *Family Linen,* she recalled:

> I had in my mind for a long time certain characters who would tell their stories. But for a while I didn't have what I wanted to have, a central mystery for everything to center on. Then I read this wonderful story of a murder which happened in North Carolina, 'The Outhouse Murder.' . . . The profound mystery that is at the heart of how any family ever works is there for this family in the question whether or not this very upstanding lady did, in fact, kill her first husband. That's the whole vehicle for the story.[36]

Her story, though recognizably similar, has its key differences. In *Family Linen* the murder occurs in 1940, not 1944, and Sybill sees a large dark figure, not definitely her mother, chopping up a man's body in the yard while a March storm rages. Later, Sybill sees her father's face in the well rather than the privy. In the news account Winnie Cameron leaves a confession and commits suicide; in the novel Elizabeth Hess dies of a stroke and leaves a mystery. Most important, the news account provides no insight into family relationships, whereas the novel explores them. The news account gives

35. Greensboro (N.C.) *Daily News,* December 15, 1979, Sec. B., p. 1 ; December 16, 1979, Sec. A, pp. 1–2; December 21, 1979, Sec. A, p. 10.

36. Hill, "Interview," 18–19.

no indication what happened to the family after the revelation about their mother; the novel becomes a saga in exploring implications of the mystery. The backyard murder becomes only the launching point for the family explorations to follow.

Before she involves the family in its crises, though, Smith is careful to describe a modern southern family, ordinary by Sybill's characterization and immersed in popular culture. Although they hardly recognize it, each member defines himself or herself in relation to the mother who is the mysterious center of the ordinary. The oldest daughter Sybill is clearly what Elizabeth might have become if she had never married. Sybill's life, as she sketches it for hypnotist Dr. Bob Diamond, is one of genteel precision, modern style.[37] Second sister Myrtle Dotson, conventional wife of dermatologist Dr. Don Dotson, shows what her mother might have become with a conventional husband. Although Myrtle's life is traditional in form, she takes her values from popular culture rather than from family past. Third sister Candy Snipes, beautician and widow of a soldier killed in Vietnam, represents the style of life rejected by her genteel mother. She lives in the same town with Elizabeth but in a different world. Of Elizabeth's other two children, the youngest daughter Lacy is most like her mother in her love for poetry and in their parallel experiences of being abandoned by their husbands. Son Arthur, divorced and nurser of a "weak heart," has been an active rebel against his mother's values. Brought up more by Nettie, Elizabeth's sister, than by his mother, he has followed his lust all his life and played in rock groups while his mother "rose above" such outrages.

In the generation of the children's children, the sons and daughters, though in rebellion, ironically feel more respect for family than do their parents. Although Sean, Myrtle and Don's fourteen-year-old son, thinks Magnum on television is more real than his family, he half-consciously hopes for a real family as he sits outside his grandmother's house and remembers how she made chocolate cakes, corrected his manners, and made paper cutouts of little boys holding hands. He is surprised to learn that Jewell Rife was his grandmother's first husband and, stretching his family memory, realizes his middle name Bird was his grandmother's maiden name when he carves his initials, SBD, on the video machine after winning a game (63–66, 143–46). Lacy's daughter Kate can taunt her mother with modern mores by asking what she would do if Kate became pregnant, but on her

---

37. Lee Smith, *Family Linen* (New York, 1985), 20, 29–30.

video game at the Piggly Wiggly store she tries to rescue the "Last American Family" from the "Nuclear Holocaust" (79–80).

Members of Elizabeth's own generation likewise show how the modern southern family has lost its coherence in the welter of popular culture. Her sister Fay, seen as crazy by Elizabeth's children and shunned by Elizabeth, lives more with television, movie, and tabloid personalities like Kenny Rogers, Lady Di, Natalie Wood, and the "Dallas" stars than with her own family. In place of family stories about how ancestors met and married, she turns to "The Wacky Way I Met My Mate" (37, 83–84, 88). Long alienated from Elizabeth and seen as "not a lady" for her tomboyish ways when young and for her irregular arrangements with men when older, Nettie not only lives on the edge of town but has a marginal existence as an embarrassing relative of Elizabeth Hess, lady and leader of the town's poets' circle (193, 220, 237, 251).

In this medley of moderns, it is ironic that the nonblood members are more alert to family loyalties than are the core members. Myrtle's husband Don, orphan and man so without family models in his youth he has to attend "parenting" seminars to learn how to be a father, is the most conscious of needing to keep family matters within the family. He welcomes the chance to keep Elizabeth's house in the family, where it has been for what he estimates as "almost a hundred years" but is actually only seventy-seven (112, 199–20, 255). Nettie's retarded stepson Clinus further acts as family chronicler by broadcasting news of family crises on his sign at the One Stop. So full of contemporary markers is the narrative that one wonders if *Family Linen* is read fifty years hence whether readers will require a steady stream of footnotes to identify references to contemporary popular culture such as yellow pages, "active listening," BMW, "Love Boat" and "Fantasy Island," Rexall, Dr. Thomas Noguchi, and VW bug.

This is the "ordinary" southern family who, in their pastless present, undergo three crises and thereby learn they have a past. In the process of discovering the lingering effect of Elizabeth's genteel power and possible monstrosity, the family demonstrate also how their story has the classic cluster of conventions arranged in the system of the family saga. In the first crisis of Elizabeth's stroke, the family can still think of themselves as ordinary. At the hospital Myrtle can feel ambivalent sorrow at her mother's smallness and fragility while gloating at her mother's helplessness and her memory of how Elizabeth never thought what her children did was good enough (57). Lacy's ambivalence comes from recognizing how much she and her mother are alike and how Elizabeth, always aloof, never really knew her own husband Verner or her children (69). Arthur's response is denial of the seriousness of Elizabeth's condition and, when she dies, shock because he always expected her to get better. His denial further takes the form of lust as he makes a pass at nurse Palucci (92, 106, 110). Candy the beautician tries to take away the marks of mortality by touching up her mother's hair but recognizes that, with her kind of work, she has a special viewpoint on the town's tragedies and, like an artist, offers the image rather than the explanation of why suffering comes (61, 121).

The second crisis, the possibility that the ordinary family might have the dark secret of a genteel mother who is a monster, is prompted by Sybill's memory of seeing their "mother" kill Jewell Rife with an axe and seeing him down the well. Like the Sibylline figures for which she is named, she delivers a cryptic oracle that must be interpreted. Scared about the family's reputation, Myrtle and Don refuse to think about Sybill's accusation, and Myrtle, afraid of revelation of her affair with exterminator Gary Vance, says no exterminators are wanted and no death (67, 156, 163). Lacy wonders if Sybill is correct and thinks that if Elizabeth could kill Jewell for leaving her, she could kill her husband Jack. After hearing Elizabeth's careful arrangements for her own funeral and bequests, though, Lacy realizes that Elizabeth was too much in control of herself to kill Jewell and that the real family secret is Verner Hess's worship of Elizabeth as a lady (131, 162). Although Fay thinks Elizabeth mean, she confuses news of Elizabeth's departure with her own memory of planning to run away with Jewell (84, 125). Arthur feels dismay at Candy's touching up their dead mother's hair but is mystified by Clinus' remark that Candy is not Elizabeth's child (138, 155). At the same time that Candy is glad to see prim Sybill shaken and thinks everybody is crazy sooner or later, she believes Elizabeth had a full life and was too much a lady in life, as in death, to kill Jewell (113, 119, 123).

The family's insistence that Elizabeth was always the lady, however, leads to Lacy's discovery of the family past in Elizabeth's genteel and romantic memoir, self-consciously titled "Days of Light and Darkness." Like the commissary ledger Isaac McCaslin reads to find the secrets of the past, Elizabeth Bird's memoir, read by Lacy, who has no doubt read Faulkner's account of Isaac's discoveries, reveals both the family attribute and the matriarchal-patriarchal struggle of the past. The memoir provides for Lacy a record of the original identity of the Bird family as Lem Bird removed from the Virginia mountains and Mary Davenport came from the Eastern Shore to begin the Bird family in 1906 at Booker Creek. It recounts the family's divided heritage between the gentility of matriarch Mary and the violence of patriarch Lem. During their initial love idyll, Lem's raw emotions are held in check by Mary's gentility, but when Mary dies early from a ruptured appendix, Lem's raw nature begins to emerge and the family decline begins. After chronicling his violent and scandalous behavior, his genteel daughter sees his younger daughters Fay and Nettie repeat his pattern in their wildness. Her voice emerging out of the past through the memoir adds another viewpoint struggling to tell the family story. This voice, as she explains at the opening of the memoir, is that of a questing knight searching through the dark mansion of the past, determined to open every door while armed with Honesty, Courage, and Love (165), and her matriarchal vision is confirmed in her acceptance of Grace Harrison's admonition, "Remember your mother" (180). The divided heritage is embodied in the two talismanic objects left in Elizabeth Bird Rife Hess's desk: the genteel memoir and Lem Bird's revolver. Keeping that heritage divided, Lacy saves the memoir for her daughter Kate and gives the revolver to Myrtle's son Sean.

If Elizabeth is the voice of genteel romance, Nettie is the Cassandra figure who knows the dark side of the inheritance but cannot tell or, if she does tell, cannot be believed. Her memory of past events is reviewed for the reader but apparently is never told to the rest of the family. Remembering Elizabeth's early infatuation with Jewell Rife, she foresaw what had to come but did not warn anyone because "you have to hold your tongue and bide your time if you want to go on living in this world" (213–14). Her Cassandra code finds its limits, though, when Jewell disappears, Elizabeth collapses, and Fay is clearly pregnant with Jewell's child.

The third crisis, Fay's death from a heat stroke while waiting in Clinus' car for Jewell to take her to Florida, precipitates Nettie's recognition that "she must have done it, then, Fay." Nettie realizes, "I never knew it all these years" and "*She* didn't know it either," and by she, "I mean Elizabeth" (255). Although Nettie's conclusion is a product of inference rather than knowledge, her conclusion becomes a family truth, welcomed, no doubt, because it clears Elizabeth. Since Nettie will say no more, Lacy recognizes that with the mystery of Jewell's death perhaps solved but Nettie's knowledge untold, "it's more of a mystery than ever" (255). Neither she nor the rest of the family knows how much Fay understood, nor how much

Clinus, with his eyes "wild and strange," comprehended, because "with a retarded person, you can't tell how much they know, or what they feel, or see" (256). In her way, Lacy responds for the family when she feels recent developments are like a play or a movie and this supposedly ordinary family is revealed as "this odd gaggle . . . teetering here on the brink of the past" (255).

Of the saga conventions not clustered in Elizabeth's memoir, the role of the narrator-historian is the most prominent. While she was beginning to write *Family Linen* and well before she knew how it would work out, Smith said in September, 1983, "Increasingly I've been interested in the technical possibilities that are opened up by manipulating point of view, and I think in my new book I'm going to have it told by different narrators." Manipulate she does, as the point of view changes thirty-two times, with frequent shifts from first to third person and from individual members to the collective family. The shifts to first person also involve shifts in style, from Fay's stream-of-consciousness mix of tabloid and television names, memories of Jewell, and hazy awareness of current happenings in the family to Elizabeth's prim memoir. Smith noted that Elizabeth's mannered and pretentious style, like Richard Burlage's in *Oral History,* was a half-mocking tour de force for her, a voice she liked to assume but could not do straight.[38] The result of multiple narrations, however, is that no central auditor in the family hears all the stories, and the actions and motives of the disparate family remain to them, as Lacy sees, more of a mystery than ever.

In contrast with her miscellany of viewpoints, Smith makes the type scene of the family gathered at the kitchen table the unifier of generations. The kitchen table conference is the scene where the Bird-Hess-Dotson family faces its crises. In the past, the kitchen in Elizabeth's house was where Elizabeth and Jewell began their courtship while Bascom watched with misgivings (218), where Nettie saw Jewell have sex with Fay (233), and where after the catastrophe Nettie and Millard drank coffee and pondered what to do about Fay and Elizabeth (241). In the present it is where Myrtle, Don, and Sybill gather to discuss Sybill's strange accusation (67), where Sean sees the family act "real zooey" as it argues to keep Sybill's suspicion within the family (141), where, after Elizabeth dies without answering Sybill's charge, Sybill and Candy openly argue over Elizabeth's bedroom sets and silently debate who was most in Elizabeth's favor (58), where after Elizabeth's

38. Arnold, "Interview with Smith," 252; Hill, "Interview," 13.

funeral Lacy joins Candy and Arthur in temporary truce by eating together, and where Myrtle finds Elizabeth's shopping list and thinks how she and Elizabeth have made the kitchen the site of rituals they live by (209). In centering family rituals in the kitchen, Smith again asserts the power of matriarchy. Rituals, "any sort of thing that is a celebration of the passing of time, and making an occasion out of things," she says, are the deep subjects women write about and are "as important as slogging through some battle." [39]

Ritual likewise becomes the basis of Smith's comic resolution of the potentially tragic "Outhouse Murder." She makes Candy, the beautician and artist, the chief custodian of rituals. That Candy is the agent of reconciliation can be seen in the way she remakes people while passing on family news. Sybill gets a new hairstyle as she becomes reconciled to giving up Edward Bing as the last Mr. Right, becomes friendly and relaxed, and helps with Karen and Karl's wedding reception. Myrtle accepts becoming forty, gets a "young grandmother" hairdo, and begins to sell real estate. Lacy's Kate gets a pink streak in her hair crown for the family party. Perhaps the greatest reconciliation comes when Candy, Myrtle, Sybill, and Lacy show their new view of Elizabeth by agreeing that their mother, who before thought her children could never do things right, would have approved the wedding and reception they arranged (271).

If realigning actors into reconciled couples is one sign of comic resolution, even more a sign is their dancing and drinking at the reception beside the swimming pool built at Elizabeth's renovated house. While Lacy's Kate and Myrtle's Theresa dance the can-can and Lacy's Bill does fancy dives, the family celebrate on top of the site of the old axe murder and burial in the well. Like Clinus' sign at the One Stop telling Karen and Karl that "today is the first day of the rest of your life," the family tacitly agree that the past cannot be known and turn instead to the future. For them, an ambiguous past is better left unexplained and forgotten. They agree with Smith and L. P. Hartley in the epigraph: "The past is a foreign country: they do things differently there."

To the extent that they are representative of third-generation family sagas, Lee Smith's *Family Linen* and *Oral History*, like Reynolds Price's *Surface of Earth* and *Source of Light*, demonstrate a kind of postmodern skepticism about narration. Although they employ multiple points of view and multiple narrators, they provide no central narrator-historians who

39. Hill, "Interview," 16.

have access to all viewpoints and can assemble coherent views of the generations. Like the multiple lines of narrative in Genesis, the contradictory or conflicting viewpoints sit side by side, giving their partial views of the past and waiting for readers as the ultimate narrator-historians to make meaning as they can.

7

SAGAS, AUTHORS, AND AUDIENCES

Once the family saga is published, it becomes the reader's rather than the author's. Few authors take the opportunity for a second say in their sagas about what they meant or intended, though Allen Tate did so in his revised ending of *The Fathers* in 1977, thirty-nine years after the original. In the hands of readers, the family saga then becomes a matter of assimilation and interpretation, and one issue that arises is whether the saga exists in the world of contemplation as a work of autonomous art or in a pragmatic relationship with its audience. Readers may, for example, be prompted to find or develop their own family histories, as apparently happened after publication of Alex Haley's *Roots* and especially after its televised version. Or they may see the family saga as a political document calling for a political response, such as joining a public demonstration in the manner of Jane Pittman's march on the courthouse in Bayonne. When that happens, the family saga becomes less a reflection on history than a part of history. In such cases the question further arises as to whether the saga was intended for a particular audience or was adopted by its audiences according to their special needs.

In the minds of their audiences, family sagas then become objects of both exegesis and interpretation. Characters in sagas may continue to live in the memories of readers as well as of authors and may become focal points of further speculation as they are adopted into a tradition of the author's, or of the genre's, memorable characters. Cruxes left unresolved in the sagas, such as the puzzle about Jane Pittman's agreement with Jules Reynard's speculations on what went on between Tee Bob Samson and Mary Agnes LeFabre, remain for readers to ponder. Gaps left in the narrative require readers to supply their own explanations and interpretations, about why, for example, Buck McCaslin stopped running from Sophonsiba Beauchamp and married her after the Civil War or about what made Roth Edmonds become aware of his heritage and turn against Henry Beauchamp. Those initiated in expectations of the saga genre likewise are left to ponder the abortive courtship of Buck and Sophonsiba as a variation on the convention of the meeting with the betrothed.

In the task of interpretation readers need to settle in their minds matters of judgment and evaluation raised either explicitly or implicitly by the sagas. Does Isaac McCaslin speak for Faulkner when he reviews a heritage of guilt and renounces it for a life of humility and poverty? And if he does speak for the author, is that decision viable in the developing history of the South and the nation? Readers are similarly left to judge whether the world of Shellmound in Welty's *Delta Wedding* is teetering on the edge of change or remains viable as a legend of happiness beyond historical circumstance. When making such judgments, readers need either to confront the problem of determining the author's intended meaning, if it can be recovered, or to interpret the narrative in light of readers' interests in a later time, as in the case of later views of race relations and women's status. Not least is the need for readers to understand how meanings are conveyed, what techniques are used to present the narrative evidence, and how the saga is managed: what conventions are emphasized or muted or omitted and why.

One answer to such problems comes from the authors themselves, speaking postsaga as sensitive and perhaps privileged readers on what is by then a matter of public record. Acting within the practice of recorded interviews, a phenomenon of mid- and late twentieth-century literary life, they speak as reader to reader about a literary artifact external to them both. As members of the interpretive community, they face the problem of the validity of their memory about their own work and thus, while exceptionally informed about the literary artifact, are subject to verification. One wonders, for example, about the reliability of Faulkner's response when he says Cass Edmonds is Isaac McCaslin's uncle in "Was" or if Lee Smith is remembering something edited out of the novel when she refers to "the wild alcoholic housesitter in *Family Linen*." [1]

For a writer who works from distilled and transmuted memory, like Katherine Anne Porter, talking about a work completed is to open it again to the agony of composition and revision. "I think everyone lives a story three times over," she says. "The first time is when the events occur . . .

---

1. Gwynn and Blotner, eds., *Faulkner in the University*, 38; Hill, "Interview," 11.

then when you remember them . . . and the third time is when you begin to put them into art." Porter explains further what happens when the writer interprets his or her own work: "And there is a fourth time when they ask artists to explain themselves. Tracing the art through the labyrinth of experience . . . is really an impossible undertaking, a little like tapping one's own spinal fluid." To explain symbols, she says, is to expose "something so deep in your own consciousness" that the writer has to become another person, one who sees symbols unthought of as symbols when they were written.[2]

In any case, writers of sagas, speaking their dialogues from within a synchronic limbo, agree that interpretation is the reader's role. When they speak as interpreters, they speak as readers of their own works. Again and again they say with Shirley Ann Grau: "What the writer meant to say is irrelevant. It's what is out there, so that whatever you [the reader] see in it is truly there. . . . There is no one meaning to it. It means whatever the reader sees in it. You [the author] can't put meaning in it anymore than anybody else, any other reader. It means different things to different people, which is of course why you can go back and read it over and over again." Eudora Welty recognizes that "a story writer hopes to suggest all kinds of possibilities" and that a possibility suggested to a reader but not intended by the author is still legitimate: "No, it doesn't bother me one bit if someone interprets something in a different way. . . . The only way I think to err is to completely be out of tone or out of scope of the story or its intention." Toni Morrison says her work expects and demands reader participation in supplying "some of the color, some of the sound." Her writing, she adds, "has to have holes and spaces so the reader can come into it." Reynolds Price acts as his own critic when he explains connections between the epigraph of *Surface of Earth* and the role of blacks as angel messengers in the novel by invoking public knowledge about angels, "not . . . at all in the supernatural sense but in the literal Greek sense of 'messengers.'" And Faulkner has cited multiple examples of his expectations that readers will add meanings, shape them, and even provide editorial decisions. In the interviews at Charlottesville, he recognized that "when the reader has read all these thirteen different ways of looking at the blackbird [*Absalom, Abslom!*], the reader has his own fourteenth image of that blackbird which I would like to think is the truth." When reading "The Bear" as a story separate from *Go Down, Moses,* he insisted, one should regard the

2. Givner, ed., *Porter Conversations*, 36, 54.

hunt for Old Ben as "a dangling clause" in the descriptions of Isaac Mc-
Caslin and recognize Parts IV and V are parts of the novel but not of
the short story; thus, "the way to read that is to skip that when you come
to it." To Malcolm Cowley he said in answer to the problem of the relationship of "Pantaloon in Black" to the McCaslin saga that "Rider was
one of the McCaslin Negroes." Like other readers, Cowley wanted to respond, "Why didn't you say so?"[3]

If Faulkner thought he wrote for a book-reading northern audience
more than for a tale-telling southern one, Ernest Gaines has said on more
than one occasion he hopes for an audience of black youth in the South.
In particular, he wants to encourage black men to regain their confidence
after years of being separated from their paternal place and authority. Morrison, by contrast, believes she writes out of the perspective of black women
for white and black women. Saying she sees more difference between the
perceptions of black women and those of white women than between
black and white men or between black men and women, she wants to show
how black women, used to aggressive behavior, "seem able to combine
the nest [of domestic life] with the adventure [of life outside the home]."
In concurrence, Haley noted that readers' letters in response to the *Reader's
Digest* condensation of *Roots* were 90 percent from white readers. That is,
he confirmed the greater similarity between perceptions of black male writers and those of whites, at least in his case. Price, however, notes that sexual differences among readers of *Surface of Earth* are minor in that both
sexes recognize the dangers of Thanatos inherent in Eros, but women respond in sympathy to the possibility of death in childbirth and men in
guilt.[4]

Acting as their own interpreters, but at a higher and more abstract
level, Price and Grau recognize that their sagas, like most fiction, call for
readers to grapple with larger questions of understanding and spiritual
survival. Since early times, Price says, stories have provided a sense of order through "sequential, even causal patterns," and "the more clearly a

3. Canfield, "Conversation with Grau," 46; Jo Brans, "Struggling Against the Plaid: An
Interview with Eudora Welty," in *Conversations with Welty,* ed. Prenshaw, 300–301; Claudia
Tate, ed., *Black Women Writers,* 125; Price and Ray, *Conversations,* 69; Gwynn and Blotner,
eds., *Faulkner in the University,* 136, 274, 273; Malcolm Cowley, *The Faulkner-Cowley File:
Letters and Memories, 1944–1962* (New York, 1966), 113.

4. Mary Ellen Doyle, "A *MELUS* Interview: Ernest J. Gaines—'Other Things to Write
About,'" *MELUS,* XI (1984), 61; Rowell, "This Louisiana Thing," 50; Claudia Tate, ed., *Black
Women Writers,* 122; "*The Black Scholar* Interviews: Alex Haley," *Black Scholar,* VIII (1976),
39; Price and Ray, *Conversations,* 39, 75.

creature comprehended time and cycle, the stronger [were] his chances for moving with the massive flow of nature, therefore living longer." Seeing narrative as a transaction between teller and audience, Price thinks that a narrative is "an account of something known, especially by the narrator but partially by his audience (their response to total *news* could only be bafflement)" and that "a majority of readers when asked to define *story* will include themselves as audience in their answers." His reading of Old Testament stories convinced him that readers demand "an ultimately consoling effect" and that "only the story which declares our total abandonment [by God] is repugnant and will not be heard for long." Grau likewise views the goal of fiction generally "to make more understandable, more bearable, if you will, the muddle of human life" and in *Keepers of the House* particularly to explore "the evil that good men do"; she says, "I wanted to show the alternative of love and evil" and "the self-destructiveness of hatred."[5]

At the more pragmatic level, saga writers may discuss ex post facto their sources and intentions as part of the meaning readers are to understand but discuss them often in wry knowledge that the intended meaning was not fully realized. Faulkner remembered the dog he used as the model for Lion in "The Bear" as a faithless and savage creature that never performed a heroic action: "There's a case of a sorry, shabby world that don't quite please you, so you create one of your own, so you make Lion a little braver than he was. . . . I'm sure that Lion could have done it, and maybe at times when I wasn't there to record the action, he did do things like that." Margaret Walker admitted she did not realize her character Vyry in *Jubilee* was a close portrait of her great-grandmother, known to her only in family stories, until her mother told her so. Walker thought she had modeled Vyry on her own grandmother, who had told her the stories. In effect, part of her audience knew her story better than the author did. Although she makes them less sympathetic characters than others in *Oral History,* Smith admits that Jennifer with her tape recorder and Richard Burlage with his journal are more like her than is anyone else in the book.[6]

Like other readers, authors as audience provide interpretations of their

5. Price, *A Palpable God,* 15–16, 25–27; Grau, "Essence of Writing," 16; Nancy Campbell, "Miss Grau Eyes Her Novel," New Orleans *Times-Picayune,* June 27, 1965, Sec. 3, p. 5.

6. Gwynn and Blotner, eds., *Faulkner in the University,* 59–60; Phanuel Egejuru and Robert Eliot Fox, "An Interview with Margaret Walker," *Callaloo,* II (1979), 30; Arnold, "Interview with Smith," 250; Hill, "Interview," 16.

sagas in retrospect and in response to other readers. Having made their characters and stories, they get to talk about them as something now external to themselves and sometimes reveal that their interests as readers do not always match their emphases as authors. Smith, for example, says that her favorite character in *Family Linen* is Candy the beautician. Although Candy's perspective is examined through fewer shifts of viewpoint than, say, Myrtle's, Sybill's, Lacy's, or Arthur's and through less extended narrations than Elizabeth's or Nettie's, she represents to Smith "the most successful person in the book . . . an artist figure" who "prepare[s] everybody for every ritual that happens in the town," acts as psychiatrist to her customers, and disseminates the news. And to explain why Myrtle has an affair with the sleazy pest exterminator, Smith the reader provides a psychological reason she could not make explicit, indeed kept ambiguous in the novel: "Often suburban women will yearn for the liberation they imagine to be found in a lover from a lower class." [7]

In Welty's view, houses, like people, have characters to be revealed in the progress of sagas. Both Shellmound in *Delta Wedding* and the Renfro cabin in *Losing Battles* are important: "[They] have a value in the work of fiction because they convey, I hope, the kind of person, the kind of background to which they belong. It is just as evocative to a knowing reader as saying 'they never went to school,' 'they make so-and-so a year,' or 'they are poor whites,' or 'they are ambitious people on the make.'. . . I think it is important, not strictly that you see the house in your mind's eyes, but rather that you know these facts." Like Smith, she could also critique her characters as a reader, providing an emphasis in exposition that was muted in narration. To Welty the reader, Julia Mortimer in *Losing Battles* is the epitome of the teacher in the pre–World War II South, maker of the web of connections tying the generations of Renfros, Beechams, and Vaughns together.[8] Other characters in the action are remarkable to her for the way they first appear as flat and typical but become more complex as they respond to events: Aunt Beck, though gentle, hurts without intending to; Lexie grows through the torments of nursing Julia Mortimer; Judge Moody becomes interested in the kind of people he intended to

7. Hill, "Interview," 19, 17; Ann Jones, "World of Lee Smith," 121.

8. Jan Nordby Gretlund, "An Interview with Eudora Welty," in *Conversations with Welty*, ed. Prenshaw, 214–15; Louis D. Rubin, Jr., "Growing Up in the Deep South: A Conversation with Eudora Welty, Shelby Foote, and Louis D. Rubin, Jr.,"in *The American South*, ed. Rubin, 67.

avoid; and Jack Renfro shows himself to have deeper feelings than does Gloria, who claims to be sensitive about Julia.[9]

Although Price says he does not continue inventing what his characters did after the close of their stories, it is clear with him, as with other saga writers, that these characters continue to live in the imaginations of their creators-as-readers. In his role as reader after finishing *Surface of Earth*, Price speculated in 1975 on the later significance of Hutch Mayfield. That view became central in *Source of Light* in 1980: "It does seem to me that Hutch has either learned or inherited genetically or been given perhaps by the grace of God certain forms of knowledge and control and understanding which were not previously visible in any other member of his family in the past three or four generations."[10] By the time of *Source of Light,* that view, first sensed by the author as reader, becomes the basis for making Hutch the potential narrator-historian of the family vision.

Clearly his own characters continued to live in the imagination for Faulkner. He could speculate on their motives, meanings, and afterlife with other readers twenty and more years after the stories were written. When asked what was the significance of Sophonsiba's presenting the ribbon to Buck McCaslin in "Was," Faulkner invoked backgrounds not explicitly present in the story. Besides noting, as other readers can, that she saw her brother as claimant to the Earldom of Warwick, Faulkner also imagined that "Miss Sophonsiba lived on Walter Scott, probably, and she had nothing to do, and she would read the fine flamboyant tales of chivalry where the maiden cast the veil to the knight in the tournament." When Cynthia Grenier called Isaac McCaslin her favorite character because "he rejected his inheritance," Faulkner answered as reader more judgmentally than he did as author: "And do you think it's a good thing for a man to reject an inheritance? . . . Well, I think a man ought to do more than just repudiate. He should have been more affirmative instead of shunning people." When asked what Isaac means when he says his wife is lost, "was born lost," Faulkner turned to her historical and social time to answer that for her, "sex was something evil, that it had to be justified by acquiring property." According to him, "she was ethically a prostitute," and "sexually she was frigid," and Isaac knew she was incapable of love: "That's probably what he meant." Why does the wife laugh? Because she knows Isaac is serious in his intent to give away his inheritance and she intends to

9. Gretlund, "Interview with Welty," in *Conversations with Welty,* ed. Prenshaw, 223.
10. Price and Ray, *Conversations,* 74.

make him suffer. "Yes, I'm sure she was convinced of that, no matter what he might have said." [11]

Commenting on the enigmatic *Absalom, Absalom!*, Faulkner adopted the reader's wish to have answers in contrast with his author's role in muting answers. Despite his work in revising the novel to render the "facts" contingent and speculative, as a reader he could make Sutpen's motive in his design more explicit than could the speculating narrators: "He wanted to take revenge for all the redneck people against the aristocrat who told him to go around to the back door. He wanted to show that he could establish a dynasty too—he could make himself a king and raise a line of princes." As a reader Faulkner could also extrapolate on Sutpen's harshness to say that if Sutpen thought Charles Bon would destroy his design by exposing that he had a half-Negro son, Sutpen "would have destroyed Bon just as he would have destroyed any other individual who got in his way." Notable in the answer is Faulkner's recognizing Bon as Sutpen's son, a recognition never made certain in the saga. Was Bon in reality part Negro, and if so, when did that identification become important to him? Again, what is contingent in the novel becomes fact in the interpretation: "I think that Bon knew all the time that his mother was part Negress, [but] that wasn't too important [in the Indies and New Orleans]. . . . It became important only when Bon realized it was important to his father." Did Bon know Sutpen was his father? "I should think that his mother dinned that into him as soon as he was big enough to remember, and that he came deliberately to hunt out his father, not for justice for himself, but for revenge for his abandoned mother." By contrast, no narrator in the saga knows if such a woman existed. Did this suppositious woman have a lawyer other than in Shreve's imagination? Faulkner thought so: "There probably was a lawyer. . . . That sounds too logical in Mississippi terms. Yes . . . there was a little lawyer there." Why did Goodhue Coldfield retreat into the attic when the war started? To answer, Faulkner again appealed to general history rather than to the specifics of the narrative: "I think he was probably a Unionist. He probably came from eastern Tennessee where people were Unionists at that time. . . . He had no agrarian tradition behind him in which slavery was an important part of it." Is the Quentin Compson of *Absalom, Absalom!* consistent with the Quentin of *The Sound and the Fury?* "To me he's consistent" but equally erroneous

---

11. Cynthia Grenier, Interview, in *Lion in the Garden*, ed. Meriwether and Millgate, 225; Gwynn and Blotner, eds., *Faulkner in the University*, 275–76.

in both stories, said Faulkner. Making judgments as a reader that he shunned as a novelist, Faulkner thought Shreve "had a truer picture of Sutpen" and "Quentin was still trying to get God to tell him why" in both books.[12] What the reader must do, these saga writers say, is to complete the vision within the saga by supplying coherence to the elements created by the writer, in effect becoming the writer's silent coauthor.

For all their concern with the world inside their sagas, however, these authors have had to recognize that readers look for connections between that world and their own. As readers, they respond to that search for connections, sometimes militantly, sometimes defensively. The external implications of sagas have been cultural and political, often both in the same writer, the perspective varying with time. That is, according to their own testimony as readers, saga writers in the South have been first concerned with getting right the southern reality, its place, customs, and language, and then with recognizing the implications of what they have written. "I have been told that *Jubilee* makes a strong political statement," Walker says, "of which I was not quite as aware as I have been made aware." *Jubilee*, she first thought, was more protest against the historic and literary depiction of black women than militant statement. Evidently, readers helped reshape the author's view of her own work. For Welty in 1956 the value in Faulkner's created world of Yoknapatawpha was its "carefullest and purest representation" heightened to "twice as true as life." By 1972, though, after getting night telephone calls asking her to use her novelistic powers to protest injustices in the South, she could say she had always been writing about injustice, about "love and hate and so on," for "they are human characteristics which [she] had certainly been able to see long before it was pointed out to [her] by what happened in those years." She had been writing about them "from the inside," and the political dimension "stated from the outside . . . seemed to [her] so thin and artificial."[13]

For southern writers, getting the culture right was primary, getting the politics right only incidental. And language was the key. They divided, though, on whether southern culture in their sagas was monolithic or diverse. Price noted that though the South is larger than France, more

---

12. Gwynn and Blotner, eds., *Faulkner in the University*, 97–98, 272–73, 93, 274–75.

13. Egejuru and Fox, "Interview with Walker," 29; Eudora Welty, "Place in Fiction," in *The Eye of the Story: Selected Essays and Reviews* (New York, 1978), 126–27; William F. Buckley, Jr., " 'The Southern Imagination': An Interview with Eudora Welty and Walker Percy," in *Conversations with Welty*, ed. Prenshaw, 100.

similarity exists between Durham, North Carolina, and Jackson, Mississippi, eight hundred miles distant, than between Durham and Philadelphia, four hundred miles to the north. In Philadelphia they speak "an utterly different dialect." His writing reflected, he thought, "the way men and women have talked in the South in the last fifty or sixty years." Going to another place would require one having to learn "a kind of second language." To Welty, southern sense of place and language is so local that Tennessee and Virginia are different from Mississippi, and Alabama, parts of Georgia, and Louisiana are "totally different," but "they all have their own truths," she saw. For Morrison, black culture and language rather than southern, were the common bond. Whether in Maine, Ohio, or points south, what is important remains the same: "I know what the language will be like. . . . You can change the plate, but the menu would still be the same." [14] From her perspective after the great migration, her people are southern blacks rather than black southerners.

Most saga writers have abjured working with political purposes in mind. Gaines has noted that he wrote *Autobiography of Miss Jane* "when Mr. [S. I.] Hayakawa let the cops on campus" at San Francisco State University and realized "most people thought I should be writing something more contemporary" than a book about a hundred-year-old woman in rural Louisiana. But political purpose is dangerous to an author trying to get the story and characters right. "The writer should be very detached from his work," like a heart surgeon in an operation. "To write well, you can't be crying as you're cutting someone's heart out." Grau similarly thought political and literary intentions should be separated, nonfiction articles for social criticism, fiction for storytelling: "When I do nonfiction, I've got an ax to grind. When I do fiction, I've got a story to tell." Welty remarked that crusading put the editorial writer on the opposite side of language from the novelist: "The only thing at stake is the proper use of words for the proper ends." The crusader, having started with generalities, must end with generalities and judgment; the fiction writer produces climaxes rather than judgments. [15]

In contrast, Walker sees that "everything is political," that "everything you do has political connotations." Citing W. E. B. DuBois' doctrine of

14. Price and Ray, *Conversations*, 24, 217; Gretlund, "Interview with Welty," in *Conversations with Welty*, ed. Prenshaw, 215; Claudia Tate, ed., *Black Women Writers*, 119.

15. Doyle, "Gaines—Other Things to Write," 60; Jeanie Blake, "Interview with Gaines," 5; Carlton Cremeens, "Exclusive Interview," 22; Eudora Welty, "Must the Novelist Crusade?," in *Eye of the Story*, 147, 149.

the twoness of black Americans, she takes "political" to mean consciousness of cultural pluralism and resistance to the idea of assimilation. Randall Ware's ideas in *Jubilee,* she says, were not ahead of his time; they have
always been part of the black mind. Beyond characterization of Ware's
ideas, though, Walker had more specific purposes. One was to enable her
readers to reshape their images of black women from powerless and ex-
ploited stereotypes in previous fiction, from "the mammy, the faithful
retainer, the pickaninny, Little Eva and Topsy, the tragic mulatto, the con-
jure woman or witch, the sex object, the bitch goddess, the harlot and
prostitute and, last but not least, the matriarch," into active and resourceful
presences like Vyry. The second was to change her readers' sense of class
for blacks and to recognize that black women, like Walker herself, can be
middle-class professionals: "I'm a third generation college graduate. Society doesn't want to recognize that there's this kind of writer. I'm the
Ph.D. black woman. That's horrible." Walker's third purpose was to show
that traditional black religion has been a tool of the system and has op-
pressed blacks. Gaines supported that purpose when he observed that "the
Christian religion" has failed to bring black fathers and sons together or
give the black father "a political position or any position of authority" to
bring back sons. If religion cannot, then literature should have its chance.
Indeed, Gaines considered literature as the instrument for promoting black
self-worth. He hoped the people he wrote about would realize that life in
rural Louisiana is a meaningful part of the larger world: "I'm trying to
write about people I feel are worth writing about, to make the world aware
of them, make them aware of themselves. They've always thought literature is written about someone else, and it's hard to convince them they
are worthy of literature." Haley likewise noted that *Roots* has implications
for new social and political consciousness among blacks. Telling the saga
of his family, he said, is telling the saga of all black people, and he expected
them to recognize their larger world in that of his family.[16]

Clearly, the social and political climate of the 1970s promoted political interpretations of black family sagas whether or not their authors intended them originally. The same can be noted for family sagas written
in other times of political and social stress. If his political meanings were
secondary, or at least diffused, as he struggled to write *The Grandissimes*

16. Egejuru and Fox, "Interview with Margaret Walker," 29–31; Claudia Tate, ed., *Black
Women Writers,* 201–204; Egejuru and Fox, "Interview with Walker," 30; Rowell, "This
Louisiana Thing," 40; Doyle, "Gaines—Other Things to Write," 60–61; "*The Black Scholar*
Interviews," 40.

in the 1870s, after a decade of polemics on the cause of the freedman George Washington Cable could say in "My Politics" in 1889, "I meant to make *The Grandissimes* as truly a political work as it has ever been called." During the Depression in 1935, after he had completed his Vaiden trilogy, T. S. Stribling actively promoted his fiction as propaganda. Propaganda persuades by emotion, not reason, he said, and the emotions in fiction could act as "enfilading fire" on readers' convictions "to persuade somebody to change his mind." Propaganda, including fiction, he thought, was "the only instrument that will move a democracy." [17]

The political context, however, is only one within which family sagas are read and interpreted. Having a context is the important consideration in reading sagas and is apparently the reason the literary tradition of family sagas is alive and well. Within the South, a region still biblically oriented in memory if not in working detail, the operative context is still some version of Providential Order. The mysterious and perhaps divine will yet operates through human agency, and the family saga, with its long reaches of time and memory, affords glimpses of purpose beyond the daily struggles of generations. It is those moments of vision to which readers turn as much as to the dismaying, sometimes violent, sometimes sardonically humorous acts of people caught in the grip of immediate life. Because family sagas afford a long view of history rendered in terms of individual people, not abstract forces, readers can contrast the new with the old; see, if not totally understand, actions of the patriarchs and matriarchs; observe the repeated scenes of the ancestors; hear their voices echo through time; and, like minor gods, preside over it all. Like Jack Burden in *All the King's Men* overlooking the crowds on the capitol lawn during impeachment proceedings against Willie Stark, readers of family sagas can view present events with history past and future looking over their shoulders:

> I felt like God, because I had the knowledge of what was to come. I felt like God brooding on History, for as I stood there I could see a little chunk of History right there in front. . . . Over beyond the statues, there were the people who weren't History yet. Not quite. But to me they looked like History, because I knew the end of the event of which they were a part. Or thought I knew the end.

17. Turner, ed., *Negro Question*, 15; Piacentino, *T. S. Stribling*, 126; Eckley, *T. S. Stribling*, 111.

BIBLIOGRAPHY

PRIMARY SOURCES

Cable, George Washington. *The Grandissimes: A Story of Creole Life.* 1880; rpr. New York, 1957.

Caruthers, William Alexander. *The Cavaliers of Virginia, or The Recluse of Jamestown.* 2 vols. 1834; rpr. Ridgewood, N.J., 1968.

———. *The Knights of the Golden Horseshoe: A Traditionary Tale of the Cocked Hat Gentry.* 1845; rpr. Chapel Hill, 1970.

Faulkner, William. *Absalom, Absalom!* 1936; rpr. New York, 1951.

———. *Go Down, Moses.* 1942; rpr. New York, 1951.

Gaines, Ernest J. *The Autobiography of Miss Jane Pittman.* New York, 1971.

Gordon, Caroline. *Penhally.* 1931; rpr. New York, 1971.

Grau, Shirley Ann. *The Keepers of the House.* New York, 1964.

Haley, Alex. *Roots.* New York, 1976.

Lytle, Andrew. *A Wake for the Living: A Family Chronicle.* New York, 1975.

Morrison, Toni. *Song of Solomon.* New York, 1977.

Porter, Katherine Anne. *The Collected Stories.* New York, 1965.

———. *Pale Horse, Pale Rider.* New York, 1939.

Price, Reynolds. *The Source of Light.* New York, 1981.

———. *The Surface of Earth.* New York, 1975.

Smith, Lee. *Family Linen.* New York, 1985.

———. *Oral History.* New York, 1983.

Stribling, T. S. *The Forge.* Garden City, N.J., 1931.

———. *The Store.* New York, 1932.

———. *Unfinished Cathedral.* New York, 1934.

Tate, Allen. *The Fathers and Other Fiction.* Edited by Thomas Daniel Young. Baton Rouge, 1977.

Walker, Margaret. *Jubilee.* Boston, 1966.

Welty, Eudora. *Delta Wedding.* New York, 1946.

———. *Losing Battles.* New York, 1970.

SECONDARY SOURCES

Books

Alter, Robert. *The Art of Biblical Narrative*. New York, 1981.

Armens, Sven. *Archetypes of the Family in Literature*. Seattle, 1966.

Bishop, Freeman. *Allen Tate*. New York, 1967.

Botkin, B. A. *A Treasury of Southern Folklore*. New York, 1949.

Boyers, Robert. *Excursions: Selected Literary Essays*. Port Washington, N.Y., 1977.

Brinkmeyer, Robert. *Three Catholic Writers of the Modern South*. Jackson, 1985.

Brooks, Cleanth. *William Faulkner: The Yoknapatawpha Country*. New Haven, 1963.

Cable, George Washington. *Old Creole Days: A Story of Creole Life*. 1879; rpr. New York, 1957.

Calhoun, Arthur W. *A Social History of the American Family from Colonial Times to the Present*. Vol. III of 3 vols. 1917; rpr. New York, 1977.

Cowley, Malcolm. *The Faulkner-Cowley File: Letters and Memories, 1944–1962*. New York, 1966.

Creighton, Joanne V. *Faulkner's Craft of Revision: The Snopes Trilogy, "The Unvanquished," and "Go Down, Moses."* Detroit, 1977.

Davenport, F. Garvin, Jr. *The Myth of Southern History: Historical Consciousness in Twentieth-Century Southern Literature*. Nashville, 1970.

Davis, Curtis Carroll. *Chronicler of the Cavaliers: A Life of the Virginia Novelist Dr. William A. Caruthers*. Richmond, 1953.

Dekker, George. *The American Historical Romance*. New York, 1987.

DeMouy, Jane Krause. *Katherine Anne Porter's Women: The Eye of Her Fiction*. Austin, 1983.

de Rougemont, Denis. *Love in the Western World*. Translated by Montgomery Belgion. New York, 1940.

Devlin, Albert J., ed. *Welty: A Life in Literature*. Jackson, 1987.

Dollarhide, Louis, and Anne J. Abadie, eds. *Eudora Welty: A Form of Thanks*. Jackson, 1979.

DuBois, W. E. B. *The Souls of Black Folk*. 1903; rpr. New York, 1969.

Dupree, Robert S. *Allen Tate and the Augustan Imagination*. Baton Rouge, 1983.

Eckley, Wilton J. *T. S. Stribling*. Boston, 1975.

Ekström, Kjell. *George W. Cable: A Study of His Early Life and Work*. Cambridge, Mass., 1950.

Evans, Elizabeth. *Eudora Welty*. New York, 1981.

Fain, John Tyree, and Thomas Daniel Young, eds. *The Literary Correspondence of Donald Davidson and Allen Tate*. Athens, Ga., 1974.

Fleishman, Avrom. *The English Historical Novel: Walter Scott to Virginia Woolf*. Baltimore, 1971.

Fowler, Alastair. *Kinds of Literature: An Introduction to the Theory of Genres and Modes.* Cambridge, Mass., 1982.

Frazier, E. Franklin. *The Negro Family in the United States.* Rev. and abr. ed. Chicago, 1966.

Freistat, Rose Anne C. *Caroline Gordon as Novelist and Woman of Letters.* Baton Rouge, 1984.

Frye, Northrop. *The Great Code: The Bible and Literature.* New York, 1982.

Gaines, Francis Pendleton. *The Southern Plantation.* New York, 1924.

Gaudet, Marcia, and Carl Wooten, eds. *Porch Talk with Ernest Gaines: Conversations on the Writer's Craft.* Baton Rouge, 1990.

Gill, Richard. *Happy Rural Seat: The English Country House and the Literary Imagination.* New Haven, 1972.

Girouard, Mark. *Life in the English Country House.* New Haven, 1978.

Givner, Joan. *Katherine Anne Porter: A Life.* New York, 1982.

――――, ed. *Katherine Anne Porter: Conversations.* Jackson, 1987.

Gossett, Louise Y. *Violence in Recent Southern Fiction.* Durham, 1965.

Gray, Richard J. *The Literature of Memory.* Baltimore, 1977.

――――. *Writing the South: Ideas of an American Region.* New York, 1980.

Gunkel, Herman. *The Legend of Genesis: The Biblical Saga and History.* Translated by W. H. Carruth. New York, 1964.

Gwynn, Frederick L., and Joseph L. Blotner, eds. *Faulkner in the University: Class Conferences at the University of Virginia, 1957–1958.* New York, 1965.

Henderson, Harry B. *Versions of the Past: The Historical Imagination in American Fiction.* New York, 1974.

Hendrick, Willene, and George Hendrick. *Katherine Anne Porter.* Rev. ed. Boston, 1988.

Hicks, Jack. *In the Singer's Temple.* Chapel Hill, 1981.

Hill, Dorothy Combs. *Lee Smith.* Boston, 1992.

Hobson, Fred. *Tell About the South: The Southern Rage to Explain.* Baton Rouge, 1983.

Hoffman, Fredrick J. *The Art of Southern Fiction: A Study of Some Modern Novelists.* Carbondale, 1967.

Hubbell, Jay B. *The South in American Literature, 1607–1900.* Durham, 1954.

I'll Take My Stand: The South and the Agrarian Tradition. 1930; rpr. New York, 1962.

Irving, Washington. *Bracebridge Hall, or The Humourists.* Edited by Herbert F. Smith. 1821; rpr. Boston, 1978.

Kennedy, John Pendleton. *Swallow Barn, or A Sojourn in the Old Dominion.* Rev. ed. New York, 1852.

Kent, Thomas. *Interpretation and Genre: The Role of Generic Perceptions in the Study of Narrative Texts.* Cranbury, N.J., 1986.

Kimball, Sue Laslie, and Lynn Veach Sadler, eds. *Reynolds Price, From "A Long and Happy Life" to "Good Hearts," with a Bibliography.* Fayetteville, N.C., 1988.

Kreyling, Michael. *Eudora Welty's Achievement of Order.* Baton Rouge, 1980.

———. *Figures of the Hero in Southern Narrative.* Baton Rouge, 1986.

Lee, Harper. *To Kill a Mockingbird.* Philadelphia, 1960.

Lucas, Mark. *The Southern Vision of Andrew Lytle.* Baton Rouge, 1986.

Lytle, Andrew. *The Hero with the Private Parts.* Baton Rouge, 1966.

MacKethan, Lucinda. *The Dream of Arcady: Place and Time in Southern Literature.* Baton Rouge, 1980.

Mailloux, Steven. *Interpretive Conventions: The Reader in the Study of Narrative Texts.* Ithaca, 1982.

Manning, Carol S. *With Ears Opening Like Morning Glories: Eudora Welty and the Love of Storytelling.* Westport, Conn., 1985.

McClung, Willam Alexander. *The Country House in English Renaissance Poetry.* Berkeley, 1977.

Meriwether, James B., and Michael Millgate, eds. *Lion in the Garden: Interviews with William Faulkner, 1926–1962.* New York, 1968.

Muhlenfeld, Elisabeth, ed. *William Faulkner's "Absalom, Absalom!": A Critical Casebook.* Jackson, 1984.

Nance, William L., s.m. *Katherine Anne Porter and the Art of Rejection.* Chapel Hill, 1964.

O'Brien, John, ed. *Interviews with Black Writers.* New York, 1973.

Piacentino, Edward J. *T. S. Stribling: Pioneer Realist in Modern Southern Literature.* New York, 1988.

Porter, Katherine Anne. *The Collected Essays and Occasional Writings of Katherine Anne Porter.* New York, 1970.

———. *The Days Before.* New York, 1952.

Prenshaw, Peggy Whitman, ed. *Conversations with Eudora Welty.* Jackson, 1984.

———, ed. *Eudora Welty: Critical Essays.* Jackson, 1979.

Price, Reynolds. *A Palpable God.* New York, 1978.

———. *Things Themselves: Essays and Scenes.* New York, 1972.

Price, Reynolds, and William Ray. *Conversations: Reynolds Price and William Ray.* Memphis, 1976.

Ragussis, Michael. *Acts of Naming: The Family Plot in Fiction.* New York, 1987.

Randisi, Jennifer Lynn. *A Tissue of Lies: Welty and the Southern Romance.* New York, 1982.

Reed, John Shelton. *The Enduring South: Subcultural Persistence in Mass Society.* Chapel Hill, 1974.

———. *One South: An Ethnic Approach to Regional Culture.* Baton Rouge, 1982.

———. *Southern Folk, Plain and Fancy: Native White Social Types.* Athens, Ga., 1987.

Ridgely, Joseph V. *John Pendleton Kennedy*. New York, 1966.

Rollyson, Carl E. *Uses of the Past in the Novels of William Faulkner*. Ann Arbor, 1984.

Rooke, Constance. *Reynolds Price*. Boston, 1983.

Rubin, Louis D., Jr., ed. *The American South: Portrait of a Culture*. Baton Rouge, 1980.

Rubin, Louis D., Jr., and C. Hugh Holman, eds. *Southern Literary Study: Problems and Possibilities*. Chapel Hill, 1975.

Schleuter, Paul. *Shirley Ann Grau*. Boston, 1981.

Schoenberg, Estella. *Old Times and Talking: Quentin Compson in Faulkner's "Absalom, Absalom!" and Related Works*. Jackson, 1977.

Scholes, Robert. *Structuralism in Literature: An Introduction*. New Haven, 1974.

Scholes, Robert, and Robert Kellogg. *The Nature of Narrative*. New York, 1966.

Shoumantoff, Alex. *Mountain of Names: A History of the Human Family*. New York, 1985.

Speiser, E. A. *The Anchor Bible Genesis*. Garden City, N.Y., 1964.

Squires, Radcliffe. *Allen Tate: A Literary Biography*. New York, 1971.

Stewart, John L. *The Burden of Time: The Fugitives and Agrarians*. Princeton, 1965.

Stone, Elizabeth. *Black Sheep and Kissing Cousins: How Our Family Stories Shape Us*. New York, 1988.

Stuckey, William J. *The Pulitzer Prize Novels: A Critical Backward Look*. Norman, 1981.

Tate, Allen. *Collected Poems, 1919–1976*. New York, 1977.

———. *Essays of Four Decades*. Chicago, 1968.

———. *Memoirs and Opinions, 1926-1974*. Chicago, 1975.

Tate, Claudia, ed. *Black Women Writers at Work*. New York, 1983.

Tavuchis, Nicholas, and William J. Goode. *The Family in Literature*. New York, 1975.

Taylor, William R. *Cavalier and Yankee: The Old South and American National Character*. New York, 1961.

Teubal, Savina J. *Sarah the Priestess: The First Matriarch of Genesis*. Athens, Ohio, 1984.

Tobin, Patricia. *Time and the Novel: The Genealogical Imperative*. Princeton, 1978.

Trelease, Allen W. *White Terror: The Ku Klux Klan Conspiracy and Southern Reconstruction*. New York, 1971.

Turner, Arlin. *George W. Cable: A Biography*. Baton Rouge, 1966.

———, ed. *Critical Essays on George W. Cable*. Boston, 1980.

———, ed. *The Negro Question*. Garden City, N.Y., 1958.

Unrue, Darlene. *Truth and Fiction in Katherine Anne Porter's Fiction*. Athens, Ga., 1985.

Vande Kieft, Ruth M. *Eudora Welty.* New York, 1962.

Waldron, Ann. *Close Connections: Caroline Gordon and the Southern Renaissance.* New York, 1987.

Watt, Ian. *Rise of the Novel: Studies in Defoe, Richardson and Fielding.* Berkeley, 1957.

Welty, Eudora. *The Eye of the Story: Selected Essays and Reviews.* New York, 1978.

Westling, Louise. *Sacred Groves and Ravaged Gardens: The Fiction of Eudora Welty, Carson McCullers, and Flannery O'Connor.* Athens, Ga., 1985.

Williams, Raymond. *The Country and the City.* New York, 1973.

Young, Thomas Daniel, and Elizabeth Sarcone, eds. *The Lytle-Tate Letters: The Correspondence of Andrew Lytle and Allen Tate.* Jackson, 1987.

Zeitlin, Steven J., Amy J. Kotkin, and Holly Cutting-Baker, eds. *A Celebration of American Family Folklore.* New York, 1982.

Articles, Essays, and Stories

Adamowski, T. H. "Isaac McCaslin and the Wilderness of the Imagination." *Centennial Review,* XVII (1973), 92–112.

Ahlport, Daniel B. "Tate's *The Fathers* and the Problem of Tradition." *Southern Studies,* XIX (1980), 355–64.

Andersson, Theodore. "The Displacement of the Heroic Ideal in the Family Sagas." *Speculum,* XLV (1970), 575–93.

Andrews, William L. "'We Ain't Going Back There': The Idea of Progress in *The Autobiography of Miss Jane Pittman." Black American Literature Forum,* XI (1971), 146–49.

Arnold, Edwin T. "An Interview with Lee Smith." *Appalachian Journal,* XI (1984), 240–54.

Baker, J. F. "*PW* Interviews: Alex Haley." *Publisher's Weekly,* September 6, 1976, pp. 8–9, 12.

Barker, Stephen. "From Old Gold to I.O.U.'s: Ike McCaslin's Debased Genealogical Coin." *Faulkner Journal,* III (1987), 2–25.

Behrens, Ralph. "Collapse of Dynasty: The Thematic Center of *Absalom, Absalom!" PMLA,* LXXXIX (1974), 24–33.

Benert, Annette. "The Four Fathers of Isaac McCaslin." *Southern Humanities Review,* IX (1975), 423–33.

"*The Black Scholar* Interviews: Alex Haley." *Black Scholar,* VIII (1976), 33–40.

Blake, Jeanie. "Interview with Ernest Gaines." *Xavier Review,* III (1983), 1–13.

Blake, Susan. "Folklore and Community in *Song of Solomon." MELUS,* VII (1980), 77–82.

Boatright, Mody C. "The Family Saga as a Form of Folklore." In *The Family Saga and Other Phases of Folklore,* edited by Mody C. Boatright, with Robert B. Down and John T. Flanagan. Urbana, 1958.

BIBLIOGRAPHY

Boyd, Herb. "Plagiarism and the *Roots* Suit." *First World,* II (1979), 31–33.

Bryant, Jerry H. "Ernest J. Gaines: Change, Growth, and History." *Southern Review,* n.s., X (1974), 851–64.

Buloski, Anthony. "The Burden of Home: Shirley Ann Grau's Fiction." *Critique,* XXVIII (1987), 181–93.

Callahan, John. "Image Making: Tradition and the Two Versions of *The Autobiography of Miss Jane Pittman*." *Chicago Review,* XXIX (1977), 45–62.

Campbell, Nancy. "Miss Grau Eyes Her Novel." New Orleans *Times-Picayune,* June 27, 1965, Sec. 3, p. 15.

Canfield, John. "A Conversation with Shirley Ann Grau." *Southern Quarterly,* XXV (1987), 39–52.

Carpenter, Lynette. "The Battle Within: The Beleaguered Consciousness in Allen Tate's *The Fathers*." *Southern Literary Journal,* VIII (1976), 3–23.

Carson, Barbara Harrell. "Winning: Katherine Anne Porter's Women." In *The Authority of Experience: Essays in Feminist Criticism,* edited by Arlyn Diamond and Lee R. Edwards. Amherst, 1977.

Chappell, Fred. "A Choice of Romantics: Allen Tate's *The Fathers*." *Shenandoah,* XL (1990), 30–42.

Cheatham, George. "Literary Criticism, Katherine Anne Porter's Consciousness, and the Silver Dove." *Studies in Short Fiction,* XXV (1988), 109–15.

Chicatelli, Louis W. "Family as Fate in Reynolds Price's *The Surface of Earth* and *The Source of Light*." *Mid-Hudson Language Studies,* V (1982), 129–36.

Cremeens, Carlton. "An Exclusive Tape-Recorded Interview with Shirley Ann Grau." In *Writer's Yearbook.* New York, 1966.

Dalke, Anne French. "'Love ought to be like religion, Brother Milt': An Examination of the Civil War and Reconstruction Trilogy of T. S. Stribling." *Southern Literary Journal,* XIV (1981), 24–31.

Davis, Thadious. "'Be Sutpen's Hundred': Imaginative Projection of Landscape in *Absalom, Absalom!*" *Southern Literary Journal,* XIII (1981), 3–14.

De Arman, Charles. "Milkman as the Archetypal Hero: 'Thursday's Child Has Far to Go.'" *Obsidian,* VI (1980), 56–59.

Doyle, Mary Ellen. "A *MELUS* Interview: Ernest J. Gaines—'Other Things to Write About.'" *MELUS,* XI (1984), 59–81.

Egejuru, Phanuel, and Robert Eliot Fox. "An Interview with Margaret Walker." *Callaloo,* II (1979), 29–35.

Ferris, Sumner. "Chronicle, Chivalric Biography, and Family Tradition in Fourteenth-Century England." *Studies in Medieval Culture,* XIV (1930), 25–38.

Flanders, Jane. "Katherine Anne Porter and the Ordeal of Southern Womanhood." *Southern Literary Journal,* IX (1976), 47–60.

Flora, Joseph M. "Fiction in the 1920s: Some New Voices." In *The History of Southern Literature,* edited by Louis D. Rubin, Jr., *et al.* Baton Rouge, 1985.

Gaines, Ernest J. "Miss Jane and I." *Callaloo,* I (1978), 23–38.

Garrett, Kim S. "Family Stories and Sayings." *Publications of the Texas Folklore Society,* XXX (1961), 273–81.

Gaudet, Marcia, and Carl Wooten. "An Interview with Ernest J. Gaines." *New Orleans Review,* XIV (1987), 62–70.

Gerber, David A. "Haley's *Roots* and Our Own: An Inquiry into the Nature of a Popular Phenomenon." *Journal of Ethnic Studies,* V (1977), 87-111.

Gibbon, Kay. "Planes of Language and Time: The Surfaces of the Miranda Stories." *Kenyon Review,* n.s., X (1988), 74–79.

Going, William T. "Alabama Geography in Shirley Ann Grau's *The Keepers of the House.*" *Alabama Review,* XX (1967), 62–68.

Gordon, Caroline. "Always Summer." *Southern Review,* n.s., VII (1971), 430–45.

———. "Cock-Crow." *Southern Review,* n.s., I (1965), 554–69.

Grau, Shirley Ann. "The Essence of Writing." In *The Writer's Handbook, 1977,* edited by A. S. Burack. Boston, 1977.

———. "Shirley Ann Grau." In *World Authors, 1950–1970,* edited by John Wakeman. New York, 1975.

Greensboro (N.C.) *Daily News,* December 15, 1979, Sec. B, p. 1; December 16, 1979, Sec. A, pp. 1–2; December 21, 1979, Sec. A, p. 10.

Haley, Alex. "Epilogue." In *The Autobiography of Malcolm X.* New York, 1973.

———. "Foreword." In *From Freedom to Freedom: African Roots in American Soil,* edited by Mildred Bain and Ervin Lewis. New York, 1977.

Harris, A. Leslie. "Myth as Structure in Toni Morrison's *Song of Solomon.*" *MELUS,* VII (1980), 69–76.

Harris, Trudier. "'I Wish I Was a Poet': The Character of the Artist in Alice Childress's *Like One of the Family.*" *Black American Literature Forum,* XIV (1980), 24–30.

Hicks, Jack. "To Make These Bones Live: History and Community in Ernest Gaines' Fiction." *Black American Literature Forum,* XI (1977), 9–19.

Hill, Dorothy Combs. "An Interview with Lee Smith." *Southern Quarterly,* XXVIII (1990), 5–19.

Holman, C. Hugh. "*The Fathers* and the Historical Imagination." In *Literary Romanticism in America,* edited by William L. Andrews. Baton Rouge, 1981.

Jones, Ann Goodwin. "The World of Lee Smith." *Southern Quarterly,* XXII (1983), 115–39.

Jones, Suzanne W. "City Folks in Hoot Owl Holler: Narrative Strategy in Lee Smith's *Oral History.*" *Southern Literary Journal,* XX (1987), 101–12.

Kane, Patricia. "An Irrepressible Conflict: Allen Tate's *The Fathers.*" *Critique,* X (1968), 9–16.

Kaufman, Wallace. "'Notice I'm Still Smiling': Reynolds Price." In *Kite-Flying and Other Irrational Acts,* edited by John Carr. Baton Rouge, 1972.

Kinney, Arthur F. "'Topmost in the Pattern': Family Structure in Faulkner." In

BIBLIOGRAPHY

New Directions in Faulkner Studies, edited by Doreen Fowler and Ann J. Abadie. Jackson, 1984.

Klotman, Phyllis R. "Oh Freedom: Women and History in Margaret Walker's *Jubilee.*" *Black American Literature Forum,* XI (1977), 139–45.

Klotz, Marvin. "Procrustean Revision in Faulkner's *Go Down, Moses.*" *American Literature,* XXXVII (1965), 1–16.

Krause, David. "Reading Bon's Letter and Faulkner's *Absalom, Absalom!*" *PMLA,* XCIX (1984), 225–41.

Kreyling, Michael. "Motion and Rest in the Novels of Reynolds Price." *Southern Review,* n.s., XVI (1980), 853–68.

Ladd, Barbara. "'An Atmosphere of Hints and Allusions': Bras Coupé and the Context of Black Insurrection in *The Grandissimes.*" *Southern Quarterly,* XXIX (1991), 63–76.

Law, Richard. "'Active Faith' and Ritual in *The Fathers.*" *American Literature,* LV (1983), 345–66.

Lensing, George S. "The Metaphor of Family in *Absalom, Absalom!*" *Southern Review,* n.s., XI (1975), 109–14.

Lytle, Andrew. "Caroline Gordon and the Historic Image." *Sewanee Review,* LVII (1949), 560–86.

———. "Jericho, Jericho, Jericho." *Southern Review,* 1st ser., I (1936), 753–64.

———. "Mister McGregor." *Virginia Quarterly Review,* XI (1935), 218–27.

Mickelson, David. "The Campfire and the Hearth in *Go Down, Moses.*" *Mississippi Quarterly,* XXXVIII (1985), 310–27.

Mizener, Arthur. Introduction to *The Fathers,* by Allen Tate. Chicago, 1960.

Morehead, Martha H. "George W. Cable's Use of the Bible in His Fiction and Major Polemical Essays." Ph.D. dissertation, University of North Carolina, Greensboro, 1980.

Othow, Helen Chavis. "*Roots* and the Heroic Search for Identity." *CLA Journal,* XXVI (1983), 311–24.

Pinsker, Sanford. "Magic Realism, Historical Truth, and the Quest for a Liberating Identity: Reflections on Alex Haley's *Roots* and Toni Morrison's *Song of Solomon.*" In *Studies in Black American Literature I: Black American Prose Theory,* edited by Joe Weixlmann. Greenwood, Fla., 1984.

Pirie, Bruce. "The Grammar of the Abyss: A Reading of *The Fathers.*" *Southern Literary Journal,* XVI (1984), 81–92.

Price, Reynolds. "Given Time: Beginning *The Surface of Earth.*" *Antaeus,* XXI (1976), 57–64.

Reuter, M. "Doubleday Answers Haley: Denies All Charges." *Publisher's Weekly,* September 6, 1977, pp. 34–35.

———. "Haley Settles Plagiarism Suit, Concedes Passages." *Publisher's Weekly,* December 25, 1978, p. 22.

————. "Two Writers Question the Originality of 'Roots.'" *Publisher's Weekly*, May 2, 1977, p. 20.

————. "Why Alex Haley Is Suing Doubleday: An Outline of the Complaint." *Publisher's Weekly*, April 14, 1977, p. 25.

Rocks, James E. "T. S. Stribling's Burden of History: The Vaiden Trilogy." *Southern Humanities Review*, VI (1972), 221–32.

Rollyson, Carl E. "Faulkner as Historian: The Commissary Books in *Go Down, Moses.*" *Markham Review*, VII (1978), 31–36.

Rooke, Constance. "On Women and His Own Work: An Interview with Reynolds Price." *Southern Review*, n.s., XIV (1978), 706–25.

Rowell, Charles T. "Poetry, History, and Humanism: An Interview with Margaret Walker." *Black World*, XXV (1975), 4–17.

————. "'This Louisiana Thing That Drives Me': An Interview with Ernest Gaines." *Callaloo*, I (1978), 39–51.

Schultz, Elizabeth. "African and African-American Roots in Contemporary Afro-American Literature: The Difficult Search for Family Origins." *Studies in American Fiction*, VIII (1980), 127–45.

Simms, L. Moody, Jr. "Albion W. Tourgée on the Fictional Use of the Post-Civil War South." *Southern Studies*, XVII (1978), 399–409.

Skaggs, Merrill Maguire. "*Roots:* A New Black Myth." *Southern Quarterly*, XVII (1978), 42–50.

Smith, Lee. "Oral History." *Carolina Quarterly*, XXXIII (1981), 75–84.

Spallino, Chiara. "*Song of Solomon:* An Adventure in Structure." *Callaloo*, VIII (1985), 510–24.

Sprengnether, Madelon. "*Delta Wedding* and the Kore Complex." *Southern Quarterly*, XXV (1987), 120–30.

Stephens, Robert O. "Cable's Bras-Coupé and Mèrimée's Tamango: The Case of the Missing Arm." *Mississippi Quarterly*, XXXV (1982), 387–97.

Stout, Janis P. "Miranda's Guarded Speech: Porter and the Problem of Truth-Telling." *Philological Quarterly*, LXVI (1987), 259–78.

"A Symposium on *Roots.*" *Black Scholar*, VIII (1977), 36–42.

Walsh, Thomas F. "Miranda's Ghost in 'Old Mortality.'" *College Literature*, VI (1979), 57–63.

Warren, Robert Penn. "T. S. Stribling: A Paragraph in the History of Critical Realism." *American Review*, II (1934), 463–86.

White, Ellington. "A View from the Window." In *The Lasting South: Fourteen Southerners Look at Their Home*, edited by Louis D. Rubin, Jr., and James J. Kilpatrick. Chicago, 1957.

Young, Thomas Daniel. Introduction to *The Fathers and Other Fiction*, by Allen Tate. Baton Rouge, 1977.

INDEX

Absalom, Absalom! (Faulkner): narrative
style of, 12, 52–55, 65; compared with
Stribling's Vaiden trilogy, 51–52;
narrator-historian in, 52–55, 65; authorial entries into narrative of, 53–54; author's writing process for, 53; dynastic
potential of Sutpens in, 54–55; family
attributes in, 55–56; removal motif in,
55; displacement of inheritance in, 56;
family decline in, 56–57; matriarchal-
patriarchal conflict in, 57–58; homeplace in, 58–59; talismans in, 58–60;
type scenes in, 58; history in, 60–61; visionary moments in, 61–62; author's
comments on, 204, 209–10
Addison, Joseph, 18, 19
African, The (Courlander), 148
Agrarians, 74–75, 82
All the King's Men (Warren), 100, 213
"Apology to Florence" (Stribling), 42
Aubert, Alvin, 158–59
Augustine, St., 183
Austen, Jane, 18
Autobiographies, 12
Autobiography of Malcolm X, The (Haley),
149–50
Autobiography of Miss Jane Pittman, The
(Gaines), 12, 155–62, 202, 211

"Bear, The" (Faulkner), 64, 68, 72,
204–205, 206

Beauchamp, Thomas, 14–15
"Belles Demoiselles Plantation" (Cable),
28–29
Bennett, John, 165
"Bibi" (Cable), 29–30
Bible: as paradigm for family saga, 3–6,
11–12; narrative style of, 5–6, 150, 201;
Faulkner's use of, 11–12, 63, 65; Ca-
ble's use of, 30, 39; women in, 101; in
Price's works, 173, 174–75
Birth of a Nation, The, 145*n*
Birthright (Stribling), 41
Black family sagas: development of, 142;
Walker's *Jubilee* as, 143–47; matriarchy
in, 146–47; Haley's *Roots* as, 147–55;
patriarchy in, 154–55; Gaines's *The Autobiography of Miss Jane Pittman* as,
155–62; Morrison's *Song of Solomon* as,
162–70; and legend, 163–70
Black folklore, 145–46, 160
Blacks: family stories of, 8, 141–42; in Cable's works, 28, 38, 43; in Faulkner's
works, 43, 63, 66, 68; in Kennedy's
works, 43; in Stribling's works, 43,
44–45, 51; in Grau's works, 133–34,
135; in Price's works, 175–76; Gaines's
writing for, 205, 212; Morrison's writing for black women, 205; Morrison on
culture of, 211. *See also* Slavery
Bloodline (Gaines), 156
Botkin, B. A., 1, 165